Islam in Modern Turkey

The New Edinburgh Islamic Surveys
Series Editor: Carole Hillenbrand

edinburghuniversitypress.com/series/isur

Islam in Modern Turkey

Kim Shively

EDINBURGH
University Press

Edinburgh University Press is one of the leading university presses in the UK. We publish academic books and journals in our selected subject areas across the humanities and social sciences, combining cutting-edge scholarship with high editorial and production values to produce academic works of lasting importance. For more information visit our website: edinburghuniversitypress.com

Edinburgh University Press Ltd
The Tun – Holyrood Road
12 (2f) Jackson's Entry
Edinburgh EH8 8PJ

Typeset in 11/13pt Baskerville MT Pro by
Servis Filmsetting Ltd, Stockport, Cheshire

A CIP record for this book is available from the British Library

ISBN 978 1 4744 4014 1 (hardback)
ISBN 978 1 4744 4015 8 (paperback)
ISBN 978 1 4744 4016 5 (webready PDF)
ISBN 978 1 4744 4017 2 (epub)

Published with the support of the University of Edinburgh Scholarly Publishing Initiatives Fund.

Contents

Figures

Acknowledgements

I am humbled by the fact that so many friends and colleagues have been willing to read and comment on drafts of chapters and provide interesting insights into the issues discussed in this book. While I drew on the wisdom of many researchers who have studied Islam in modern Turkey, I especially want to thank Mustafa Kaya, Halim Çalış, Züleyha Çolak, Hikmet Kocamaner and Fabio Vicini for their input into various parts of the manuscript and for answering my many questions about matters large and small. I am also indebted to my student assistant, Greg White, who checked the clarity of the prose and copy-edited a number of the chapters. I cannot thank enough my many Turkish friends and interlocutors who have helped me at various stages of my research in Turkey – some of them appear under pseudonyms in this book. I will forever be grateful for their boundless wit, wisdom, kindness and hospitality.

I wish to acknowledge the institutions who supported me in my research and writing. Various components of my research in Turkey were made possible by grants from the Wenner-Gren Foundation for Anthropological Research, the Institute of Turkish Studies, the Sachar International Scholarship of Brandeis University and the Research Committee at Kutztown University. I am furthermore grateful to Kutztown University for twice awarding me sabbatical leave, once for conducting research in Turkey and a second time to work on completing this book. Nicola Ramsey at Edinburgh University Press has been especially helpful with the project as she approached me with the idea for the book and has been kind and supportive throughout the editing process. I thank my children, Emre, Benjamin, Evren and David, for tolerating my absentmindedness and occasional lapses into obsession as I researched the material for this book. Finally, I am grateful to my husband, Deniz, not only for supporting me in the writing process, but also for being willing to hunt down information, find images and double-check facts. I dedicate this book to him.

Note on Turkish usage

Since 1928 Turkish has been written in a modified Latin alphabet, rather than in the Arabic script that was used during the Ottoman Empire. The modern Turkish alphabet consists of twenty-nine letters, including most of the letters of the English alphabet plus six additional letters to indicate and distinguish particular sounds. Turkish spelling does not use *q*, *w* and *x*. The beauty of modern Turkish writing is that every letter is pronounced consistently from one word to the next, which means every Turkish word is pronounced how it is spelled. The following is a guide to the pronunciation of certain Turkish letters:

c   a hard *j* sound, as in *j*udge
ç   a *ch* sound, as in *ch*urch
g   always pronounced as a hard *g*, as in *g*oat
ğ   mostly silent but used to lengthen the preceding vowel
ı   an *eh* sound, as in doz*e*n
i   always pronounced *ee*, as in t*ee*
j   a soft *j*, as in plea*s*ure
o   a long *o*, as in h*o*me
ö   pronounced like the French *eu*, as in monsi*eu*r
ş   a *sh* sound, as in *sh*oe
u   as in p*u*t
ü   pronounced like the French *u*, as in t*u*

Glossary

aşık	a Turkish bard; an Alevi musician who provides music for the *cem* rituals
Aşure	(Arabic: *ashura*), for Shi'a Muslims and Alevis, the day in the month of Muharram (in the Islamic calendar) when Imam Hüseyin was killed at the Battle of Kerbala in 680 CE.
bağlama	a long-necked lute, also known as a *saz*
batini	a search for deeper meaning in texts
bid'a	unlawful innovation in Islam, especially in Islamic law
Buyruk	'Decree': the sacred book of the Alevis
caliph	(Turkish: *halife*), literally, the 'representative' of the Prophet Muhammad. The leader of the global Sunni Muslim community
çelebi	gentleman; title of the leader of a *Tarikat*
cem	the central ritual of Alevis, combining dancing, recitation and music
cemaat	a religious organisation, usually made up of followers of a particular religious leader
cemevi	a building, usually in a city, where the *cem* is performed
Cumhuriyet Bayramı	Republic Day, a national holiday commemorating the founding of the Turkish Republic, celebrated annually on 29 October
cuz	(Arabic: *juz'*), one-thirtieth of the Qur'an. During the thirty days of Ramadan, it is customary for Muslims to read one *cuz* of the Qur'an each day
dede	a senior member of a *Tarikat*; in Alevism, a holy man whose ritual authority is derived from his descent from Haci Bektaş Veli
dergah	dervish lodge or *tekke*
dernek	association or club
dershane	a tutoring and test-preparation school
dervish	(Turkish: *derviş*), member of a *Tarikat*
Diyanet	short for Diyanet İşleri Başkanlığı (Directorate of Religious

	Affairs), a bureaucratic division that handles religious affairs in Turkey
dua	an invocation prayer in Islam
ezan	(Arabic: *adhan*), the call to prayer
fetva	(Arabic: *fatwa*), a legal decision by an Islamic judge or *alim*
gecekondu	'built at night': a squatter house or settlement
görgü	a complex set of Alevi rituals designed to mediate conflicts in the community
haci	one who has been on the *hajj*
hadith	(Turkish: *hadis*), an account of the Prophet Muhammad's sayings or actions
hafiz	one who has memorised the Qur'an
hajj	(Turkish: *hac*) a pilgrimage to Mecca; one of the Five Pillars of Islam
Hakikat	full realisation of the divine, which is the ultimate goal of Sufi and Alevi ecstatic ritual. In Alevism, it refers to the 'oneness of being'.
hatip	a Muslim preacher
Hidrellez	a popular spring festival celebrated on 6 May to commemorate the day when two especially righteous Prophets, Hızır (Khidr) and Ilyas (Elijah), were believed to have met on earth
hijra	the migration of the original Muslim community from Mecca to Medina in 622 CE; it marks year one of the Islamic calendar
hizmet	service; the name of the service organisation associated with the Gülen movement
hoca	master, teacher, leader
iftar	the meal that breaks the fast during Ramadan
imam	a prayer leader; also a successor to the Prophet recognised by Shi'i Muslims and Alevis
irşad	the propagation of Islamic knowledge
jihad	religious striving or warfare
kalam	Islamic theology
Kandil günleri	five holy nights relating to the life of the Prophet Muhammad when special prayers are said
kaymakam	mayor
Kırklar Semahı	'Dance of the Forty Saints': an Alevi *semah* dance
Kızılbaş	a popular movement in the eastern Ottoman Empire whose members aligned themselves with the Shi'a Shahs of the Safavid Empire against the Ottomans
Kurban Bayramı	(Arabic: *Eid al-Adha*) the feast of sacrifice held at the end of the *hajj*

Kurmanji	a dialect of the Kurdish language
meclis	an assembly; a parliament
medrese	religious secondary school
mehter	Ottoman military band
mescit	a small mosque, not used for Friday communal prayers
mevlit	A Turkish poem recounting the birth of the Prophet Muhammad, recited at special events, such as weddings, circumcision ceremonies and death anniversaries
mihrap	a niche in a mosque wall indicating the direction of Mecca
millet	originally an autonomous community, in modern Turkish refers to a nation
minber	a pulpit reached by a straight set of stairs
miraç	the nocturnal ascent of the Prophet Muhammad to heaven
muezzin	one who calls the *ezan*
Muharram	first month of the Islamic calendar; on the tenth (*ashura*) of Muharram Shi'as and Alevis commemorate the Battle of Kerbala and the death of Imam Hussein
mürid	a disciple in a *Tarikat*
mürşid	a spiritual guide or master in a *Tarikat*
namaz	(Arabic: *salah*), the five daily prayers of Islam
nefs	the material or carnal self
niyet	intention
oruç	(Arabic: *sawm*), Islamic fasting
Padişah	Sultan
pardesü	a long overcoat worn by women to maintain modesty standards
pir	a master or sheik in a *Tarikat*
rabıta	the master-disciple relationship in Sufi orders
Ramadan	(Turkish: *Ramazan*), the ninth month in the Islamic calendar, the month in which the Prophet Muhammad received his first revelation
Ramazan Bayramı	(Arabic: *Eid al-Fitr*), the festival celebrating the end of fasting during Ramadan; also known as the Sugar Festival (*Şeker Bayramı*)
sadaka	any charitable giving beyond the requirements of *zekat*
Safavid	the enemy Shi'a Empire east of the Ottoman Empire
saz	a long-necked lute, also known as a *bağlama*
sazende	a bard who plays the *saz*
secde	the kneeling part of the Islamic ritual prayer
semah	dancing performed during the Alevi *cem* or during the rituals of some Sufi orders
şeyh	sheikh; a master in a *Tarikat*

Şeyhülislam	the Grand Mufti, the leader of the muftis
shahada	the Muslim declaration of faith; the first Pillar of Islam
Shari'ah	(Turkish: *şeriat*), Islamic law
silsile	spiritual genealogy of the masters of Sufi orders
site	apartment complex
siyer	literature about the life of the Prophet Muhammad
sohbet	a sermon or conversation
sünnet	generally, Turkish for *Sunnah* (the sayings and deeds of the Prophet Muhammad); more particularly, ritual circumcision of boys following Muslim custom
surah	a chapter of the Qur'an
takva	love of and obedience to God
talip	student; in Alevism, a follower of a *dede*
Tanzimat	reforms, especially the centralising reforms of 1839–1973
Tarikat	a Sufi order or brotherhood (Sunni Islam); ritual practice and moral conduct (Alevism)
tasavvuf	Sufism, Islamic mystic traditions
tawhid	the unity of God
tefsir	Qur'anic interpretation
tekke	lodge of a *Tarikat*
tesettür	clothing that conforms to Islamic standards of modesty
tespih	string of beads used to keep count of prayers or for reciting phrases of praise
tuğra	an ornate signature of an Ottoman sultan, designed to resemble a bow
türbe	religious shrine or tomb of a Muslim saint
Türk Dil Kurumu	Turkish Society for the Study of Language
Turnalar Semahı	'Dance of the Cranes': an Alevi *semah* dance
ulema	(singular: *alim*) scholars of Islamic law
umre	(Arabic: *umrah*), visiting the sites of the *hajj* during non-*hajj* times of the year
vaiz	(feminine: *vaize*), a preacher
vakıf	(plural: *evkaf*; Arabic: *waqf*), a pious charitable foundation
vali	governor of a province or region
varoş	immigrant neighbourhood
zahiri	a superficial, literal interpretation of a text
zaviye	a shrine to a Muslim saint or venerable person
Zaza	a language spoken by some Kurds in Turkey
zekat	(Arabic: *zakat*), alms given to the poor and needy; the third Pillar of Islam
zikir	(Arabic: *dhikr*), repetition of the names of God or formulas of praise

Commonly used acronyms

CHE	Council of Higher Education (*Yüksek Öğretim Kurulu*, YÖK)
DP	Democrat Party (*Demokrat Partisi*, DP)
ECHR	European Court of Human Rights
HBVV	Haci Bektaş Veli Anatolian Culture Foundation (*Haci Bektaş Veli Vakfı*)
IHH	Foundation for Human Rights and Freedoms and Humanitarian Relief (*İnsan Hak ve Hürriyetleri ve İnsani Yardım Vakfı*), an aid organisation
ISHAD	Association of Solidarity in Business Life (*İş Hayatı Dayanışma Derneği*), a business networking organisation associated with the Gülen movement
JDP	Justice and Development Party (*Adalet ve Kalkınma Partisi*, AKP)
KYM	*Kimse Yok Mu* (literally 'Is anyone there?'), an aid organisation associated with the Gülen movement
MÜSİAD	Association of Independent Industrialists and Businessmen (*Müstakil Sanyici ve İşadamları Derneği*)
NOM	National Outlook Movement (*Milli Görüş*), the Islamic political movement overseen by Necmettin Erbakan
NSC	National Security Council (*Milli Güvenlik Kurulu*, MGK)
PKK	Kurdistan Workers' Party (Kurdish: *Partiya Karkerên Kurdistanê*), a militant Kurdish separatist movement in Turkey
RPP	Republican People's Party (*Cumhuriyet Halk Partisi*, CHP), the original party of Mustafa Kemal Atatürk
TÜSİAD	Organisation of Turkish Industrialists and Businessmen (*Türk Sanayicileri ve İş İnsanları Derneği*)
TUSKON	Turkish Confederation of Businessmen and Industrialists (*Türkiye İşadamları ve Sanayiciler Konfederasyonu*), a business networking organisation associated with the Gülen movement
VP	Virtue Party (*Fazilet Partisi*, FP)
WP	Welfare Party (*Refah Partisi*, RP)
YPG	People's Protection Units (Kurdish: *Yekîneyên Parastina Gel*), Kurdish military units in northern Syria fighting the regime of Bashar al-Assad

Preface

Historically, surveys of Turks have reported high levels of religiosity. In all my travels and research in Turkey, I only occasionally heard anyone openly admit that they were atheist, at least until recently. Almost everyone who talked to me about religion readily declared that they were indeed Muslims, because they believed in God and that the Prophet Muhammad is God's messenger. This was the case whether the individual was a self-declared secularist who rarely performed ritual prayer (*namaz*) or was a devoted member of one of Turkey's religious organisations (*cemaat*). Research backed up the importance of Muslim identity in Turkey. In a survey conducted in Turkey in 2006, sociologists Ali Çarkoğlu and Binnaz Toprak found that 98.4 per cent of their 1,492 respondents identified themselves as 'Muslim' (2007: 41). This number requires some interpretation, however, since in Turkey Muslim identity may often be part of the national identity, in that the construction of the modern Turkish nation was often couched in terms of Muslim Turks vs non-Muslim, largely Christian enemies. Muslim identity for some may be more about being Turkish than about being religious. It is nevertheless remarkable that only 1.6 per cent of the population declared that they professed faith in no religion.

Furthermore, over 90 per cent of the 2006 sample identified themselves as 'religious', though what 'religious' meant in this context seemed to vary somewhat. Certainly in my own fieldwork, people would label themselves as observant or serious about Islam if they fasted during Ramadan and prayed on holidays. Others argued that real religiosity meant following all of the Five Pillars of Islam (see Chapter 2), as well as following dietary and clothing regulations and so on. In their study Çarkoğlu and Toprak attempted to gauge respondents' self-perceived religiosity by asking each person to place themselves on a ten-point scale from 'secularist' to 'Islamist'. Almost 50 per cent identified themselves on the Islamist end of the scale while only 20 per cent placed themselves at the secularist end. The rest put themselves in the middle, at point 5. In a separate question on identity, 45 per cent of the respondents – by far the most – described themselves first and foremost as Muslim, rather than as Turkish, Kurdish or even as a citizen of the Turkish Republic, suggesting that religious identity is often more important than national identity (Çarkoğlu and Toprak 2007; this discussion is taken from Shively 2013: 205–6).

Yet, a recent (2018) survey[1] found that the level of religiosity in Turkey declined between 2008 and 2018. The survey of 5,800 people found that 51 per cent of respondents described themselves as 'religious', down from 55 per cent in 2008, though the authors of the survey do not explain what was meant by 'religious'. In the 2018 survey, those who called themselves 'atheists' increased to 3 per cent, up from 1 per cent in 2008, and those who identify as 'non-believers' rose to 2 per cent from 1 per cent. There have been reports of young people in particular turning away from the religious practices they grew up with in their families. The reasons for the shift in attitudes towards religion are a matter of speculation, but some social scientists have suggested that the current Turkish government's increasing emphasis on creating religious institutions and encouraging religious practices – while the regime itself has displayed high levels of corruption and nepotism (see Chapter 8) – has created a backlash and a sense that religious discourse does not lead to ethical behaviour.[2] Even with this decline in religiosity, the 2018 survey indicates that 97 per cent of the Turkish population has some sort of religious belief, superficial or otherwise. Clearly, religion has been important in Turkish society, and the study of Islam in modern Turkey is essential to understanding the country's culture and history.

My background

While I began to visit Turkey in 1992, the field research that I allude to in this book began in late 1997 at a time of considerable political and social upheaval in the country. In February 1997, Turkey underwent what many have called a 'soft coup' or 'post-modern coup d'état' when Turkey's Islamic-oriented government was pressured by the secularist military to step down if it did not want to face outright military action. The coalition government, headed by the Welfare Party (WP) prime minister Necmettin Erbakan, cooperated and resigned, soon after which the WP was dissolved by the Constitutional Court and Erbakan was banned from politics for life. Until 2002, with the rise of the Justice and Development Party (JDP), the coalition governments that formed after the coup were weak and ineffectual, and Turkey suffered economic instability that was exacerbated by a devastating earthquake in the Istanbul region in 1999. These developments will be discussed at greater length in Chapter 5.

The focus of my original research was the formulation of secularism in Turkey and how it affected the lives and thinking of pious groups in Turkey's cities. Most of my research took place in Ankara – especially in the Sincan neighbourhood north-west of the capital city – but I spent some time in Istanbul as well. My research subjects consisted primarily of a network of families related by blood or by marriage who had all migrated from the same Black Sea province to Ankara and Istanbul. Most of the members of this extended family were deeply pious – they read and studied the Qur'an regularly, attended mosque, performed the Five Pillars to the best of their ability (though none had yet had a chance to go to Mecca), and observed the dietary, modesty, and other rules of traditional Turkish Islam. However, there were also members of the family who had strongly secularist views and were critical of what they saw as the excessive piety of their kin. In short, there was tension within the extended family on questions of religion and politics.

Some of these family members will appear in the various chapters of this book. In particular, one young woman, Meryem,[3] and her family were important to my research and were (and still are) very good friends. Meryem's family was not only deeply pious but also studious and articulate about their understandings of Islam. They also were willing to discuss the difficulties they experienced being devout Muslims in a secular society like Turkey, which has sometimes tried to control the public display of religious symbols in ways that many devout Turks have found problematic. Meryem and both her parents had reputations for piety and wisdom in their community, and they each regularly gave sermons and taught the Qur'an in their Sincan neighbourhood. Meryem's father in particular was renowned for his beautiful voice and was often hired to recite the Qur'an and the *mevlit*[4] for special occasions. Even though my dissertation fieldwork ended in 1999, I return to Turkey almost every year, sometimes for weeks or months at a time, to conduct new research projects. When there, I try to see Meryem – now married with two children and living in Istanbul – and her family back in Sincan, just as I try to visit other members of the extended family and groups of friends that I have kept in touch with over the years. All of these experiences have allowed me to gain a good understanding of the experience of being Muslim in modern Turkey.

The organisation of the book

The topic of Islam in modern Turkey is very broad, and putting together a shorter, more accessible book such as this required making sometimes difficult decisions about what to include and what to leave out. Because the book is looking at historical developments over the span of more than a century, I will emphasise national developments and the rise and transformation of various institutions in the late twentieth and early twenty-first centuries, while neglecting more localised, popular practices. The first chapter presents an overview of the role Islam played in the foundation of the modern Republic of Turkey, focusing particularly on how the secularising reforms of Turkey's founder, Mustafa Kemal Atatürk, affected the development of religious institutions and practices throughout the history of the country. Chapter 2 examines the formation of the Directorate of Religious Affairs (*Diyanet İşlerleri Başkanlığı*), which, along with religious education courses in the public schools, is the primary governmental institution that has effects on the practice of Islam in modern Turkey. The chapter also looks at some of the basic aspects of Sunni Muslim practice in Turkey and points out the ways in which these practices are influenced or controlled by the Directorate of Religious Affairs. Chapter 3 provides a description of Alevism, an important religious minority in Turkey that has often experienced discrimination and hardship in the face of the Sunni Islam promoted by the state. Chapter 4 surveys some of the Sufi orders (*Tarikat*) and religious organisations (*cemaat*) that have been important to popular Islam in Turkey from the time of the Ottoman Empire to the present day. Chapter 5 examines the strengthening of Islamic political parties in Turkey, especially after the 1980 military coup, when the military leaders sought to promote Islamic interests as a way to counter the influence of communism in Turkish political and social life. Both formal and informal modes of religious education is the topic of Chapter 6, while Chapter 7 discusses the effects that policies promoting economic liberalism have had on religious institutions and practices. While I do not discuss in any depth local popular practices, such as the visitation of saints' tombs and local permutations of religious festivals, I do provide a vignette of my field research at the beginning of many of the book's chapters in order to give the reader a sense of the lived experience of religion in Turkish society.

The decision to organise the book thematically – where I focus each chapter on a different aspect of Turkish religious life – rather than purely historically was driven by two concerns. First of all, certain religious institutions and practices played important roles in Turkish society at different times in the country's history, and the organisation of the chapters reflects that pattern to some degree. An extended examination of the Directorate of Religious Affairs begins early in the book because for much of modern Turkish history, that institution has intensely influenced the development of policy and the public practice of Islam in Turkey up to the present. The Sufi orders and religious organisations, the Islamic political parties, as well as institutions of religious education, have had profound effects on religious life. The complexity of these subjects require chapter-length discussions – indeed, books have been written on each of these topics.

There are other important topics that I regret not being able to cover in greater detail. For example, I only discuss in passing the position of modern Turkey in the global order and Turkey's relationships with other countries, including those countries where there is a significant Turkish diaspora. Of course, how Turkey as a country represents itself to the rest of the world affects religious policy and public practice at home. As such, I will discuss international relationships, but only to the extent that they shape Islam within modern Turkey. I will not go into the situations of the Turkish diaspora, even though in certain countries, such as Germany, the Turkish communities are quite large.

Another issue that I do not explore extensively is the position of the Kurdish minority in Turkey. The 'Kurdish question' is an ongoing political concern that has been important to understanding Turkish politics in the past and the nature of Turkey's relationships with its neighbours to the south and the east. The reason for this omission is that Turkey's problems regarding its Kurdish minority have largely revolved around ethnic, territorial and historical issues rather than religious differences. Both Turks and Kurds identify as Muslim, though the Alevi minority is disproportionately composed of Kurds. Still, most Alevis are ethnically Turkish, and religion plays a relatively small role in the tensions between Turks and Kurds. Indeed, the Kurdish separatist movement, the PKK (Kurdistan Workers' Party), involved in the long-standing armed conflict with the Turkish military in the south-east of the country, is a communist party that rejects religion altogether.

Problems of categories

As an aid to the reader, I provide a glossary of Turkish words and acronyms that appear throughout the text (see pp. x–xiii). There are, however, a couple of terms that have complex meanings that need more discussion than that provided by a dictionary definition. For example, I will repeatedly use 'Kemalist' to describe the secular state and its supporters that dominated the Republic of Turkey from its founding in 1923 until the end of the twentieth century. Kemalists are those who adhere to 'Kemalism', which is the English term referring to the principles and revolutions (*ilke ve inkilap*) of Mustafa Kemal Atatürk. In Turkish, a Kemalist is an *Atatürkçü* and Kemalism is *Atatürkçülük*. While I will describe Kemalism in some detail in Chapter 1, for now I want to emphasise that Kemalism is the label for a form of secularism particular to Turkey, in which the state exerts control over religious expression as a means of maintaining a secular (non-religious) public sphere. It is hard to overstate the importance of Kemalism in the development of the Turkish Republic over its almost century of existence, as we will see. Even so, we should not think of Kemalists as composing a homogeneous political and social unit. Certainly the Kemalist establishment, which includes the twentieth-century Constitutional Court, the Council of State, the past military generals and secularist politicians, such as members of the Republican People's Party, articulate fairly consistent sets of beliefs about the role of religion in society and the inviolability of the Kemalist reforms and revolutions, among other things. Yet conversations with those who identify themselves as 'Kemalist' reveal a wider range of attitudes and beliefs both about Atatürk and about Islam than the 'official' party line would suggest. Generally, when I refer to the Kemalist position, I am indicating those who articulate general support of the political discourse of the establishment, even if their support may be sometimes ambivalent.

And just as Kemalists are not a unified group, neither are pious Muslims. When I refer to pious Muslims or religiously observant individuals, I am referring to those who conscientiously adhere to the beliefs and practices of Islam – as they understand them – even though that adherence may vary considerably in content and intensity. I am reluctant to label religiously observant or pious individuals as 'conservative', since there are many different kinds of conservatism in Turkey. Indeed, Kemalism itself seems to be a form of conservatism in Turkey, in that the Kemalist establishment has been resistant to change and movements towards political and social liberalisation in the decades since the 1960s (Yavuz 2009: 153–6). In this context, I use terms such as 'observant', 'devout' or 'pious' to describe those Turkish Muslim practitioners who see themselves as participating in a more conscious and rigorous form of Islam than do Kemalists. But, as indicated above, most Turks, no matter their political orientation, see themselves as Muslim in that they believe in the basic principles of Islam.

Notes

1. https://interaktif.konda.com.tr/tr/HayatTarzlari2018/ (in Turkish). A discussion of the survey in English can be found at https://www.al-monitor.com/pulse/originals/2019/01/turkey-becoming-less-religious-under-akp.html
2. There has been some degree of discussion of declining religiosity in Turkey. For reflections from Turkish social scientists, see the Georgetown University Berkeley Forum 'Politics and Piety in Turkey' of 15 April 2019 at https://berkleycenter.georgetown.edu/posts/politics-and-piety-in-turkey
3. All names of my research interlocutors are pseudonyms.
4. The *mevlit* is a distinctly Turkish ceremony that includes a long Turkish poem recounting the birth of the Prophet Muhammad. It is held at special events, such as weddings, circumcision ceremonies and death anniversaries.

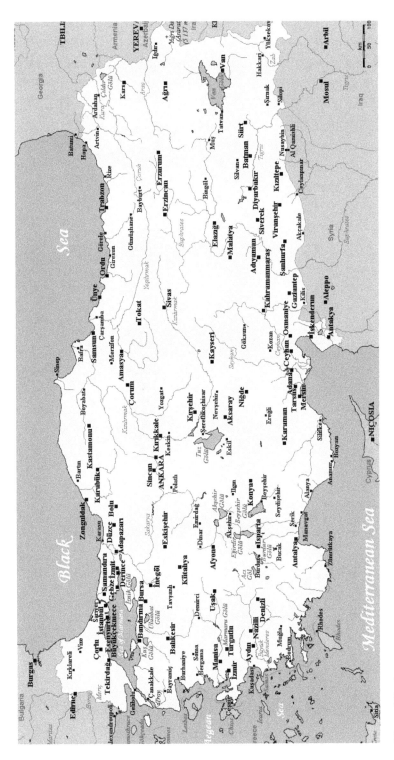

Map of Turkey

Islam and the formation of the modern Turkish Republic

An oral history

World War I (1914–18) is sometimes known as the 'Great War' or the 'War to End All Wars'. Even though more people died during World War II, the First World War represented something entirely new, both because the war unleashed tremendous technologies of destruction on the global population, and because it brought to an end some of the great empires that had dominated the world for centuries. The Russian, Austro-Hungarian and Ottoman Empires all collapsed in the course of or soon after World War I, reshaping political boundaries and relationships around the world. In the case of the Ottoman Empire, its demise transformed the Middle East, leading eventually to the establishment of many of the Middle Eastern countries that exist now. The modern Republic of Turkey is the nation that succeeded the Ottoman Empire, and it now occupies the old Ottoman heartland in Anatolia (Asia Minor) and eastern Thrace (see Map). The creation of the modern Turkish nation was an often painful process in which the founders of the new Republic attempted to establish a state that was based on principles, practices and traditions different from those that formed the basis of the empire. This chapter will focus on the emergence of the modern Turkish Republic and the role that Islam played in the formation of the new state. Given the centrality that Islam had in the organisation and functioning of the Ottoman state, I will pay special attention to the ways in which the founders of the Turkish Republic simultaneously rejected most Ottoman religious institutions and supported other Ottoman religious traditions, including the Ottoman willingness to legislate public religious matters. And as we will see over the course of the book, the spectre of the Ottoman Empire and the early Republic will 'haunt' the imagination of Turks throughout the history of the twentieth and twenty-first centuries.

The reforms introduced by Turkey's founding government were extensive, as this chapter will make clear, but the population of the new nation experienced the reforms to differing degrees. For many rural peasants, for example, life continued much as it had for generations, whereas those in larger cities felt the changes in institutional and political arrangements more immediately. For some Turkish women, the reforms brought new opportunities for education and public roles, since part of the modernisation programme of Turkey was targeted at liberalising women's position in society. While many or even most women could not take advantage of these changes, I had the opportunity to collect an oral history of one woman, Zehra Hanım, who was able to move from a provincial town, where religious devotion was taken for granted, to Turkey's largest city, Istanbul, in order to be trained as a nurse in an expanded nursing programme. Zehra Hanım was born before the War ('in the time of the *Padişah* [sultan]', as she put it) in the Black Sea town of Safranbolu and had vivid recollections of life during and just after the Great War and during the early years of the Republic. She was the youngest child, born in 1911 to a relatively well-to-do knife-maker (*bıçakçı*) in Safranbolu.

She recollects:[1]

> My father went to Kayseri to join the army ... When my father was in the military, there was a typhoid fever outbreak, and he caught the typhoid fever and died. In 1915 the news of my father's death arrived. I don't remember my father at all. At that time, we had three houses: the one in the city [Safranbolu], a *bağ evi* [an orchard house] and there was a house in the garden. There was a lot of fruit, you know, and there were a lot of cows. My father also left money when he went to the military ... My father's store went to my brother.

> [After the death of the father,] my mother took care of the cows in the garden and she cooked. She made food for weddings. Eighteen different kinds of food were made ... We were an abundant community. Since the war didn't come [to Safranbolu] there were a lot of rich people, there was a lot of gold. In the summer we would go to the *bağ evi*, and in the winter we would live in the Safranbolu house. We made yogurt. In the winter, we would dry mulberries broken from the limb. We made *pekmez* [a molasses made from grapes]. We never wasted anything. There were a lot of plums. In the garden, there were fifteen to twenty different kinds of plums. We would make prune juice and *pestil* [sheets of dried fruit pulp]. The women of Safranbolu had a lot of work.

I asked her what religious life was like in Safranbolu at the time. Zehra Hanım was not a very religious person when I knew her, but she described her mother and sister as devout Muslims:

> My mother was very religious, devoted to religion. In the summers during the school holidays she would send us for three months to the *hoca* [instructor]. He was teaching the Qur'an. From that I can read the Qur'an very well, and I know some *surah*s by heart. It's in Arabic, so I don't know the meaning, but by reading I learned it. I could recite from memory the 'Amme' [Surah 78, *An-Naba*'], 'Tebareke' [Surah 67, *Al-Mulk*] and 'Yasin' [Surah 36].[2] I memorised the prayers. Later I also became a Qur'an *hoca* and I also gave Qur'an courses. In the summers I read the *mevlit*. But I don't like *sofuluk* [extremeness or strictness in the practice of religion] ... Before the sun rose my mother would pray early in the morning. My mother prayed a lot, and she would call me to pray too. She

Figure 1.1 Safranbolu houses

would get me up out of sleep. They would fast (during Ramadan). I can't stand being hungry and because of that I would secretly eat during the fast.

Zehra Hanım had been a nurse, and her family and neighbours held her in high esteem as an educated and capable woman. She described her educational experience:

> I was seven years old when I started school. At that time we read in the old alphabet. In 1928 the new letters came out.[3] Atatürk had come. In those times I had taken private lessons. I loved to read, as I told you. I went and learned [the letters] from the government. Together with the civil servants, I took an exam on the new letters and I passed. Later I taught a course on the new letters. That is, I taught the [new] Turkish letters to those who knew the Arabic script. Then I taught 4th grade. There in Safranbolu I was a teacher, I loved to read very much.

Zehra Hanım's daughter later explained that because Zehra Hanım was so successful in school, Safranbolu's *kaymakam* (mayor) supported her by arranging a teaching position for her. However, an inspector from the state (*müteffiş*) came to watch her and judge her to see if she would qualify to become a permanent teacher. This official disapproved of her and judged against her, so she couldn't become a teacher. After this, the *kaymakam* helped Zehra Hanım go to Istanbul to become a nurse. He organised a whole group of young women to go and register for nursing school in Istanbul, an opportunity that was made possible by the reforms of the early Republic. Zehra Hanım remembers her trip to Istanbul vividly:

> I was eighteen years old when I wanted to go to Istanbul. My mother didn't want to send me. She wanted me for [to be married to] a grocer. The man's wife had

Figure 1.2 Zehra Hanım's house in Safranbolu, with her oldest son, Erol

died and there was a child. There was a mother-in-law and father-in-law, too.
My mother introduced me to them as a [potential] daughter-in-law. I didn't
want this. I struggled and struggled with my mother, then I went off to Istanbul.

Her trip was quite harrowing, requiring her to travel to the Black Sea coast to
wait for a ferry and bus to take her to the big city. She had never seen electricity
or indoor plumbing before arriving in Istanbul. Yet she successfully completed
her studies at nursing school:

I had prepared my papers for entering nursing school. I walked to school, entered the exam and passed. A month later I started school. I studied at the 'Nursing School' – they said 'Nurse' [in English]. After I finished nursing school – of course I had acquired a circle of friends, I had got to know people, so I stayed in Istanbul. I transferred to Zeynep Kamil's place [a hospital]. I became acquainted with a doctor's family when I was looking after sick people. Zeynep Kamil Hospital was the biggest maternity hospital in Üsküdar [a district of Istanbul]. The Zeynep Kamil hospital had just opened then, and they sent me there as head nurse. From there I was transferred to the Haybeli Ada Sanatorium. From Heybeli the director of my [nursing] school brought me to the school as a teaching nurse.

After she married a military officer, Zehra Hanım left nursing and began to have children. But during World War II, while her husband was on active duty, she returned home to Safranbolu and took up nursing again:

I also came to Safranbolu at that time. There were few nurses then. Safranbolu's hospital was right on the hilltop in the most beautiful part of town. I had myself transferred there, and I worked there for a year. Later my husband would not let me do nursing. I said, 'Let me be a midwife.' In Beyazit [a district in Istanbul] at the university there was a school of midwifery. Again I applied there and studied there for two years. I have two diplomas – one from a nursing school and one from a school of midwifery. So I also practiced midwifery. In Safranbolu I delivered many children, in Kemerburgaz [a neighbourhood in Istanbul] I delivered a number of children, too. Wherever we went I practised midwifery. I delivered babies – countless babies.

The end of empire

In many ways, the life trajectory of Zehra Hanım – her transformation from a provincial girl to a capable, professional woman – reflects the aspirations that the founders had for creating a modern, developed state with a well-educated population. One of the most difficult issues the new nation faced is the role that Islam would play in social and political life, an issue citizens of Turkey debate to this day.

The Ottoman Empire – the imperial predecessor to the modern Turkish Republic – has loomed very large in the Turkish national imagination, for better or for worse. The empire indeed had a magnificent run, founded by the descendants of Osman (the Turkish word for Ottoman is Osmanlı, that is, 'those of Osman') in the thirteenth century after the Mongol invasions destroyed the empires in Asia Minor that had preceded it. It grew through successive military conquests over the Byzantine Empire (and others) to dominate first the peninsula of Asia Minor and the Balkans, culminating in the Fatih Sultan Mehmet's (Mehmet the Conqueror) conquest of the Byzantine capital, Constantinople, in

1453. The empire continued to expand under the descendants of Fatih Mehmet until it reached its greatest expanse in 1683 when it stretched from Mesopotamia in the east to what is now Algeria (North Africa) in the west, and from Poland in the north to the Holy Lands of Arabia and the Levant into the Sudan in the south. In the years after 1683 until its dissolution in 1923, the Ottoman Empire shrank gradually, losing territory to competing powers or to independent movements – an experience typical of the empires that disappeared in the nineteenth and twentieth centuries. As it struggled to survive, the Ottomans attempted to reform the state, especially in the nineteenth century, to create institutions that could compete with the increasingly powerful nation-states of the North Atlantic region. Ultimately, however, those reforms failed, and when the Ottoman Empire suffered a defeat in the First World War, it could no longer survive.

The basic political events surrounding the birth of the Turkish Republic from the ashes of the Ottoman Empire can be summarised in a brief outline. Because the Ottoman Empire allied with the Axis powers in World War I, it shared in the Axis defeat in 1918. The fate of the empire was in the hands of the victorious Allies who negotiated the Treaty of Sèvres with the Ottoman Sultan, Mehmed (VI) Vahideddin. This treaty allowed the Allied forces – in particular, Greece, France, Italy and the UK – to partition and control the remaining territory of the Ottoman Empire, leaving only a small state in central Anatolia for the Turks (McMeekin 2012: 41–3; Zürcher 2004: 143–7). Against this, a group of revolutionaries, including army officer and military hero Mustafa Kemal (later called Atatürk), led a Turkish national movement that fought what came to be known as the War of Independence (1919–23) in which the Turkish forces were able to push the various European powers out of the Anatolian peninsula and Eastern Thrace. The 1923 Treaty of Lausanne concluded the hostilities and granted the Turks sovereignty over most of the territory of present-day Turkey (Zürcher 2004: 152–65). Thereafter, Atatürk and his nationalist followers established the Republic of Turkey, whose primary political authority rested in the Turkish parliament in the new capital, Ankara.

Of course, the process of nation-building was considerably more complex than this one-paragraph summary would suggest. Rather than go into the details of this process – there are many excellent books on the topic – I instead focus on a few issues essential for understanding the development of Islam in modern Turkey. First of all, there were many political factions with differing interests and goals vying for power in the post-war years up to and following the founding of the Turkish Republic. But it was the Turkish nationalists led by Mustafa Kemal Atatürk who came to dominate the government and were essential to shaping the republican nature of the emerging state. The 'Kemalists' (those who followed the principles of Atatürk) imagined that they were creating a modern nation based on ethnic (Turkish) and religious (Muslim) uniformity. This stood in contrast to the multi-ethnic, multi-religious character of the Ottoman Empire. Religious minorities (i.e., non-Muslims) in the Ottoman Empire had, since the reign of Fatih Mehmet II, been organised into *millets*, which were communities defined by religion. These communities were generally autonomous, collecting taxes, overseeing education and dealing with legal issues, such as inheritance and marriage, within the *millet* community. The *millets* were ultimately subservient to the Sultan and paid the special 'head tax' (*cizye*) to the Empire, but they were largely left alone (Imber 2002: 130–1). Those Ottoman subjects who were Muslim were conceptualised as members of the 'community of Muhammad' and were subject to direct Ottoman law and administration.

By the nineteenth century, however, the Turkish term *millet* had come to describe a national political entity or nation-state. This reflected the influence of European nationalism, which presumed that states could be defined by ethnic and linguistic distinctiveness (e.g., France is for 'the French', and so on).[4] In the case of Turkey, Atatürk and his supporters envisioned that the new Turkey would be for Muslim Turks. This ethno-nationalist push to create such a supposedly homogeneous state was facilitated by the fact that by the end of World War I, most of the Ottoman population was actually Muslim. The non-Muslim populations of the Empire – who outnumbered Muslims for most of Ottoman history – had, in the early twentieth century, either migrated out, been expelled or 'exchanged' from Ottoman lands, or were now citizens of new countries created from former Ottoman territories after the Great War.[5]

During Turkey's War of Independence, the leaders had drawn on religious nationalism to rally the Anatolian people to support the independence movement. For example, the nationalists – with the aid of provincial religious leaders – invoked the theme that the Sultan-Caliph in Istanbul was a prisoner of the Allied (Christian) forces and that the nationalists were fighting for the preservation of the Muslim Empire. At the opening of the First Grand National Assembly (parliament) in 1920, Atatürk held a ceremony in which the presiding officials offered public prayers calling on God to save the sultanate and caliphate (Toprak 1981: 64). Religious leaders were able to stir up popular resistance by issuing *firmans* or *fetvas* (legal orders) that called for jihad (fighting for the faith) in support of the Sultan. In effect, the nationalists used the Muslim identity of Turks as a political tool in their quest to create a unified, modern Turkish nation willing to defend itself against hostile forces.

This view of religion as politically 'useful' would become a sustaining feature of official attitudes and policies regarding the role of Islam in the early years of the Republic. Many Kemalists accepted Islam as a means of creating social solidarity in what had been a fractured post-war society. But if not properly controlled, religion could also serve as a rallying cry for those who opposed the new government and its revolutionary policies. Furthermore, the early reformers viewed the Ottoman Empire as a failed state, and they tried to create a nation that rejected many of the organising features of the old empire. Since Islamic institutions had been a centrepiece of Ottoman imperial rule, Turkey's new leaders viewed their continued existence as harmful to the goals of the Republic, so they set about abolishing or transforming these institutions with the goal of creating a modern democratic secular state. That is, even though Atatürk and his supporters saw Islam as important for creating national unity, they ultimately wanted to establish a nation-state in which religion would be separated from and subordinated to the Turkish government.

Creating a secular state

The process of creating a secular state required the Kemalist reformers to either eliminate state institutions once controlled by religious authorities or transform them into institutions managed by non-religious bureaucrats. There were many such institutional transformations, but perhaps one of the most dramatic secularising changes to occur in the first years of the Republic was the abolition of the sultanate and the caliphate. For much of the history of the Ottoman Empire, the Ottoman monarch had served as both Sultan, the military and political imperial ruler, and Caliph, the successor to Muhammad and supreme leader of the global Muslim community, known as the *umma* (Imber 2002: 115–17). The marriage between religion and state – *din ü devlet* – endowed significant legitimacy on Ottoman imperial authority since Muslim subjects could view the state not only as pursuing mundane political goals, but as serving God as well.

But the early republicans came to see first the sultanate and then the caliphate as barriers to their democratic nationalist goals. They feared that the Sultan Mehmed VI Vahideddin would act as an alternative source of power around which an opposition to the nationalists could mobilise. In an attempt to discredit Sultan Mehmed VI, nationalists claimed the Sultan had not been a victim of Western designs on Ottoman lands (as they had claimed during the War of Independence) but had actually been a Western dupe willing to cooperate with the invading Christian authorities in the hope of saving some of the Anatolian territories in a compromise. And they were not entirely wrong. Mehmed VI had in fact opposed the efforts of the nationalists to protect the Anatolian heartland from the European powers. He and his supporters had viewed the nationalist War of Independence as a threat to the foundation of the empire because the nationalists wanted to establish a parliamentary system that would limit the power of the Sultan. The Sultan believed he could keep the empire intact with the support of the victorious Allied powers, and he had willingly signed the harshly punitive Treaty of Sèvres in 1920. When Atatürk and his followers prevailed in the War of Independence, the government of the new Republic abolished the sultanate in 1922, sending Mehmed VI into permanent exile. In a further rejection of the Ottoman imperial past, the republican government moved the capital to Ankara and established the Grand National Assembly as an alternative government to the imperial seat in Istanbul.[6]

After the elimination of the sultanate, the nationalist government initially maintained the caliphate as a ceremonial position to be occupied by Mehmed VI's heir and cousin, Abdülmecid Efendi. But the power relationship between the National Assembly and the caliphate was not clearly defined, and many in the new power elite viewed the Caliph as a potential rival to Mustafa Kemal Atatürk and his government. So in March 1924, just a few months after the founding of the Republic of Turkey, the government abolished the caliphate and ordered all members of the Ottoman dynasty to leave the country (Zürcher 2004: 166–8). The Sunni caliphate was at an end. The abolition of the caliphate affected Muslims around the world, since the Caliph was the religious leader of the global Sunni Muslim community. Muslims were alarmed by the termination of the caliphate in Istanbul as there was no replacement, a situation that has not changed.

The republican government did not just eliminate the position of the Ottoman ruler but also took steps to eliminate the traditional bureaucracy of the empire. The Ottoman bureaucracy had been largely run by a class of religious elite – the *ulema* (singular: *alim*) – who had been its beating heart. The *ulema* was made up of men from elite families who were formally educated in classical Islamic sciences and rituals. Led by the *Şeyhülislam* (the Grand Mufti), the *ulema* were responsible for managing a number of essential Ottoman institutions and regulating religious practices and other aspects of Ottoman life. Most importantly, almost all of the legal system and much of the education system were in the hands of the *ulema*, at least until the nineteenth century when some non-religious and non-Muslim institutions gained strength. In any case, the *ulema* along with the Sultan-Caliph had an essential role in shaping and promulgating Muslim orthodoxy throughout Ottoman history.

But, like the Sultan-Caliph, Atatürk and his government viewed the *ulema* as an impediment to Turkey's modernisation project, and they feared that the members of the *ulema* could serve as a potential source of opposition to the new government. In order to bring the *ulema* under control, the republican government abolished the office of the *Şeyhülislam*, the official head of the *ulema*, and closed down institutions over which the *ulema* had exerted extensive control. One especially important institution was the traditional Ottoman legal system, which had been based on *Shari'ah* (*şeriat* in Turkish). The word *Shari'ah* is often translated as 'Islamic law' in English, but *Shari'ah* is not a legal code in the Western sense. It is instead a process of interpreting foundational Muslim texts, such as the Qur'an and *hadith*. The interpretations that emerged historically from the various legal schools (*madhhabs*) provide guidance for proper, pious behaviour and ultimately seek to establish a just and peaceful moral society that conforms to God's will. The government of Atatürk rejected *Shari'ah* and the court system that depended on it and replaced it with secular legal codes – more specifically, with Italian penal codes and Swiss civil codes. The introduction of Swiss civil law was especially aimed at the secularisation of family law, enabling the state to enact reforms, such as the elimination of polygyny (permitted under *Shari'ah*) and making marriage a civil ceremony, not a religious one, as it had been before (Anscombe 2014: 188–9).

The republican government also eliminated the Ottoman *medrese* (school) system and replaced it with a new centralised public education system. To that end, the government created the 1924 Unity of Education law (*Tevhid-i Tedrisat Kanunu*), putting all education under the control of the new Ministry of Education, which developed a nationally unified curriculum to be shared by all students of the new nation. The Unity of Education law also made primary schooling universally compulsory for both boys and girls. In the Ottoman context, most education was directed towards boys – usually elite boys – who would take up positions in the bureaucracy. There had previously been some schools for girls, but the republican government emphasised the education of women (Zehra Hanım was able to take advantage of these new opportunities), though this emphasis was based on the assumption that women's education was necessary for bringing up educated and knowledgeable children (Gök 1995).[7]

Education was an essential way in which the Turkish state could push for a unified culture and ethnic identity that were supposed to define the new nation. Though the education ministry made some provisions for non-Muslim students, the Turkish identity promoted in the national curriculum was that of the Muslim Turk. The national curriculum was also created to instil a sense that all Muslims in Turkey are Turks who speak the Turkish language (Kaplan 2006: 39). This emphasis on Turkish ethnic nationalism denied the ethnic and linguistic distinctions of Turkey's substantial Kurdish population. In fact, the push to 'Turkify' the Kurds – that is, enforce on them a Turkish identity and language – has been a consistent feature of republican governance. The Treaty of Lausanne – the treaty that concluded the War of Independence against European forces and helped to establish the Turkish state – only recognised and extended some rights to non-Muslim minorities in Turkey. But because Kurds are primarily Muslim, the Treaty offered them no rights as a minority group (Oran 2007). The result has been that Kurds have been subject to a number of unwanted assimilation projects over time, including forced population movements (to dilute the concentrations of Kurds in any particular area), educational policies that deny the history of the Kurdish ethnic group, lack of political representation and severe restrictions on the use of Kurdish language, not only in publishing and broadcasting but privately too. Kurds have met this repression with a range of reactions from acquiescence to political engagement to armed conflict.

The Sufi orders

Beyond secularising government institutions, Turkey's secularisation project also involved the disbanding of the various Sufi brotherhoods (*Tarikats*) that had been popular throughout the history of the Ottoman Empire. 'Sufism' is a broad term referring to communities organised around charismatic religious leaders, some of whom promoted mystical engagement with the divine. While many of the orders were primarily focused on spiritual attainments and building community engagement, there had been certain important brotherhoods that were involved with political factions and sometimes even opposed the Sultan's power militarily. I will discuss the state of the Turkish Sufi orders and other religious communities in the twentieth century in Chapter 4. Suffice it to say here that after the establishment of the Republic, many Sufi orders had become sources of opposition to the secularising reforms of the Kemalists. So, Atatürk and his supporters came to see the brotherhoods in general as impediments to the secularisation and Westernisation of the new nation. Atatürk himself made repeated appeals to the general public to oppose the supposedly dangerous reactionary aspects of the *Tarikats*. He regularly appropriated religious discourse to argue for the relinquishment of the old ways for new ones (*Tarikat* literally means 'way'), thereby creating a sense that the goals of modernisation and science would replace the 'backwardness' of traditional religious practice as uniting forces in Turkish society. For example, Atatürk argued (in Lewis 1961: 405):

> The whole nation must know, and know well, that the Republic of Turkey cannot be the land of *şeyhs*, dervishes, disciples, and lay brothers. The straightest, truest Way (*Tarikat*) is the way of civilization. To be a man, it is enough to do what civilization requires. The heads of the brotherhoods will understand this truth that I have uttered in all its clarity, and will of their own accord at once close their convents, and accept the fact that their disciples have at last come of age.

The abolition of the Sufi orders not only entailed the closure of Sufi lodges (*tekke*), but also involved the shuttering of shrines (*türbe*) of Sufi saints, which had been the focus of much popular piety (though many remained open or reopened at later times). The reforms also targeted non-Sufi religious leaders. Imams, preachers and other teachers were forbidden from wearing religious clothing other than when performing religious duties, and traditional religious titles, such as *haci* (one who has been on the *hajj*), *hafiz* (one who has memorised the Qur'an) and *molla* (a highly ranked religious judge or theology teacher), were prohibited by a 1934 law. The 1938 'Law of Associations' made illegal the formation of independent societies based on religion, sect and *Tarikat*, as well as societies formed for the purposes of religious prayer and practice. That is, the government of Atatürk attempted to eliminate all popular forms of religious leadership and community, with the explicit goal of establishing centralised institutions that would promulgate an acceptable form of Islam that would 'not challenge state sovereignty or the state's governmental priorities' (Kocamaner 2019: 4).

To that end, the Turkish government established the Directorate of Religious Affairs (*Diyanet İşleri Başkanlığı* – the 'Diyanet' hereafter) as a bureaucratic division under the direct control of the Prime Ministry.[8] According to the 1924 law (No. 429) that established the Diyanet, the fundamental purpose of the directorate was to provide for the 'implementation of all provisions concerning faith and worship aspects of the religion of Islam, and the administration of religious institutions'.[9] The Diyanet was designed to replace the old Ottoman office of the Grand Mufti and was ideally supposed to create a centralised religious authority that could compete with the old Sufi brotherhoods. As we will see in Chapter 4, the Sufi communities proved to be too pervasive and popular to stamp out and would continue to function in modified forms throughout the history of modern Turkey into the present moment.

The Diyanet would eventually grow into a large and powerful branch of government, but during the early 'one-party' era, it was small and largely ineffectual. The one-party era (1923–46) is the period when Atatürk's Republican People's Party (RPP) controlled the government while suppressing voices of opposition. This exclusive control allowed the RPP to establish political, social and economic institutions and programmes that would shape the country according to Kemalist principles. Eventually, the government did allow opposition parties to form, as long as those parties did not stray far from Kemalist principles, such as secularism and nationalism. The Diyanet was not a priority for the RPP, who starved it of cash and personnel. For example, the government failed to provide an adequate system to train new religious professionals at the same time that Atatürk was disqualifying many of the traditional leaders who could lead prayers, bury the dead and educate the populace in Islamic knowledge. This led to such a severe shortage of religious personnel that citizens began to complain to state officials. Iren Ozgur (2012: 36–7) recounts that, by the 1940s,

> many people had begun to voice their grievances against the state for the lack of religious functionaries who could 'lead them in prayer' and 'bury their dead.' Hamdullah Suphi Tanrıöver, a member of government, brought these complaints to Parliament, when he read a letter that said: 'There is only one imam who serves six villages. We have to keep the bodies of the deceased waiting for days before the imam can come to bury them. If you do not send us more imams, the bodies of our dead will decompose in the open like those of animals.'[10]

This shortage only began to be resolved with the advent of multi-party politics in 1946 when competing political candidates had to win over voters with policy proposals that would satisfy the needs and aspirations of different groups of citizens. One especially powerful voting group that politicians had to appeal to was the large rural population, which had been long neglected by the RPP government in favour of the urban bureaucratic elite who benefited from the

Westernising Kemalist reforms. As Banu Eligür noted (2010: 50), the government's economic policies of the one-party era

> made the government deeply unpopular among the large majority of Turkish
> citizens by the end of World War II. The rural population did not see any great
> improvement in their standard of living with respect, e.g., to health, education,
> infrastructure, or communications.

Moreover, the rural peasantry felt alienated by the secularist policies of the
RPP, such as the requirement that the call to prayer be broadcast in Turkish
rather than the traditional Arabic. New politicians who emerged after 1946
loosened some of the restrictions on religious practice and education and established institutions within and alongside the Diyanet to produce more religious
officials to serve the needs of the population. Yet, as we will see in future
chapters, these state institutions remained dedicated to producing a particular
type of Islam that served the needs of the secular state in creating a modern
and rational society.

On the surface, the idea that a secular state takes upon itself the promotion of
religion can seem paradoxical. But secularism takes many forms, and as Turkish
political scientist Ahmet Kuru (2009) has suggested, we can analyse secularism
in Turkey according to its place on a spectrum from passive to assertive forms
of secularism. Secularism in the United States, for example, is relatively passive
in that it presumes that the government should maintain neutrality towards
religion, and it strives (at least ideally) for a separation of 'church and state'.
Turkish secularism is 'assertive secularism', or what is known as 'laicism' (after
laïcité in French). This is a form of governance in which religion is not free from
the state but is directly under its control. A central idea of laicism is that religion
should not be in the hands of a powerful and independent clerical elite that can
rival government power, as the *ulema* had during the Ottoman Empire. Rather,
religious institutions should be subordinated to the non-religious (*laicist*) state,
where they no longer pose a potential threat to government hegemony (Davison
2003: 341). As such, Turkish secularism – or laicism – does not make assumptions of religious neutrality or objectivity in the public sphere; instead, religion is
legally subordinated to the political establishment. The Turkish state controlled
the exercise of public religion primarily through the institution of the Diyanet.

Furthermore, Atatürk and his supporters distrusted certain aspects of religious practice, such as the Sufi orders and the conservative *ulema*, because these
elements could impede and disrupt the early state's modernisation agenda. Still,
many republican leaders saw Islam as playing an essential role in creating a
unified national identity, especially after existential crises, such as the collapse
of the Ottoman Empire, created a need for national solidarity and strength.
The republican government dealt with its ambivalence towards Islam by extol-
ling and celebrating Islam as part of national identity while simultaneously

controlling public religious practices and religious education to ensure that Turkey's Islam conformed to the Kemalist agenda. As Anscombe put it (2014: 188):

> The fundamental content of Turkishness thus did not really change from the religious element that had shaped Ottoman identity, but the practical import of the relabeling of religious as national identity was great. The state would henceforth be the only permitted channel for the expression of the identity and would police aggressively all alternative paths for formation and demonstration of social awareness. Atatürk's republic nationalized Islam.

How has the Kemalist state, through the Diyanet, defined proper, 'permitted' Islam? Basically, the Turkish state has followed Western European practices by promoting the notion that religion can be separated out from other types of social activities, including politics, which allows for the creation of supposedly neutral, non-religious public spaces and institutions (Asad 2003). In the case of Turkey, a laicist public sphere is one in which the state has the power to curtail and sometimes prohibit unauthorised Islamic symbols and practices. Such an interpretation of Islam rests on the assumption that there is one essential, apolitical Islam that the state appropriately articulates and enforces through policy and practice. Other religious practices are deemed in violation of Turkish secularism, and the state, especially the military and judiciary, has established itself as a protector of secularism, and therefore has the right to limit these practices in the public sphere. To be fair, the Turkish state has largely left people to practise religion as they please, but it has sometimes stepped in to curtail practices that seem politically problematic – the closing of the Sufi orders is a case in point. In any case, Kemalist officials can claim that religious freedom is maintained in Turkey because they are not necessarily condemning the unauthorised practices altogether, but are simply excluding them from the public realm. The practices may be performed in the privacy of the family home or to some extent in designated places of worship, so that they do no harm to the secular political order. As we will see, the state's attempt to establish a particular type of Islam in the public sphere in Turkey has been somewhat successful, but there has been consistent pushback from many different segments of the Turkish population regarding religious affairs. The relationship between state policy and popular expressions of Islamic belief will be an important topic in this book.

Disenchanting daily life

The Kemalist reforms not only disestablished religion from the political arena and removed the *ulema* from state bureaucracy, but they also emphasised the secularisation of daily life and the transformation of gender roles and relations in Turkish society. The reforms were numerous and often quite dramatic, but they tended to affect different segments of Turkish society to different extents. That is, citizens accepted, accommodated, negotiated or ignored the reforms according to their own needs, situations and desires, as Hale Yılmaz has made clear (2013). What I want to demonstrate here is that the Kemalist reforms endeavoured to reorganise space and time in ways that explicitly worked to secularise and Westernise the Turkish public sphere while simultaneously trying to create 'modern' worldviews in Turkey's citizens.

Reorganisation of time

Until the nineteenth century, the Ottoman Empire used the traditional Islamic calendar[11] to accommodate religious holidays and events, and to coordinate state activities. But because the Islamic calendar is lunar, the months move backward through the solar year and have little relationship to seasons, which made organising modern economic activities cumbersome, especially modern forms of tax collection. As far back as the late eighteenth century, Ottoman reformers attempted to create a hybrid lunar-solar calendar for state use, but it wasn't until 1916 that the Ottoman government decided to use the European Gregorian calendar for affairs of government while leaving the Islamic calendar for religious affairs. One effect of this shift was the adoption of the Western 'weekend', with Sunday as the day of rest, even though the weekly holy day in Islam is Friday. This meant that while civil servants, students and other workers often had Saturday and Sunday off, they had to take time out of their Friday work or school day to attend Friday communal prayers and the weekly sermon. Similarly, telling time was secularised when the state adopted the Greenwich clock as its standard in 1926, though the five daily calls to prayer still follow the traditional Islamic time schedule based on the movement of the sun in the sky. In both the calendar and telling the time, the state separated secular and religious time; the state functionally adhered to the former and religious activities followed the latter.

These changes had significant effects on the regimentation of work and leisure in urban and provincial contexts, especially for those engaged with the administrative and educational institutions of the republican state. But for those living in rural areas and engaged in agricultural labour, the official reorganisation of time had only minimal effects, at least during the first few decades of the new state. Turkish farmers traditionally followed the seasons – and not a calendar – to manage the annual planting and harvesting of crops, the births of animals and so on. In villages, weddings and circumcision ceremonies and other lifecycle rituals might not take place in 'June' (a calendric unit) but 'after the planting' or 'after the harvest', that is, according to the rhythms of agriculture. Similarly, the hours of the clock would be less important than the movement of the sun across the zenith. Farmers would rise at first light for the morning prayers (that is, according to Islamic time) and begin the day's labour soon after.

They would perform the necessary tasks – ploughing, hoeing, milking, cooking and so on – until those tasks were completed for the day, stopping to pray, rest or socialise according to custom. So many aspects of rural life would have been left untouched by the reforms in timekeeping. Still, some aspects of the reforms did leave their mark on Turkish villagers, especially through institutions of education, taxation and – later – national media, especially radio and television.

Another way in which the Turkish Republic tried to reorganise and create secularised time was to 'invent' national secular holidays and festivals that were celebrated alongside the religious holidays. The most important traditional religious holidays are still recognised and promoted by the state. The two major Muslim festivals, *Ramazan Bayramı* (Ramadan Festival; Arabic: *Eid al-Fitr*)[12] and *Kurban Bayramı* (the feast of sacrifice; Arabic: *Eid al-Adha*),[13] are official state holidays in modern Turkey, and schools and public offices are closed during these times as people travel to gather with their families to celebrate the holy days. The state mosques also recognise other minor religious holidays, such as *Kandil* nights (five Islamic holy nights relating to the life of the Prophet Muhammad) and provide special religious programming on those days as well.

As part of building a modern secular nation, the early Turkish state established new national holidays that fell on particular dates in the Western calendar. For example, in 1927 Atatürk established 23 April as National Sovereignty and Children's Day, and 29 October became Republic Day (*Cumhuriyet Bayramı*), which commemorates the declaration of the Republic on 29 October 1923. Hale Yılmaz has pointed out that this invention of tradition helped to create and maintain 'a collective historical memory and a shared identity. By marking important moments in the recent, or distant, past of the nation, they [the national holidays] provide an opportunity to remember those events collectively and interpret them in a national context' (2013: 180). The republican government designed these and other national holidays to be inclusive and participatory, though the holidays often emphasised Muslim Turkish identity over other religious or ethnic identities. For the Turkish majority, these national observances are still very popular and widely celebrated.

The Alphabet revolution, language reform and a re-imagined past

As early as 1851, Ottoman reformers proposed that the Arabic script of Ottoman Turkish be converted to a Latin-based (or even Cyrillic-based) alphabet to make it easier to learn to write and to boost literacy rates. But such a dramatic change met with a lot of resistance, some of which was based on religious concerns (Lewis 1999: 28–30). For many Ottoman Turks the use of the Arabic script connected the Turkish language to the Arabic language of the Qur'an, even though Turkish and Arabic are unrelated languages. Arabic was – and still is – seen as a language with divine significance, and turning away from its beautiful written form suggested a degree of impiety. Moreover, critics of the reform efforts

Figure 1.3 Schoolchildren dressed for a folk dancing performance on National Sovereignty and Children's Day, Istanbul, 1998; behind the children is a portrait of Atatürk with the text of his 'Speech to the Youth' on one side and the text of the Turkish national anthem (İstiklal Marşı) on the other (photograph by author)

argued that the change from Arabic script to Latin script represented a turn towards Christianity and a denial of Turkish Muslim history.

The many reforms that were introduced after the establishment of the Turkish Republic included a revived effort at alphabet reform. Atatürk and his supporters believed that the Arabic alphabet used to write Ottoman Turkish was a difficult script that emphasised class divisions, since it took years of study to learn the script – something available only to the elite. Based on the arguments of sociologist Ziya Gökalp, Atatürk claimed that the alphabet and language reforms were a healthy renunciation of the cultural heritage of the Ottoman elite – including their script and classical languages – in favour of a system of writing and language that would be accessible to all classes of society. The alphabet reform had other political goals as well: the transition to Latin letters would also make the language of the Qur'an less accessible to the Turkish masses, further signifying the secularising aspects of the language reform process (Lewis 1999: 153). And the reformers openly discussed the fact that they saw the adoption of the Latin script as an opportunity to align Turkey with the West and away from its identification with Islam and the Middle East (Lewis 1999: 40).

Atatürk himself worked with others to develop a Latin-based alphabet for Turkish, which was introduced in 1928 and was taught in the new public school system. Atatürk also took part in the education efforts to spread knowledge of the new script to the people, going before various audiences to demonstrate the use of the Latin letters (Lewis 1999: 30–8). Kemalists spread out into the provinces to teach the alphabet – as we saw in the oral history at the beginning of this chapter, Zehra Hanım learned the new alphabet at that time and was one of the teachers of the new writing system in her provincial town of Safranbolu. Even as the new alphabet was introduced in Turkey's reformed educational system, use of the old script was allowed to persist until 1930, though some citizens continued to use it well beyond the 1930 deadline (Yılmaz 2011).

The Kemalists also took up the Young Ottoman and Young Turk project of removing Arabic and Persian words and grammatical structures from the Turkish languages. In 1932, Atatürk established the Turkish Society for the Study of Language (*Türk Dil Kurumu*), which was charged with purifying the language by creating Turkish neologisms to replace the expunged words. Also in 1932, the Diyanet ordered all mosques to broadcast the call to prayer (*ezan*) not in the canonical Arabic but in Turkish (Lewis 1999: 45–7). This radical break with Muslim orthodoxy sparked considerable resentment and protest, which was sometimes violently suppressed. When the *ezan* was again permitted to be broadcast in Arabic in in the 1950s, people openly rejoiced to hear the old sounds (Toprak 1981: 79).

One effect of the alphabet and language reforms is that present-day Turks cannot read historical documents or monuments created before the reforms (that is, prior to 1928 or so) unless they are especially trained in Ottoman Turkish. The language reforms created a 'nation of forgetters' (Toprak 1981: 42) in that they made it difficult for the average citizen to access Turkey's common Ottoman past. This national 'amnesia' was deliberately created and gave Atatürk and the reformers the opportunity to change the reference and meaning of Turkish heritage. Rather than emphasise the Ottoman past, Atatürk extolled the pre-Islamic Turkish past as a more genuine basis of national identity. Atatürk and other nationalists rewrote Turkey's pre-Islamic history, creating an elaborate set of national myths extending far back in time. For example, they propagated the ethnic nationalist idea that the indigenous inhabitants of Anatolia were always ethnically Turkish, so that when the Turkoman tribes intermixed with these people in the period of early migration from the Abbasid Empire and Central Asia, they were merely mixing with their ethnic brethren. The Turks, in other words, were 'purely' Turk, with not a trace of the Greek, Armenian, Arab (and so on) mixing that might have happened during the multi-ethnic Ottoman period. This is an interesting example of the re-imagining of history that takes place in nationalist movements, in which the nationalism 'takes pre-existing cultures and turns them into nations, sometimes invents them, and often obliterates pre-existing cultures' (Hobsbawm 1990: 110).

This national mythology was accompanied by an equally intense form of linguistic jingoism that was embodied in the so-called 'Sun-Language Theory' (*Güneş-Dil Teorisi*). In this doctrine, the Turkish nationalists argued that all ancient civilisations and languages, most notably those of the Hittites and Sumerians, originated in Central Asia and were ultimately based on primitive Turkic society and language. These Central Asians had spread out into Anatolia, Europe and Northern Africa to form the great civilisations of history. Thus, the languages of these civilisations were precursors to modern Turkish, and Turkish could be seen as the language that binds all languages.[14] The languages and cultures of Anatolia and Europe were just derivatives of an imagined original Turkish culture. These nationalist ideologies reconciled the incompatible goals of Westernisation (looking to Europe as a model for the new nation) and Turkish nationalism. It justified Westernisation by arguing that Western civilisation has its real roots in Turkic Central Asia. In essence, Atatürk not only promoted the Orientalist view that Westernisation was the only viable method of modernisation, but he also created an ideology in which Westernisation was, in the end, a return to 'genuine' Turkish roots that the Ottoman Empire had obscured (Toprak 1981:42–3). Historians outside and inside Turkey criticised these nationalist myths as lacking any foundation in evidence, and the myths eventually faded away, especially the Sun-Language Theory.

Clothing reforms
In creating a modern state, the administration of the new Republic sought to change the appearances of their citizens to match their imagined national goals. The Ottoman Empire had long regulated clothing, though these 'regulations generally served to reinforce or maintain existing ethnic, religious, gender or social distinctions by making those differences visible in dress' (Yilmaz 2013: 23). But the early republican clothing reforms encouraged Turks to wear European-style clothing with the hope that such changes would help create a

unified Turkish population that would 'erode old social and communal distinctions and . . . create and promote new social distinctions and identities' (Yilmaz 2013). Because the reforms represented the state's effort to create a new type of citizenry, they were largely top-down efforts, in that the leadership either established laws and regulations determining what Turks should wear or they exerted a great deal of social and political pressure to ensure conformity to European clothing practices.

One of the most consequential of the republican clothing reforms was the 'Law on the Wearing of the Hat' (*Şapka İktisâsı Hakkında Kanun*) passed on 25 November 1925, which required male citizens to forfeit what had come to be considered the 'traditional' fez in favour of Western-style hats. Though the fez had been a part of the traditional Turkish male wardrobe only since 1829,[15] by the early twentieth century it had come to signify the wearer's allegiance to Islam and to the Ottoman imperial past. The 1925 Hat Law elicited objections from many pious Muslims since the newly required hats had rims that prevented the worshipper from touching his head to the ground during daily prayers, as required by Muslim tradition. In fact, for Muslims, 'to wear a hat' (*şapka giymek*) had been an idiomatic expression that meant to apostatise and become a Christian, and even in the late nineteenth century, the sight of a brimmed hat could provoke a hostile reaction among Muslims (Norton 1997: 158).

Atatürk began the hat reform by banishing the fez from the military uniform and then conducted a political-type campaign for the brimmed hat. On 24 August 1925, for example, he attacked the fez in a famous speech in the conservative province of Kastamonu, and, four days later, in the port town of Inebolu, he continued his campaign to 'civilize' Turkish appearance (Lewis, in Norton 1997: 159–60):

> A civilized, international dress is worthy and appropriate for our nation, and we will wear it. Boots or shoes on our feet, trousers on our legs, shirt and tie, jacket and waistcoat – and, of course, to complete these, a cover with a brim on our heads. I want to make this clear. This headcovering is called 'hat'.

There were many who willingly accepted the change in headgear, especially supporters of the Kemalist reforms. Others put up resistance, even in the face of potential punishment for non-conformity. But, as Yılmaz has described in detail (2013: 22–77), the impact of the Hat Law was uneven, since some men found ways to adapt to the laws by wearing berets, while others lived in areas where enforcement of the Hat Law was weak or non-existent.

Just as men's clothing had received significant attention by the authorities of the early Republic, women's clothing – particularly the veil – also became an object of the reform campaigns. Women's veils were never formally outlawed, though various laws banning the veil were sometimes proposed in the early republican era. Instead, there was a great deal of propaganda directed at discouraging the use of the veil, which was linked to 'uncivilised' Muslim tradition. The Republican propaganda initiatives encouraged women to wear Western clothing by publishing images of women in 'appropriate' modern clothes (including revealing bathing suits), thus linking the 'new' woman to the creation of a new nation that was revolutionarily different from its Ottoman-Islamic predecessor (Çınar 2005: 59–67; Yilmaz 2013: 78–101). In fact, one way that the Kemalist media sought to project Turkey's new secular modernity to the outside world was by encouraging Turkish women to compete in national and international beauty contests (Shissler 2004).

Creating the new Turkish citizen

The most striking aspect of all these Kemalist reforms – secularisation of educa-tion and the government institutions, the reorganisation of time and reforms in language and clothing – is how the dispositions, practices and lifestyles of ordi-nary Turkish citizens were under the scrutiny of the state. Indeed, the bodies of the Turkish people became – and still are in many ways – the ultimate signifiers of the success or failure of Turkey's Westernisation efforts. From the Hat Law to the state's active encouragement of women to unveil, the Turkish republican establishment showed consistent interest in and some degree of power over the bodies of its citizens. Certain signs of religion, such as the veil, were to be dele-gated to the private sphere and to places of worship where it would not interfere with Turkish 'material life and worldly concerns' (Mardin 1982: 179–80). In the space of a few decades, the reformers carved out a secular sphere at the expense of public religious practices, a process of secularisation that took place over many generations in Europe. This demonstrates that Kemalist Westernisation was not an organic process of reform by which values and social priorities shifted gradually. Rather, the reforms represented the new government's top-down civi-lisational project 'by which local patterns and traditional values are dismissed and devalorized . . . [and] local Islam, which is considered alien to rationalist and positivist values, is expelled' in favour of the universalist claims and goals of 'civilization' (Göle 1996: 132–3).

As Alev Çınar has argued (2005), though, the secularisation project was not only aimed at transforming the appearances of the citizenry and of the public sphere to indicate the state's modernity. Rather, by encouraging Turks to partake in particular bodily displays, practices and language use, the state was also attempting to transform the citizens' subjective experience of national iden-tity. By making people appear modern, the hope was that they would also feel modern and personally invested in Turkey's modernisation project. To some extent, this transformation was successful in that Turkey established a secularist elite who dominated in Turkey's major institutions – such as the civil service, education and the military – into the twenty-first century. Yet there were many sectors of the Turkish population who were less committed to and/or affected by the secularising reforms of the early Republic, while others openly repudiated the reforms. For example, the promotion of Turkish ethnic identity over all others led to rebellions in Kurdish areas of eastern Turkey. Some members of the religious and political opposition, which had been harshly suppressed, attempted assassinations and coups against Atatürk and his regime. At least one violent rebellion against the religious reforms occurred in western Anatolia, which was quickly suppressed by the ever-strengthening state.

But for most citizens of Turkey outside the urban areas, the effects of the reforms were less pronounced and dramatic than might be supposed. Residents of smaller provincial towns and the rural peasantry would have experienced the reforms through the lens of the local government and elites, some of which did not change dramatically in the republican era (Meeker 2002). In many places, prohibited religious activities and language practices continued, often with only minor changes, while new religious movements grew in response to the needs of the rapidly developing society. Certainly, there have been enduring tensions between the Turkish state's civilisational projects and various sectors of Turkish society. As we will see in later chapters, the citizens of Turkey have responded to state reform programmes in different ways, by accommodating, resisting against or compromising with them as circumstances permit.

Notes

1. This narrative has been edited for space and clarity.
2. These three surahs (78, 67 and 36) are especially popular as a group since they provide an overview of life and one's destiny. They are commonly recited at funerals.
3. It was in 1928 that the Turkish government initiated the Alphabet Reform, when a reformed Latin alphabet replaced the Arabic script that had been used to write Ottoman Turkish. See below.
4. In contemporary Turkish, the word *millet* means 'nation' or 'national people'.
5. Those non-Muslim populations that remained within the empire – including Jews, Greeks and Armenians – have formally had full equal rights in the Turkish Republic, though they have often suffered from discrimination.
6. Ankara had previously been a relatively unimportant town, but its insignificance meant that the new republican government could 'start from scratch' and create a modern planned city to fit the needs of the new political order.
7. While the 1924 law required that all boys and girls be educated at primary level, enforcement was often spotty. Girls in particular often lacked schooling and had lower rates of literacy compared to boys, a situation that improved somewhat over the course of the twentieth century.
8. The fact that the Diyanet was a branch of the Prime Ministry rather than a separate ministry allowed the state to maintain direct control over religious authority, rather than letting it function as an independent political entity that could more easily challenge the executive branch.
9. Available on the English version of the Diyanet website, at http://www.diyanet.gov.tr/en-

US/. The Turkish-language version of the website is much more extensive and interactive than the English version, and the Turkish site assumes that the reader already has basic knowledge of Islam.

10. According to Muslim tradition, the dead should be buried as soon as possible, preferably within twenty-four hours of death.

11. The Islamic calendar is a lunar calendar that starts with 622 CE as year 1. The year 622 CE is the year of the *hijra*, that is, the migration of the Prophet Muhammad and the Muslim community from Mecca to Medina.

12. *Ramadan Bayramı* is held at the end of Ramadan to celebrate the ending of the fast. It is also known as *Şeker Bayramı* (sugar festival) because it is a custom to visit friends and relatives who offer sweets to their guests.

13. *Kurban Bayramı* is held at the end of the period of the hajj when an animal is sacrificed and the meat is eaten and distributed to relatives and to the poor.

14. See Chapters 4 and 5 of Lewis (1999).

15. Sultan Mahmud II had decreed in 1829 that the fez should replace the turban as a way to minimise the difference between Muslims and non-Muslims.

CHAPTER 2

Sunni Islam in Turkey: institutions and practices

The Diyanet's annual Ramadan book sale, Ankara 1999

Every year during Ramadan, the Diyanet Endowment[1] (*Türkiye Diyanet Vakfı*) hosts a religious book and education fair in some of the large urban mosques – Sultan Ahmet (the Blue Mosque) in Istanbul and Kocatepe mosque in Ankara. In January 1999 I attended the Kocatepe fair with five young women from the Qur'an course I observed. The fair was in an open courtyard, and it was exposed to the harsh winter weather except for a rather flimsy transparent 'roof' over the yard designed to protect the book stands from the frequent rains. This set-up meant that it was not much warmer inside the fair than outside, and the cold was exacerbated by the fact that the floor and walls were marble, which seemed to absorb the cold and kept the air from warming.

We roamed stalls together, and my companions all studied the offerings very carefully. The book fair was quite large as many publishing houses and magazines had representative booths in the fair, and the Diyanet featured many of its own publications and products. I saw some software that recites the Qur'an and for learning Qur'anic Arabic, and software featuring the sermons of preacher Fethullah Gülen, among other things. I bought a book about women from the booth of the women's auxiliary (*kadın kolu*) of the Diyanet. My friends bought posters and pictures as well as books, though I didn't really get a good look at the kind of books that they got. I know that the Qur'an course *hoca* (teacher), Meryam, bought a book about appropriate prayers for sickness. Hande was looking for a small Qur'an for a friend and she bought some books of prayer – one in Arabic, one in Turkish – for herself. She also bought an anti-evolution (creationist) book, a book that is associated with a conference that travels around the country. I have seen this conference – about the anti-religious motives behind the propagation of the theory of evolution – advertised in the religious newspapers.

Meryam had been looking for the books of certain authors, and she thought the authors were banned from the fair for espousing an interpretation of religion not supported by the Diyanet. She said that she had heard that Abdurrahman Dilipak (a columnist for the conservative *Akit* newspaper – now called *Yeni Akit*) and some other authors were banned and she wanted to find out about them.

Figure 2.1 Kocatepe mosque in Ankara (photograph by author)

She confronted the Diyanet Endowment director running the fair, asking why those authors weren't available and if the government had banned them. I had a hard time understanding the director's response since his voice was low and blended in with the sound of the electric heater that kept his office warm. What I could tell – and what Meryem later explained to me – was that the director said that it was not that the government had banned the authors in question, but rather that the Endowment had ordered that certain books not be sold. The man stressed that the Endowment was separate from the government. Meryem commented that the books had been available the previous year, and the man replied only that many things had changed since the previous year. He commented that people must be careful and bend with the times. It was not the policy of the fair itself to ban these books, but it was a temporary decision of the Endowment that set up the fair. Meryem was not very satisfied with this contradictory answer but she left it there. She had frequently complained about the state's attempt to control religious ideas, and she was not convinced that the Endowment was that separate from Diyanet (and state) management.

We later ran into a vendor with whom Meryem discussed the problem of the missing books. This vendor complained that the previous year they had been able to sell those books and he didn't understand why they couldn't be sold that year. He wanted to make sure that we knew that the books were available outside the fair, even if they were banned from the fair. He gave us a publishing list from his company. I asked him to mark the books that were not allowed to be sold that year, and he accommodated me. These included several books by Dilipak, as well as other famously conservative authors. Afterwards, the women and I went to the women's section of the Kocatepe mosque for noon prayers.

The Diyanet (Directorate of Religious Affairs)

One of the most important aspects of the Kemalist reforms is the establishment of modern Turkey as a laicist state. This means that rather than trying to build a wall of separation between religion and governance, Turkey instead sought to subordinate religion to the needs of the state by establishing state institutions that manage and regulate public Islamic practice. The most important of these institutions is the Diyanet (Directorate of Religious Affairs, introduced in Chapter 1) and state-mandated programmes of religious education. These institutions establish official religious doctrine, promote particular types of Sunni Muslim practice and disseminate 'official Islam' through channels of education, media production and the regulation of religious institutions, such as mosques. To be clear, most religious practices actually occur in private homes or in local communities and are conducted according to individual or family traditions and desires. (There are also religious organisations called *cemaat* that have a large presence in Turkish religious life – these will be discussed in greater detail in Chapter 4.) Even so, the Turkish state has long been involved in establishing frameworks and norms by which many Turkish citizens evaluate and engage in Muslim beliefs and practices. This chapter will explore in greater depth the state-citizen 'interface' regarding Sunni Islamic experience in the years since the founding of the Turkish Republic.

Throughout its history, the Diyanet has had the mandate to maintain and staff mosques and provide the basic training and employment of personnel to fulfil religious roles, such as prayer leaders (imams), preachers (*hatips*) and provincial religious leaders (muftis). As mentioned in the last chapter, the Diyanet was largely neglected during the early years of the Republic, as developing religious institutions and services was not a priority for the Kemalist government that remained in power until 1950. But, over time, the potential 'uses' of the Diyanet became increasingly clear to successive governments, and it was strengthened and expanded accordingly. One important ideological function the Diyanet has served has been to promote a particular type of religion, namely, Hanafi[2] Sunni Islam, over and against types of Islam that the Turkish state has considered unorthodox, too radical or otherwise dangerous to the unity and secular composition of the Turkish nation. The responsibility of the Diyanet to promote 'proper Islam' was certainly part of its original mandate, but the role became especially salient after Turkey's first military coup in 1960. This coup brought down the Democrat Party (DP), which had been the first political party to win national elections in 1950 in the multi-party era. While the DP was based on Kemalist principles – most of its leaders, including prime minister Adnan Menderes, had been members of Atatürk's Republican People's Party (RPP) – the DP was more liberal in its attitudes towards popular religious practice than many traditional Kemalists liked. For example, in 1950 the DP government permitted the call of prayer to return to Arabic, to great fanfare, and the decade of its rule saw a significant acceleration in mosque construction. Religious instruction became almost compulsory (students had to opt out of religion classes rather than opt in, as had been the case with classes introduced in 1949). Moreover, the DP was more accepting of autonomous (non-state) religious organisations and cultivated alliances with the officially illegal but still active Sufi brotherhoods in order to attract more support from brotherhood followers. In response to the DP's relaxation of laicist policies, coupled with the party's increasing authoritarianism and failing economic policies, the military launched a successful coup in 1960. Several leaders of the party, including Menderes, were executed and the DP was shut down.

One outcome of the coup was that the interim military government stipulated that the Turkish constitution be rewritten. Among many other things, the new 1961 constitution provided for the restructuring of the Diyanet and clarified its functions, many of which have remained in place to the present, though with expanded duties. The law that reorganised the Diyanet was ratified in 1965 and articulated a role for the Diyanet to unify Turkish society around 'proper' Sunni Islam. The law specifically charged the Diyanet with taking 'protective measures that maintain the loyalty of Muslim citizens to the national ideals' (Adanali 2008: 230). Furthermore, the law encouraged the recruitment of religious intellectuals who would

> have competence in scholarly studies on various religious topics and use the results of their studies to serve and enlighten society, and thus solidify the unity and integrity of the nation in matters of faith and moral principles by removing

bigotry and superstition, which were not permitted by the religion of Islam.
(Erdem 2008: 209)

That is, the role of all the personnel in the Diyanet has been *irşad* – the
propagation of 'sound knowledge' of Islam as defined by the Diyanet over and
against other widespread practices that the framers of the law thought might
threaten the supposed homogeneity of Turkish society (Bardakoğlu 2008: 178).
To that end, the new law established a division of the Diyanet to produce
publications and broadcasts on religious matters for its own personnel and
for the general public. In fact, the Diyanet has been very prolific, publishing
books, magazines, recorded media and other materials to promote a standard
Sunni Islam for the Turkish public. Diyanet bookshops became (and still are)
a common feature of many cities and towns, and the Diyanet regularly held
book and media fairs, such as the one mentioned in the opening vignette.
These fairs feature the Diyanet's own publications, as well as books and other
material published elsewhere but meeting the Diyanet's standard of 'sound
knowledge' about Islam. As is evident from Maryam's questioning of the book
fair organiser, not every publication with Islamic content meets the Diyanet's
standard, and as such the Diyanet does not promote views that the directory
considers to be 'unsound'.

Besides the publication division of the Diyanet, the 1965 law established
other new departments to oversee various dimensions of religious life in Turkey.
Some of these continued previous duties of the Diyanet, such as managing
mosques and producing sermons to be read on Fridays, as well as training and
assigning positions for imams and preachers. Among the new departments, one
was set up to supervise the production of the Qur'an to assure that all published
Qur'ans were accurate according to conventional standards (all official Qur'ans
in Turkey are still stamped with the blue seal of the Diyanet). Another department established accurate religious practice by carrying out such functions as
determining prayer times and sacred days.[3] Other departments provide for the
religious education of Diyanet personnel, manage the pilgrimage (*hajj* and *umrah*
– see below) and oversee aspects of the feast of the sacrifice (*Kurban Bayramı*). The
new law also required the formation of a 'Higher Board of Religious Affairs', an
advisory committee to the Diyanet composed of distinguished religious scholars,
both men and women. Its main function was to address religious questions
put to it by members of the Turkish public and issue answers (*fetvas*) to those
questions.[4] Finally, an entire division of the Diyanet provided religious support
to Turks living abroad (Erdem 2008: 209). The Diyanet still offers all of these
services – and more – to the Turkish public.

Another essential service that the Diyanet provides is delivering courses on
the Qur'an and religion to the wider public, usually in the context of neighbourhood mosques. Such 'Qur'an courses' had been available since the founding

of the republic, but in the early years, teachers of these courses often had little formal religious training. The 1965 laws that reorganised the Diyanet provided for the professionalisation of Diyanet personnel, requiring that they have either a diploma from a religious (*imam-hatip*) secondary school or a university degree from a faculty of theology. Over time, personnel at all levels of Diyanet hierarchy have become more educated and more highly credentialled, at the same time that the Diyanet grew in size and importance.

The 1980 coup and the 'Turkish-Islamic Synthesis'

Turkey experienced another military coup in 1980, which deeply affected state institutions, including the Diyanet, and transformed the relationship between religion and politics in Turkey for years to come. The 1970s had been a time of political rivalries between leftists (including communist and socialist groups) and rightists (including ultranationalists and religious conservatives), and these rivalries turned into increasingly pervasive and violent conflicts. Because the successive governments of the 1970s proved unable to quell the violence, the military took over the government in 1980. The post-coup military government was headed by the National Security Council (NSC) – created after the 1960 coup – under the leadership of General Kenan Evren (1917–2015). This government tried to wipe the political slate clean by outlawing all political parties and arresting large numbers of political activists on both sides of the political divide, though they came down much more harshly on the leftists.

Turkey's institutions of power, most especially the military (a member of NATO and ally with Western powers), were strongly anti-communist and took repeated steps to suppress communist and even left-leaning elements in society. After the 1980 coup, General Evren and other military leaders embraced an ideology developed in the 1970s, the 'Turkish-Islamic Synthesis' (*Türk İslam Sentezi*), that emphasised justice, morality and the notion of Turks as defenders of the Muslim faith. This ideology served to combat the communist and socialist movements that had arisen in the turmoil of the 1970s (Zürcher 2004: 288). It also continued Atatürk's earlier strategy of using religion as a way in which to unite the Turkish people in the face of internal or external threats, such as the Turkish communist groups that sympathised with the neighbouring Soviet Union. It was under the auspices of the Turkish-Islamic Synthesis that the government made religious instruction mandatory in all schools. The courses emphasised Sunni morality, love of family and country, and the notion that support of state and army was a religious duty (see also Altınay 2004).

The Diyanet became another important purveyor of the Turkish-Islamic Synthesis. Article 136 of the 1982 constitution (the constitution was once again rewritten after a coup, as it had been after the 1960 coup) stipulated that the Diyanet was to 'exercise its duties prescribed in its particular law, in accordance with the principles of secularism, removed from all political views and ideas, and aiming at national solidarity and integrity'. In other words, the religious principles transmitted by the Diyanet were to serve the needs of the state. What this meant in concrete terms was that the Diyanet continued to be responsible for Qur'an courses and Friday sermons but increased its course offerings. Between 1983 and 1990, the Diyanet taught approximately 135 Qur'an courses each year, educating almost a million students. One minister from the Motherland Party, Kazım Oksay, stated that 'these courses aimed at teaching the religion and raising children who would be loyal citizens of the state, democracy, and the secular republic' (in Eligür 2010: 125) – that is, they promoted the goals of the Turkish-Islamic Synthesis. My friend Meryam and the other women who visited the Diyanet book sale described above had all been students at various Diyanet Qur'an courses made available at their local mosques. They appreciated the fact that the Diyanet provided at least basic religious services to local communities, but some of them also complained that the courses lacked depth and the instructors did not always seem knowledgeable. To compensate for this lack, my friends would attend sermons by religious leaders functioning outside of the Diyanet system, which was technically not permitted, but popular in any case. I will discuss this more in Chapter 4.

At the same time the Diyanet expanded its course offerings, it increased its publications of religious books and journals, not only to promote the Turkish-Islamic Synthesis but also to provide an imagined moral compass during a time of rapid social changes that took place in the 1980s and 1990s. One significant change was the opening up of the media; in particular, the number of television channels and offerings increased dramatically. Until the early 1980s, there was only one government-controlled broadcast television channel in Turkey, but regulations loosened so that by the late 1980s, Turks had access to multiple public and private channels from within Turkey and from abroad. The Diyanet tried to cut through the media noise with increased print publications, as well as television, radio and eventually internet programming of its own. According to a former head of the Diyanet Publications Department, Yüksel Salman, these publications were geared towards the 'enlightenment of society through accurate knowledge that is based on authentic sources', among other things (Salman 2008: 319). The focus of the Diyanet's 'enlightenment', as promulgated through its courses, sermons and publications, was on enhancing faith, worship and morality as human experiences distinct from politics and law.

Religious Culture and Ethics courses in the national curriculum

Another major way in which Turkish citizens encounter official religious doctrine is through Religious Culture and Ethics courses that are mandated for all students in the educational system. Religious education classes have been part of the Turkish state-school curricula for most of the history of the Republic. Only during the period of one-party rule (1938–46) were the religion courses outlawed, but with the 'opening' provided by the turn to multi-party politics, the courses were reintroduced first as voluntary courses in the primary schools in 1949. Later, in 1956, the Ministry of Education added optional religion courses in the middle schools, though it was not until 1967 that optional religion courses were available at high-school level (Kaymakcan 2006: 450). By the 1960s, the religion courses proved to be relatively popular, partly because they served as a means by which to reinforce Sunni Islamic identity during the period beginning in the 1950s when more and more Turkish citizens were moving from rural areas into the big cities.

The political leaders who promoted the Turkish-Islamic Synthesis after the 1980 coup also envisaged that the public-school religion courses could serve as a source of social cohesion in the face of political and ethnic divisions. To that end, the 1982 constitution (in Article 24) stipulated that religion courses called 'Religious Culture and Ethics' (*Din Kültürü ve Ahlak Bilgisi*) would be compulsory at both primary and secondary levels. A 1982 directive from the Ministry of Education stated that these courses would impart a rational and modern Islam that would be compatible with Turkish national goals. Such an education would guarantee that children should not be unduly influenced by 'erroneous knowledge and influences' from family beliefs or other sources (Kaplan 2002, 2006: 86). According to the general secretariat of the National Security Council in 1981, Atatürk himself stated that 'religion must be taken out from the hands of ignorant people, and the control should be given to the appropriate people' – that is, those who would teach an appropriately 'harmless' form of Islam (in Kaymakcan 2006: 450).

What kind of Islam is compatible with the national interests of Turkey, according to the Turkish Ministry of Education? The Ministry of Education issued directives in favour of an 'official standard interpretation' of the Hanafi Sunni school of Islam. The curriculum and textbooks outline the fundamental beliefs and practices of Sunni Islam, as well as provide discussions of reason and revelation, ethics and values, religion and secularism, and the life of the Prophet Muhammad (Ozgur 2012: 69). The textbooks for the earlier grades focus on basics, such as the Qur'an, the duties and beliefs of Islam, and the story of the life of Muhammad. More complex topics are included in the upper level (10th–12th grades) textbooks. For example, students in the 11th and 12th grades read about other religions of the world – the Abrahamic religions in the 11th grade and the religions of South and East Asia in the 12th grades. Textbooks for advanced grades also provided some discussion of Sufism (*tasavvuf*), though until 2008 – when the JDP government revised the textbooks – the treatment of Sufism tended to be brief and presented the Sufi orders as having a corrupting influence on Turkish society (Ueno 2018).

While the courses provided basic religious knowledge, the overall emphasis of the texts has been on the inter-relationship between Islam and the Turkish nation. Like all Turkish textbooks, the Religious Culture and Ethics course textbooks open with the text of the national anthem (*İstiklal Marşı*), Atatürk's famous Speech to the Youth (*Gençliğe Hitabe*) and a portrait of Atatürk. But the Islamic nationalist character of the Religious Culture and Ethics textbooks tended to go much further than just presenting standard introductory material. For example, in his analysis of a 1987 middle-school version of the religious education textbook, Sam Kaplan (2006: 79) discerned four themes indicating Turkey's exceptional status as a modern Islamic nation. These themes are:

> First, that the Turkish people have an innate spiritual affinity to Islam; second, that the Turks contributed a great deal to both Islamic and world civilizations; third, that Atatürk successfully mediated and exemplified the relation between state, citizen, and religion; and fourth that only the state-endorsed version of Islam is compatible with both nationalism and modernity.

These themes emphasise the nation as a Turkish, Sunni Muslim entity while de-emphasising the notion that Islam is a worldwide community not restricted by national boundaries or ethnic identity. That is, the Islam of the Religious Culture and Ethics courses served ethnic national interests as much as religious ones.

Ironically, the nature of religious education in modern Turkey is to some extent a continuation of the *medrese* education characteristic of the Ottoman Empire, with its authoritarian approach to religious knowledge. Modern Turkish religious education promulgates only one interpretation of Islam – the state's version of Hanafi Sunni Islam – and does not allow for questioning or for discussion of any other interpretations, such as those held by Turkey's Alevis (Kaymakcan 2006: 456–7).[5] Deviating from the state's narrative is dangerous and subversive, potentially leading to social division and chaos. As Elisabeth Özdalga has argued (1999: 437), one goal of the Religious Culture and Ethics course, it seems, is to create a monoculture in which one form of Islam reigns, just as there is to be one culture (Turkish), one language (Turkish) and one future (progressive). Education serves to bring the people into this monoculture, so that 'order' and 'progress' are given more importance than ideas such as freedom and liberty.

Being Muslim in Turkey

The Religious Culture and Ethics courses and the Diyanet, with its programming and oversight of religion in public spaces, are important channels through which Turkish citizens encounter the interpretations of Sunni Islam promoted by the Turkish state. For those who are not particularly devout, the religion courses and the state provisions for major religious holidays may be the primary – or exclusive – way to learn about and participate in Islam in Turkey. For more observant Muslims, these institutions offer a starting place for the development of religious life, while other organisations and communities may provide for more extensive religious learning and practice. In this section, we will look at how public religious education and the programmes and institutions of the Diyanet contribute in basic ways to common religious experience in Turkey.

As indicated, most Turks identify themselves as Sunni Muslims, the most widely practised branch of Islam in the world. One cannot easily define 'Sunni Islam' in a way that would apply to all Sunnis around the world, but the Diyanet and the religion course curriculum articulate some basic Sunni beliefs and practices that are widespread in Turkey. Of course, official statements do not tell us what people actually think and do in their lives. All religious traditions are complex and how people relate to their own tradition is dependent on cultural and historical factors that vary considerably over space and time. Nevertheless, I will lay out some the principles of Islam as expressed by the Diyanet and the educational system, not because it states the genuine experiences of all Muslims, but because most Sunnis in Turkey would largely agree with the Diyanet's description of Islam. We can think of the religion courses and the Diyanet's treatment as a minimal starting point from which to understand Sunni Islam in Turkey.

Sacred texts

The Holy Qur'an is the central text of Sunni Islam and is believed by most Muslims to be the direct word of God[6] to humanity. The English-language version of the Diyanet's website begins its description of the Qur'an as such:

> The Quran was revealed in stages to the Prophet Muhammad (peace be upon him) by Allah the Almighty in Arabic. The Quran has been handed down intact from generation to generation. It is a book written in *mushafs* (copies), begins with Surah al-Fatiha, and concludes with Surah an-Nas. Reciting the Quran is one of the best good deeds a Muslim can do. Reciting the Quran is the best act of worship after the obligations [Five Pillars of Islam]. The Quran consists of 323,015 letters, 77,439 words, 6,236 verses and 114 surahs [chapters].[7]

Sunni Muslims believe that God has communicated with humanity through prophets from the beginning of time – Adam was the first prophet, followed by many others, including İbrahim (Abraham), Musa (Moses) and İsa (Jesus). But the messages transmitted through these earlier prophets were distorted over time. It is only the message delivered to the last prophet, Muhammad of Mecca in Arabia (570 CE–632 CE), in the form of the Qur'an that has remained undistorted and perfect.

A foundational belief in the Islamic world is that the Qur'an is only authentic (undistorted and perfect) in its 'original' Arabic language. Even though most Turkish citizens do not speak Arabic as a native language, the Arabic Qur'an is the centrepiece of Muslim worship and religious knowledge. Students of Islam spend a significant amount of time memorising parts of the Qur'an in Arabic, especially beloved passages such as the short *surahs* (chapters) at the end of the Qur'an or favourite verses that are most commonly used in various ritual contexts. Zehra Hanım, whose oral history was recounted in Chapter 1, had memorised especially popular *surahs*, such as 'Yasin' and 'al-Mulk' as part of her religious education – a common practice among devout Muslims. For religiously observant people, an individual's ability to memorise and recite long sections of the Qur'an is a source of esteem and is taken as a sign of the individual's piety. There are even extended courses and programmes in which enrollees learn to recite the Qur'an in its entirety – one who has memorised the whole Qur'an is known as a *hafiz*, a widely revered attainment among pious Muslims.

But for Turks, reading the Qur'an in Arabic makes it difficult to comprehend the text without guidance, and a significant part of both formal and informal religious education involves not only learning Qur'anic Arabic but also interpreting the text under the guidance of a master, whether it is a *hoca* (teacher) in a village, a leader of a religious order or a formally educated teacher with degrees in Islamic sciences from one of Turkey's faculties of divinity. Translations of the Qur'an into Turkish – called *Meali* or 'Interpretations' of the Qur'an – are also now widely available. These were first published in the early years of the Republic when a group of religiously devout nationalists worked on translating the Qur'an into Turkish. The *ulema* had resisted the translation project because they had feared that creating a Turkish version was part of 'a long-term plot to displace the Arabic Qur'an' (Wilson 2009: 419). Yet those who worked on the translation project were not trying to change the Qur'an and lead people from the true path, but were attempting to make the meaning of the Qur'an available to the masses in a way that was careful and well informed. Still, the Arabic Qur'an has remained the centrepiece of Turkish Islamic ritual and religious learning, while translations help people understand what they are reading (Wilson 2009, 2014).

Some of the essential themes of the Qur'an that provide foundations of Sunni Islamic thought are belief in the absolute oneness of God (*tawhid*) and the requirement that humans submit to God's will, which has been made known in the Qur'an and in the *Sunnah* ('Islam' means 'submission' in Arabic). The *Sunnah* is the accumulated sayings and deeds of the Prophet Muhammad, who is thought to be a perfect man. The *Sunnah* is known through accounts of the Prophet transmitted by his Companions and their followers, and these accounts were written down and collected into the *hadith* books (*hadis* in Turkish), a process that occurred in the eighth and ninth centuries CE. The Qur'an and the *hadith*, along with some interpretative traditions, form the basis of Islamic law (*Shari'ah*). Other essential features of Sunni Islam are belief in the angels who act as intermediaries between God and humans, and in the Day of Judgement when the faithful will be rewarded with an afterlife in heaven and the evil will be punished in hell.

The Five Pillars of Islam

The basic obligations of Islamic practice are summarised in the famous 'Five Pillars of Islam'. As in every religious tradition, differing interpretations of the meanings and requirements of the Five Pillars exist within and between groups of believers, and individuals may engage with the Pillars in differing degrees of sincerity or commitment – or may ignore them altogether. Many Turks are secular or are only superficially engaged with religious practice and may avoid religious practices altogether or only participate on special occasions. In any case, the Five Pillars provide only a very basic picture of Sunni Islamic practice in Turkey. They are as follows.

Shahada

Shahada refers to the confession of faith. Every Muslim should be willing to confess with sincerity that there is no God but God and that Muhammad is God's messenger (Arabic: *lā 'ilāha 'illā llāh muhammadun rasūlu llāh*). Children often learn the *shahada* from their parents or other family members and may hear it in prayers or in religious services. It is also taught in the Religious Culture and Ethics courses that begin in 4th grade.

Ritual prayer

Muslims are obliged to perform prayers (*namaz*; Arabic: *salah*) five times a day at stipulated times. The times of the prayers are established according to the position of the sun in the sky – the first prayer is at first light (before sunrise) and the last prayer is at last light (after sundown). Each prayer time is announced with the call to prayer, or *ezan* (Arabic: *adhan*), which consists of a sequence of statements called out by a special reciter called a *muezzin*. There are many recordings of the *ezan* on YouTube and other sites – for example, the Diyanet has released several videos of *ezan* being called in Istanbul.[8] In Turkey people usually pray wherever they are – at home, at work, and so on. If an individual is near a mosque or is in a building that has a *mescid* (a prayer room), they can avail themselves of that space for prayer. To be clear, while many devout Muslims do indeed pray five times every day, others – including those who consider themselves good Muslims – may only pray occasionally, perhaps only during the Friday services or for special holiday celebrations. In any case, the *namaz* prayers follow a particular sequence of recitations and bodily movement, including bowing and kneeling in the direction of Mecca, the geographical source of Islam.[9] Believers should be in a state of ritual purity while praying, meaning that before praying they must perform ablutions (*abdest*; Arabic: *wudu*). Prayers may be done individually or in groups, but the Friday midday prayer (*Cuma namazı*) is a communal prayer accompanied by a sermon (*hutbe*) given by a Diyanet-appointed preacher (*hatip*). Usually, it is the imam who actually delivers the Friday sermon, so most mosques are staffed by a personnel member who is called an *imam-hatip*. There is also a type of Diyanet-appointed preacher called a *vaiz* (feminine: *vaize*), who gives religious talks in mosques outside of the context of Friday prayers and before night prayers (*Tarawih*) during the holy month of Ramadan. These preachers may deliver sermons on a wide variety of topics, though as appointees of the Diyanet, they are expected to deliver religious messages that align with the overarching ideology promoted by the Diyanet.

As mentioned above, the preachers are not officially free to sermonise on their own but must follow the ideological guidelines of the state (Yılmaz 2005: 390). From the earliest days of the Republic until 2006, a central office in the Diyanet wrote Friday sermons that were conveyed to the regional muftis, who then gave the sermons to local preachers to deliver to congregations. In 2006 this process was decentralised, and local mufti offices could compose the sermons, though under the supervision of the central Diyanet. This change was supposedly to allow the sermons to address issues important to local communities and regions, but given the control the central Diyanet still exerted over the sermon-writing process, the local sermons tended to match the Diyanet in content and tone. As before, the Friday sermons tended to focus on general topics, such as 'national solidarity, loyalty to the state, and a rationalistic Islam devoid of folk traditions' (Watters 2018: 366–7).[10]

The way in which prayer is conducted has some gendered aspects, in that men and women observe somewhat different practices and have different expectations. Men and women both regularly pray at home, but mosques in Turkey primarily serve as prayer spaces for men. Throughout the Muslim world, prayer spaces are segregated by gender, and in Turkey the central and largest spaces in most mosques are for men. The women's sections are either to the side of or above the men's sections, and they tend to be smaller, sometimes much smaller, than the men's sections. As I was told by many practising Turks, the spatial differences result from the fact that men are expected to pray in mosques while women most commonly pray at home since they traditionally have had household duties that kept them nearer the house. As Turkish women have begun to join the paid labour force in recent decades (though they are still under-represented in the workforce) the logic of this spatial difference does not always hold. Nevertheless, mosques still tend to be dominated by men. Prayer leaders and preachers are primarily men as well, since it is traditionally forbidden in Islam for women to lead men or mixed audiences, though men can lead women. Still, women have always had the informal (and more recently formal) authority to lead other women in prayer or give sermons (this will be discussed in greater depth in Chapter 7).

Fasting

Sunni Muslims are enjoined to fast (*oruç*; Arabic: *sawm*) during the Islamic month of Ramadan. Ramadan is the ninth month of the Islamic calendar. According to Muslim tradition, Muhammad received the first revelation of what would become the Qur'an during Ramadan, and the fast is in celebration and as a mark of respect of this. It means that from first prayer (at first light in the morning) until sunset, the believer should not take anything into the body – no food, liquid, medicine or smoking, and there should be no sexual activity. At sunset, believers can resume eating, breaking the fast with the *iftar* meal.

Ramadan does not fall at a particular time of the solar calendar – that is, it is not practised during a certain season. Since the Islamic calendar is lunar, it is about ten days shorter than the Western solar calendar, meaning that Islamic holidays occur ten days earlier in every subsequent solar year. One effect of following the Islamic calendar is that the Islamic holidays move through the seasons over the years when days – and thus the period of fasting – may be shorter or longer. When I did my research project in Turkey in 1998 and 1999, Ramadan fell over the winter solstice when the days were shortest and so the fast only lasted ten to twelve hours. But by 2014, when I stayed in Turkey for an extended period of time, Ramadan occurred during the summer so that fasting began at about four in the morning and lasted until around nine in the evening, an incredibly long amount of time. The weather was hot too, and those who fasted not only refrained from eating but also from drinking – a true hardship. Many observant friends who fasted argued that this hardship experienced during Ramadan was a way in which believers could come to understand the suffering – the hunger and thirst – of the poor and would thus be more generous to them.

Each day's fast begins at first prayer, but some people get up prior to the call to prayer in order to eat a pre-fast meal called *suhur*. In many locations, especially in cities and towns, a small band composed of a *davul* (drum) and *zurna* (a reed instrument) sometimes accompanied by a crier strolls through the streets waking people up in time to eat before the fast (Figure 2.2). After the fourth prayer at sundown, mosques broadcast a cannon blast announcing that people may break the fast with the *iftar* meal. According to custom, most break the fast first by taking a sip of water and eating a date or two, since it is believed that the Prophet Muhammad broke his fasts by eating a date. *Iftar* meals are often celebratory and families and friends will eat together. They can sometimes be elaborate feasts that feature many favourite foods, such as savoury pastries (*börek*) and baklava. Even with extensive fasting, it is not unusual for people to gain weight during Ramadan because of the almost nightly feasting. Another common practice is for those with the means to host community *iftar* meals, often in large tents, where community members or the poor can partake of a free *iftar* meal. In Turkey, too, the state, usually through the Diyanet, hosts community *iftar* meals for needy families or as part of public religious programming.

Figure 2.2 A Ramazan band collecting tips during Ramazan Bayramı, Izmir, 1999 (photograph by author)

The end of Ramadan is celebrated with a major festival, the *Ramazan Bayramı* or *Şeker Bayramı* (the Sugar Festival). This is an official holiday when schools and businesses close, lasting three days. During *Ramazan Bayramı*, it is customary for people – even the non-religious – to get dressed up in nice clothes and visit family and friends. Fasting ceases and normal eating patterns resume, with people often giving each other sweets. It is also common for people to visit the graves of deceased family members and hold memorial services. In general, Ramadan and the Ramadan holiday are festive times when individuals and groups celebrate and enjoy special programmes and events – much like the Christmas season in North America and Europe.

Alms to the needy

All Muslims who have the means are enjoined to contribute 2.5 per cent of their annual wealth as alms (*zekat*; Arabic: *zakat*) to the poor and the needy. Islamic legal traditions lay out a number of rules governing *zekat* – who gives, how much, who is eligible to receive and what the permissible forms are. For example, people are urged to pay *zekat* if they own wealth (cash, property, investments) over a basic level (*nisab*).[11] It is not always easy to determine how much *zekat* an individual should pay, but there are many institutions and organisations that offer help by providing *zekat* programmes on their websites. The Diyanet also offers *zekat* calculation services on its website (https://zekathesapla.tdv.org/), and there are even *zekat* calculator apps for smartphones.

The command to give *zekat* is so fundamental to Islam that most Muslims do not think of it as 'charity' (as in voluntary gifts to the needy) so much as paying to God what is owed to God. In their view, it is God who provides the wealth and success in the first place – the wealth is ultimately God's. God requires that this wealth be used for the support of the individual Muslim's family but also that a portion of it must go to the poor and needy in the individual's community. This provides for a just, equitable and stable society.

While *zekat* is a fundamental requirement where the believer is discharging a duty, there is also voluntary charity, called *sadaka*, which is any form of charitable giving beyond the requirements of *zekat*. According to many devout Muslims, the voluntary nature of *sadaka* means it can enable the donor to gain God's favour since the giver is sacrificing his or her own comfort for the good of others. Such sacrifice may attract God's blessings and influence the individual's well-being both in this world and in the next. The more given, the more merit earned. Both *zekat* and *sadaka* may be given informally, such as by donating food or money to those who ask for it or by contributing to local projects or causes. For example, even though mosques are managed by the state, many local mosques rely on donations for maintenance and refurbishment, such as replacing furniture and carpets, and locals can discharge their *zekat* obligation by contributing to this.

In Turkey today, the government and many charities provide formal venues by which donors can direct their contributions towards particular charitable projects. Indeed, there is a veritable marketplace of charities seeking *zekat* or *sadaka* donations. These may have distinctly religious goals, such as the construction and maintenance of religious educational programmes, whether provided through the state or through religious organisations. Other causes may be more general, such as providing for the poor and needy in Turkey and elsewhere, building schools in poor areas of Turkey and, more recently, aiding the many refugees that have flooded into Turkey in the chaotic aftermath of the Arab Spring that began in 2011. As the charitable organisations have proliferated in the last two decades (see Chapter 7), they compete with each other for Turkish lira and have subsequently developed advertising and campaign appeals typical of charitable organisations in the United States and elsewhere in Europe.

Pilgrimage to Mecca

At least once in a lifetime, a believer should make a pilgrimage (*hac*; Arabic: *hajj*) to the sacred city of Mecca during *Dhu al-Hijjah*, the last month of the Islamic calendar. For the *hajj*, Muslims from all over the world come together to perform a series of rituals that allow participants to re-enact some of the events and visit some of the sites essential to the sacred history of the religion. Some of these rituals involve commemoration of the Prophet Muhammad, but most *hajj* rituals harken back to Islam's mythic establishment through the pious actions of the Prophet Ibrahim (Abraham) and Hagar and Ishmael. Those going on the *hajj* wear a special garment called an *ihram*, which consists of two white garments for men – one similar to a wraparound skirt and the other worn around the left shoulder like a blanket – and usually a white robe and headscarf for women. Pilgrims have to put on these special garments before entering the city boundaries of Mecca. Since many pilgrims now travel to the city by air, they don the *ihram* at the airport from which they depart for Mecca. Some pilgrims from around the world fly through Istanbul on their way to the *hajj*, and so Istanbul airport has special areas for people to change clothes on their last leg of their journey into pilgrimage. The Diyanet organises trips for the *hajj* and the *umre* (visiting the sites of the *hajj* during non-*hajj* times of the year; Arabic: *umrah*) in conjunction with certain selected travel agencies. The Saudi government applies quotas on each Muslim country for the *hajj* in order to prevent dangerous overcrowding, and so the Diyanet department responsible for the *hajj* accepts applications and decides who may go. In 2017, for example, 79,000 Turks went on the *hajj*.[12]

The pilgrimage concludes with the *Kurban Bayramı* (the feast of the sacrifice), when Muslims around the world sacrifice an animal, distribute meat to the poor and eat part of the animal. The sacrifice re-enacts the story of Abraham's near-sacrifice of his son, Ishmael. In the Jewish and Christian traditions, Abraham is commanded to sacrifice his son Isaac. Abraham in his obedience takes Isaac to be sacrificed but God in his mercy replaces Isaac with a ram (Genesis 22). In the Islamic tradition, Abraham takes his son Ishmael, born to Hagar, to be sacrificed, and Ishmael is spared when God replaces the boy with a ram. In Turkey, *Kurban Bayramı* is a major holiday when schools, businesses and most government offices are closed. Even today in Turkey, families with the means will buy a sacrificial animal – usually a ram or a cow – to sacrifice at home or in a communal area following the ritual customs. Indeed, all animals for consumption by Muslims are supposed to be killed following particular ritual proceedings in which the blood is drained from the body and prayers are uttered while the animal is being killed. These rituals make the meat *halal* (permissible). The meat from the sacrificial animal is divided up among the sacrifice sponsor (that is, the person who has bought the sacrificial animal), the sponsor's family and friends, and the poor.

In keeping with its role as the 'supervisor' of religious practice in Turkey, the state readily provides for the observance of Islamic requirements and promotes the traditional Islamic holidays such as *Ramazan Bayramı* and *Kurban Bayramı*.

Circumcision

Another ritual that has religious significance is the circumcision of boys. Male circumcision is an obligation in Islam, but circumcision ceremonies in different Muslim cultures vary greatly in both complexity and range of significance. In the Turkish context, circumcision rituals are often spectacular and elaborate – families may spend considerable sums on a ceremony that lasts several days – and they employ distinctly royal symbolism that harks back to Ottoman imperial ceremonialism and to a time when the country was the centre of the Muslim world. For example, the boys to be circumcised don royal garb and are often paraded through the streets on decorated horses prior to the circumcision itself (see Figure 2.3). The Turkish rituals are performed on boys as old as twelve and may be seen as a 'coming of age' rite that transforms the participants from boys to men. The ceremony is also bound up with popular Turkish conceptions of national identity, that is, circumcision marks the boys as Muslims over and against the inhabitants of Turkey's historically unfriendly neighbouring Christian countries and internal non-Muslim minority groups, who are popularly and pejoratively referred to as 'the uncircumcised' (*sünnetsiz*). The circumcision of boys is so important to Turkish national identity that the state will pay for collective circumcision ceremonies for poor and orphaned boys.

Religious institutions and their limits

Through the Diyanet and required religious education courses, the Turkish state has been actively involved in establishing religious institutions, norms and expectations in the modern Republic, even if most of the time, religious practice and belief is conducted according to the inclinations of the private individual or family. Certainly, some secular Turks find the power of the Diyanet and the requirement of the Religious Culture and Ethics courses to be irritating or burdensome, and others argue that these institutions run contrary to Turkey's secularist principles. Some devout Muslims may appreciate the efforts of the Diyanet and the religion courses for providing the population with basic religious knowledge, but may criticise these institutions for the blandness or basicness of their messages.

The Diyanet and the religious education courses cater to the religious needs of the Sunni population, whether their efforts are appreciated or not. What they do not do is serve the needs of Turkey's religious minorities. The non-Muslim minorities, such as the Greek Orthodox, Armenian and Jewish populations, look to religious authorities and institutions from their own religious traditions

Figure 2.3 Boys in Sünnet costumes, Şanlıurfa, 2012 (photograph by author)

– this was a stipulation of the 1923 Treaty of Lausanne in which European powers recognised Turkey as an independent country after World War I. But the sizeable Alevi minority is not recognised as a separate division of Islam, and the Diyanet and religious educational institutions have done little to contribute to Alevi rituals, knowledge or publications in Turkey or anywhere else. In fact, until recently the Diyanet refused to recognise Alevism as a religion at all, let alone as a branch of Islam. The next chapter will discuss the fraught and changing situation of the Alevis in modern Turkey.

Notes

1. Established in 1975, the Diyanet Endowment receives money from the state and from private donors in order 'to be a sovereign of goodness on earth for people by means of providing institutions for financial aid, moral and spiritual support' (https://www.tdv.org/en-US/site/icerik/misyon-ve-vizyon–1039). This means that it helps to finance building and service projects that support the religious cultivation of people within and outside Turkey (Turan 2008).

2. There are four legal schools (*madhhabs*) in the Sunni Muslim tradition, one of which is based on the writings of Iraqi Abu Hanifa (d. 767 CE). The Ottomans adopted the legal tradition of Abu Hanifa – known as the Hanafi School – though judges from the other schools were also present in the Ottoman justice system. In modern Turkey, which has a secular legal system, the Hanafi influence remains in the Diyanet, which promotes Hanafi practices and beliefs. The majority of the Turkish population is, indeed, Hanafi by tradition, though there are large numbers of Sunnis and non-Sunnis who identify with other schools, most especially the Shafi school.

3. According to İzzet Er (2008: 278), there is a special department in the Diyanet that prepares the Islamic calendar every year. 'Preparation of the Islamic calendar requires enormous amount of expertise and knowledge from various related fields. This special department, by employing experts from all these related fields, determines the exact time of five daily prayers for the whole year, the start and the end of the months in the lunar Islamic calendar and the time for the religious festivals'.

4. The *fetva*s (Arabic: *fatwa*) issued by the Diyanet now are designed to answer questions concerning, for example, proper religious practice and family relationships. These modern *fetva*s are not legally binding (Öcal 2008).

5. There is a substantial minority in Turkey who identify as Alevi, a non-Sunni branch of Islam that will be described in the next chapter.

6. 'Allah' is the word for 'God' in both Turkish and Arabic. I will use the English term throughout the book except when quoting texts that use 'Allah'.

7. https://www.diyanet.gov.tr/en-US/Institutional/Detail/10370

8. For example, https://www.youtube.com/watch?v=432sv8HzYKM shows a video of the winner of an *ezan*-calling competition. This *ezan* is unusually elaborate, but it gives the viewer a real sense of the profound beauty and vocal complexity of the call to prayer.

9. There are many videos that demonstrate how to pray *namaz*. A particularly in-depth one can be found at https://www.youtube.com/watch?v=W9kTd7q1zjE

10. The Diyanet issues its Friday sermons in Turkish and English. The sermon is usually delivered by the Diyanet President. See http://www2.diyanet.gov.tr/DinHizmetleriGenelMudurlugu/Sayfalar/HutbelerListesi-Ingilizce.aspx

11. *Nisab* has not changed over time and is determined according to how much wealth the individual has relative to a set value of gold or silver. That is, if one has wealth above the current value of 87.48 grams of gold or 612.36 grams of silver, then one must pay *zekat*. The *nisab* for livestock differs according to the type of animal. For sheep, for example, the *nisab* is forty.

12. See http://www2.diyanet.gov.tr/hacveumregenelmudurlugu/Sayfalar/Anasayfa.aspx

CHAPTER 3

The Alevi minority in Turkey

Turkey has had persistent problems dealing with non-Sunni Muslim populations in its territory. The conflicts between the non-Sunni Muslim minorities
and the Sunni majority have sometimes concerned the differences between
the competing visions of 'proper' Islam. However, conflicts have often erupted
around ethno-nationalist issues that have their roots in the very founding of
the modern Turkish state. The non-Sunni Muslims, most especially the Alevis,
along with the Kurdish ethnic minority (two populations that overlap), disrupt
the Kemalist nationalist goal of creating a uniform nation-state in which the
population speaks one language (Turkish) and shares one religion (Sunni Islam).
Furthermore, the leftist, even pro-communist inclinations of many Alevis also
posed a threat – real or imagined – to Turkey's alignment to Western European
capitalism during the most intense years of the Cold War.

'Alevism' is the modern umbrella term for a collection of non-Sunni practices
that borrow from Shi'ism, from pre-Islamic Turkish beliefs and from other
sources. Those who now identify as Alevi constitute about 15 to 20 per cent
of the population of Turkey, though it is difficult to know the exact percent-
age since the Turkish state has refused to recognise them or count them as a
distinct group. Alevis cross many ethnic and linguistic boundaries. They may be
Turkish or Kurdish or belong to smaller ethnic groups, and while most speak
Turkish, a large minority speak other languages, such as Kurmanji (a Kurdish
dialect), Zaza, Arabic or Albanian – or any combination of those languages
(Erdemir 2005: 938).[1] Until the 1950s, most Alevis lived in central Anatolia in
villages or town quarters that were primarily Alevi, but as part of a large wave
of rural-to-urban migration beginning in the 1950s, Alevis migrated into the big
cities seeking better employment and educational opportunities.

Because Alevis are not a coherent group with a codified set of beliefs, any
description of Alevism can only be partial. Most Alevis do accept some of the
beliefs of Twelver Shi'ism. Like Shi'as, for example, Alevis generally believe
that Ali ibn Abu Talib, the cousin and son-in-law of the Prophet Muhammad,
should have immediately succeeded Muhammad as the caliph of the Muslim
community since Ali was a member of the Prophet's family. In the traditional
Sunni perspective, the caliphate was a position taken on by individuals with
the political and religious credentials to serve as an effective leader of the

community. For Sunnis, the first four 'Rightly Guided' caliphs – Abu Bakr (caliph from 632 to 634 CE), Umar ibn al Khattab (634–44 CE), Uthman ibn Affan (644–56 CE) and then Ali (656–61 CE) – were the legitimate successors of Muhammad, while for Shi'as, the first three were usurpers. That is, Shi'as – and most Alevis, too – believe that God commanded Muhammad to pass on special spiritual knowledge to Ali, who should have taken up the caliphate upon Muhammad's death. Ali in turn should have been succeeded by his sons, Hasan and Hüseyin, who were the grandsons of the Prophet through his daughter Fatima, wife of Ali. Their male descendants should have succeeded them since they were the bearers of the blood and spiritual genius of the Prophet. Twelver Shi'ism, which is dominant in Iran and most influential on Turkish Alevis, holds that secret spiritual knowledge passed from Muhammad to Ali (the first imam) to Ali's sons, on down to a twelfth descendant, Muhammad ibn al-Hasan.[2] These are the imams of Twelver Shi'ism, considered to be exemplary leaders who follow the *Shari'ah* perfectly and have esoteric knowledge about the meaning of the Qur'an. Shi'a Muslims, as well as some Sunnis, believe that God placed the final, twelfth imam in occultation (hiding) in 872 CE, where he remains. In the end times he will return with Jesus to destroy wickedness and bring peace and judgement to the righteous. The emphasis on esoteric religious knowledge and direct connection to the divine has meant that Shi'ism especially emphasises mystical and ecstatic practices, qualities adopted by many Alevis.

Haci Bektaş Veli and the Bektaşi order

Tracing some of the history of Alevism allows us to see the distinctive features of the group, especially in comparison to other Shi'as, such as those in Iran and Iraq. For example, the Alevis do not trace their religious genealogy back to the founding events of Shi'ism; instead, the spiritual genealogy of most Alevis derives from the teachings of a thirteenth-century Sufi dervish, Haci Bektaş Veli. Much of the information about Haci Bektaş is legendary, and there are numerous tales of his miraculous deeds and feats of wisdom, many of which have been collected in his spiritual biography, known as the *Vilayetname* (Birge 2015: 30–9). Historically, scholars believe that he is from Khurasan in Central Asia and migrated with the Turkoman tribes into Anatolia after the Mongol invasions in the twelfth and thirteenth centuries. Influenced by Central Asian mystics such as Ahmed Yesevi, Bektaş led a life of meditation and ritual dance, and became famous as a healer who eschewed some of the practices of mainstream Islam, such as praying in a mosque. He was a contemporary of the Mevlana (Jalal al-din Rumi), but where the Mevlana was well educated and lived in urban centres, Haci Bektaş was not trained in the *medreses* and left behind no written theology. His emphasis on ecstatic ritual and direct emotional experience of the divine rather than intellectualism made him popular with the people of the rural areas of Anatolia (Mèlikoff 1998).

The Bektaşis incorporated some Twelver Shi'a beliefs, including devotion to Ali, revering him as the chief of the saints. In fact, there is a popular myth that Haci Bektaş is a descendant of Ali, from whom he received esoteric knowledge directly. The most common quotation of the Prophet Muhammad popular among the Bektaşis (and frequently found over the doorways to Bektaşi lodges) is 'I am the City of Knowledge and Ali is its Gateway' (Birge 2015: 124). Still, the Bektaşis were not entirely given over to Shi'ism. For example, while the Shi'is maintained that the imam – the infallible leader – was a necessary mediator between human beings and God, the Bektaşis (like other Sufis) believed that direct communion with God is possible through one's own ecstatic experience. Furthermore, Haci Bektaş and his followers incorporated into their order certain practices stemming from pre-Islamic Turkish shamanism. The ritual dances traced back to Haci Bektaş may have originated from shamanistic ecstatic dances typical of pre-Islamic Turkish tribes. The Bektaşis – and eventually modern Alevism – also absorbed ideas and practices from a wide range of other sources, including Eastern (Nestorian) Christianity, Buddhism, Manichaeism and pre-historic Anatolian religions (Erol 2010: 376).

After the death of Haci Bektaş in the late thirteenth century and during the consolidation and growth of the Ottoman Empire in the fourteenth and fifteenth centuries, his followers created a Sufi order[3] based on what they believed were the master's teachings. They designated Haci Bektaş as the first *pir* (sheikh or Sufi leader) of the order. The subsequent *pir*s managed the organisation from Haci Bektaş village in Kırşehir province in central Anatolia, and the Bektaşi *tekke* there is still the geographic centre of Alevi/Bektaşi authority and ritual. Over time, the *pir*s implemented stricter and more exclusive methods of recruiting and initiating new dervishes to the order, though it was always possible for villagers and rural people to remain affiliated with Bektaşi lodges. Folk poetry and the use of music in Bektaşi ceremonies were also popular features of the order, and many poems have been attributed to Haci Bektaş himself or to his illustrious followers (Birge 2015: 56–8). While other Sufi orders, most notably the Mevlevis (followers of the Mevlana), also used poetry and music, the Bektaşis tended to create works that had popular appeal. And the flexible attitude the Bektaşis maintained towards different religious beliefs – they were willing to absorb folk practices into the Bektaşi tradition – made them seem welcoming to many different ethnic and religious groups that lived in the Ottoman territories.

The beliefs of the Bektaşis were complex and are difficult to summarise,[4] but there are certain Bektaşi doctrines that endure in modern Alevi communities and illuminate the appeal the order had to people both historically and today. One such doctrine was the 'Oneness of Being' (*Hakikat*), a belief that all creation is simply the manifestation of God's reality, meaning that God resides in each individual. The goal of the Bektaşi practitioners was to become conscious of this interior divinity through a process of intense introspection, leading to the realisation of the unity of humanity and all creation. Social and economic stratification is irrelevant before the Oneness of Being, and therefore social differentiation should not be maintained within the context of the Bektaşi order. The order thus provided a means by which ordinary individuals who were not a member of the privileged educated classes could become involved in a fulfilling religious community in which wealth was often shared (Faroqhi 1981: 79). The doctrine of the Oneness of Being also meant that women could be included in the activities of the order. In Sunni Islam, women are only peripheral to the activities of the mosque and are still often excluded from certain positions of religious leadership and from public roles. Among the Bektaşis, by contrast, women could participate in all ceremonies, went unveiled and conversed freely with men. Birge (2015: 265) speculated that this inclusion of women in Bektaşi life not only stemmed from the doctrinal notions of unity of creation, but may also have been an inheritance of pre-Islamic Turkish social custom. In any case, the Bektaşis provided an arena in which women could freely and openly participate in religious ritual in a way not always permitted them in mainstream Sunni Islam.

During much of the history of the Ottoman Empire, the Bektaşis had an ambivalent relationship with the imperial Sunni Muslim authorities, who viewed many Bektaşi beliefs and practices to be unorthodox, if not heretical. To be clear, members of the Bektaşi orders certainly would have their own practices as 'orthodox' or 'true', and most would not have made a conscious distinction between state-promulgated Sunni orthodoxy and the so-called heterodoxy of the Bektaşi orders. To the rural villager, who was most often poorly educated and exposed only to local customs, the local religion would have probably appeared as the norm. Still, conflicts developed between the Bektaşis and the Ottoman government beginning in the fifteenth century, mostly due to the Bektaşis involvement in some anti-government movements in eastern Anatolia. In particular, a rebellious movement known as the Kızılbaş was often associated with the Bektaşis, since the Kızılbaş shared many of their beliefs, maintained a devotion to Haci Bektaş and sometimes proclaimed themselves to be Bektaşis. But the Kızılbaş were closely allied with the hostile Shi'i Safavid Empire of fifteenth- and sixteenth-century Persia – 'Kızılbaş' means 'red head', referring to the red turbans worn by Safavid soldiers – and they maintained many Shi'i ideas that were not generally held by the Bektaşis.

Even as Bektaşis were associated with rebellious populations in the empire's east, they also established a close affiliation with the Janissaries, the elite military corps of the Ottoman Empire – Haci Bektaş was the official patron saint of the corps. The connection with the Janissaries resulted in some benefits to the Bektaşi order, since it provided a means by which the Bektaşis could exercise political influence (Faroqhi 1981: 77). But the inseparability of the Janissaries and the Bektaşis meant that the downfall of one was the downfall of the other. When Sultan Mahmud II eliminated the Janissaries in 1826 in an attempt to implement military reforms, the Bektaşi order of dervishes was also abolished. In Istanbul several Bektaşi leaders were executed, some of the order's buildings were destroyed and literature burned. However, the order, especially in its popular forms, continued to operate underground, and observers in 1849 and 1850 recorded revived *tekke*s and practices in various parts of the empire. The order remained quite strong into the twentieth century, even as the Turkish republican government sought to eliminate all Sufi orders as part of its programme of Kemalist reforms (Birge 2015: 87–91).

Becoming 'Alevi'

The adherents of the Bektaşi order became one of the more prominent subsets of what are now called Alevis, who are still sometimes referred to as Alevi-Bektaşis. But to suggest that one can draw a straight line from the Bektaşis to the Alevis is misleading. Scholars Markus Dressler (2008, 2013) and Kabir Tambar (2014) have demonstrated that the notion of Alevism as a coherent religious tradition only emerged in the nineteenth century to designate a range of non-Sunni practices present in the Ottoman Empire (Dressler 2008: 283–4). The rise of Turkish nationalism in the final decades of the empire meant that these non-Sunni populations were evaluated in a new way. In the past, the Muslim minority beliefs were problematic to the empire because of their defiance of Sunni norms that dominated state government and the potential for the non-Sunni populations to ally with the enemy Safavids to the East. But the emphasis on Turkishness as the foundation of Ottoman identity that emerged in the late nineteenth and early twentieth centuries meant that the Turkish-speaking Alevis (although not the Kurdish-speaking Alevis), who were believed to have roots in the early Ottoman and pre-Ottoman past, could function as exemplars of an idealised Turkish past. Thus, the governing Ottoman elite came to conceive of 'Alevism' as a unified set of beliefs and practices.

Alevis themselves began to accept this designation because the narrative of Alevis as fundamentally Turkish meant that they had a clear place in the Ottoman-Turkish body politic, a position not extended to Christian and Jewish communities that resided in the empire. As Tambar put it (2014: 55), at first,

> nationalist elites did not repudiate Alevis as foreigners on Turkish soil (as they did various Christian communities). On the contrary, Alevis were conceived of as integral to the nation. The governing elite viewed the community's practices as a token of the nation's past, a sign of the historical depth and perdurance of a national Turkish society. Ostensibly marking cultural difference, Alevi ritual was accepted by nationalist leaders as evidence of a historically coherent national political community.

Mustafa Kemal Atatürk and the republican nationalists took up this narrative that Alevis could serve as indicators of the depth of Turkish history – a history that preceded the Ottoman Empire – in the Anatolian heartland. It helped that both Turkish- and Kurdish-speaking Alevis widely supported the secularism of the Kemalist regime and generally maintained a left-leaning political outlook throughout republican history. Alevis had hoped that a distancing of Sunni Islam from the corridors of power would mean that old prejudices against them as a minority religion would ease somewhat – a hope that did not bear fruit. When the Kemalists and others used Sunni Islam as a way to unite and homogenise the Turkish nation, Alevis did not submit to this national programme. Many Sunnis believed that Alevis were not Muslim at all or that they practised the wrong kind of Islam, especially because Alevis do not worship in mosques, which is a hallmark of Sunni practice (at least for men).[5] Ultimately, though, Alevis were classified as Muslim in the Treaty of Lausanne of 1923. They were not given protected minority status – that was only granted to non-Muslims – and because of that lack of protection were subject to sometimes oppressive and discriminatory actions both from the Turkish government and from Sunni Muslim nationalists.

One of the most notorious instances of state repression in the early years of the Republic concerned the Alevi Kurds who lived in the Dersim region of the eastern province of Tunceli. This region was mountainous, difficult to reach and hard to control, both for the Ottoman Empire and for the Turkish state. Following a policy in which the state attempted to impose Turkish homogeneity on Anatolia's ethnically and religiously diverse population, the state bombed the region for a sustained period between 1937 and 1938. According to accounts, many thousands of residents were killed or forced to leave, making this one of the most violent and repressive campaigns of the early republican military history. Until recently, the Dersim massacre has received very little acknowledgement or discussion by those in power, to the resentment of both Alevis and Kurds (Tambar 2014: 133–7; see also Van Bruinessen 1994; Watts 2000). Other acts of repression against the Alevi minority have recurred over the course of Turkish history, as will be discussed in due course.

Alevi beliefs and practices

Given the diverse history of Alevis in Turkey, even today it is difficult to identify a unified set of beliefs and practices that all Alevis share. Still, it is probably safe to say that most Alevis hold Ali and his sons Hasan and Hüseyin in special reverence and recognise the Twelve Imams of the Twelver Shi'a tradition. For example, most Alevis glorify the birth of Ali at the time of the Islamic New Year, and many Alevi houses feature an iconic image of Ali, and sometimes of his sons too. The *Buyruk* ('Decree'), which is the most important sacred text of the Alevis, depicts Muhammad and Ali as joined together in spiritual and even physical unity (Shankland 2003: 82–4). One concept found among some Alevis is that God is triune (takes three different forms), consisting of God, Muhammad and Ali. Alevis also often commemorate the martyrdom of Imam Hüseyin at the Battle of Kerbala in 680 CE on *Aşure* (Arabic: *Ashura*) during the Islamic month of Muharram (Erdemir 2005: 938). And if Alevis fast (not all Alevis do), they may do so during the month of Muharram, rather than – or in addition to – during Ramadan. For many Alevis today, Haci Bektaş is a spiritual leader and founder of the true religion of Islam and the source of profound knowledge. He is viewed as a great Turkish leader, introducing a set of traditions more closely identified with the Turkish people than with those traditions that derive from the Arabic roots of Sunni Islam. Some even claim that the religion introduced by Haci Bektaş is the 'true' Turkish religion rooted in the shamanic past of the Turkish people, while Sunnism introduced unwanted innovations such as strict monotheism and an authoritarian God (Shankland 2003: 156–7).

Alevi rituals and traditions have evolved over time, especially with the migration of Alevis from rural areas into cities – a process that began in the 1950s but accelerated in the 1970s (see 'Migration and Alevi dynamism' below). David Shankland (2003) gives a vivid description of Alevi rituals in Anatolian villages, and I follow his account here while recognising that there are many variations in different areas of Turkey. Alevis generally minimise the importance of the Five Pillars of Islam, including praying five times a day and fasting during Ramadan. Instead of the Five Pillars, Alevis articulate a different set of religious requirements, called *Alevi'nin Şartları* ('Alevi conditions'), encapsulated in the saying 'Be master of your hands, tongue, and loins' (*Eline diline beline sahip ol!*). According to Shankland (2003: 78–9), 'Interpretations of these conditions vary, but they usually begin with the proscription: "Do not take what you have not yourself set down, do not tell falsehoods, and do not make love outside wedlock!"' These are not ideas restricted to Alevism but are part of the ethics prevalent throughout Turkish society, though for Alevis they have special status as the heart of true Islam. This sentiment is expressed by Alevi leader Dede Gazi Kara in his book *Altın Kitap Alevilik* (*Golden Book of Alevism*) (Kara 2009). He states in the first paragraph of the book: 'In Alevism you will find the essence of Islam. Islam's essence is love, tolerance and righteousness. To be Alevi is to have good morals. Good morals mean do not harm others with your hands, tongue or loins' (translation mine).

Not only do Alevis downplay the significance of the Five Pillars, but they tend not to pray in mosques. Instead, the focus of Alevi worship is on the *cem* (pronounced 'jem') ritual overseen by holy men (*dedes*), and aided by a number of assistants. The *dedes* derive their ritual authority from their descent from sacred lineages traced back to Haci Bektaş Veli (Dressler 2008: 295). Each *dede* lineage may reference legends about ancestors who demonstrated exceptional powers or wisdom, but the special status of the *dedes* bespeaks an Alevi (and Shi'i) tradition in which descent from holy individuals can bestow a degree of spirituality and closeness to God not found among those of more mundane line-ages.[6] The common Alevi belief that Haci Bektaş is a descendant of Imam Ali through Imam Cafer Sadık (the sixth of the Twelve Imams) borrows from the Shi'a notion of esoteric spiritual knowledge passed on through the lineage of the Prophet to Haci Bektaş, to the *dede*-descendants who are at the centre of Alevi religious life. The Alevi villagers whom Shankland observed (2003: 79) claimed that the *cem* ritual was actually taught to Alevis by Ali himself.

The senior male members of a *dede* lineage have priority over junior members; indeed, a son may not practise *dedelik* (being a *dede*) while his father is still alive, even if the son has more knowledge and charisma than his father. All *dedes* are expected to teach and maintain the basic tenets of Alevism, and should be fair, honest, temperate and able to mediate among quarrelling parties. This last point is especially important since a *cem* ritual may not start until all conflicts among participants have been settled (Shankland 2003: 104–6). In more tra-ditional Alevi village settings, all people belong either to a *dede* lineage or to a lineage composed of followers or students (*talip*) of a particular *dede* lineage. The relationships between the *dedes* and their followers can be complex and depend somewhat on the strength, wisdom and judiciousness of the various *dedes* in the different lineages. When the *dede*–follower relationship is solid and trusting, the conduct of the *cem* rituals proceeds through a series of steps in which the follower and *dede* demonstrate their devotion to one another. Traditionally, for example, a *cem* ritual begins when a follower lineage makes a sacrifice to their *dede*, the *dede* mediates quarrels among followers and followers maintain a bodily disposition of submission in the presence of the *dede* (Shankland 2003: 106–8; Soileau 2017: 557).

Another important aspect of being a *dede* is access to the knowledge of the *Buyruk*, the text that is a source of the religious philosophy of Alevism. Alevis generally believe that the *Buyruk* is the collected teachings of Imam Cafer Sadık, and its forty sections contain stories, parables, discussions of religious organisa-tion and hierarchy, and instructions on ritual conduct. It probably originated as an oral tradition, but it has been written down and translated into modern Turkish – there is no concern about maintaining the original language as there is with the Qur'an. Also, unlike the Qur'an the *Buyruk* is not considered a 'set' text and is not the basis of a legal code but is more a source of philosophy and inspiration. In the villages, the text is largely kept and read by the *dedes*, but they do not use it in the context of the religious ceremonies themselves. Rather, the *dedes* have absorbed the knowledge of the *Buyruk* and draw on it when comment-ing on rituals or on the songs and poetry that are an important part of Alevi life. As Shankland puts it (2003: 99), the *Buyruk* is 'a rich source of ideas, one that shapes the villagers' thoughts within the overall, mostly oral, traditions on which they found their society but is not itself constitutive of a body of dogma that must be followed'.

Alevis have also absorbed not only Shi'a ideas but many Sufi beliefs as well. In particular, they extol the Bektaşi concept of the 'Four Doors' (*dört kapı*) to God: *Tarikat, Shari'ah, Marifet* and *Hakikat*. These are all flexible ideas and I can only generalise about them here. *Tarikat* (which refers to Sufi orders in Sunni thought) means for Alevis the ritual practices associated with the *cem*, the adherence to the 'Alevi Conditions' mentioned above and attention to the knowledge associated with the *Buyruk*. *Shari'ah* for Alevis refers to the exercise of power, especially by the central government, as well as to submission to the traditional 'orthodox' tenets of Islam. For some, *Shari'ah* refers to the superficial aspects of religious practice – the willingness to follow Sunni expectations rather than oppose them. *Tarikat*, on the other hand, is the profound reality that resides below the surface and is accessible to those who strive on the path of knowledge. *Marifet* is this striving on the path of knowledge of true reality. Finally, *Hakikat* is the ultimate goal of Sufi and Alevi ecstatic ritual: unity with the divine (Shankland 2003: 84–6).[7] The striving for *Hakikat* is a central feature of the *cem* ritual.

Semah

The content of the *cem* ritual has varied over time and location. In Alevi villages of the past, the *cem* rituals took place in private homes and were generally kept out of sight and awareness of non-Alevis (perhaps for fear of persecution and in order to protect the secret knowledge expressed in the ritual). Like the Bektaşis, Alevi men and women participate together in *cem* rituals, even dancing together in the *semah*.[8] Commonly, the *cem* begins with the rituals of obeisance and reconciliation, and sometimes includes prayers and recitations of the names of the Twelve Imams. But the central part of the ritual is the songs (*deyiş*) and the dance (*semah*). The songs are viewed as deep expressions of faith and often contain stories relating to the Prophet Muhammad, Imam Ali, and the martyrdoms of Imam Hasan and Imam Hüseyin, among others. Music plays such an important part of Alevi ritual, both now and in the past, that one of the historically designated assistants to the *dede* is the musician who sings and plays the *bağlama* (a long-necked lute, also known as a *saz*). The fame of these musicians – called *zakir, sazende* or *aşık* – extends well beyond the Alevi community and the *bağlama* itself sometimes serves as a symbol of Alevism. In some Alevi communities in Anatolia, all young men of the *dede* lineages are expected to learn to play the *bağlama* (Erol 2010: 378; see also Soileau 2017).

The *semah* that accompanies the songs is generally performed by everyone present who is physically able – men and women together. There are a number of different dances, each of which varies by region, so there are no set choreographic features. The most important of these dances is the *Kırklar Semahı*

Figure 3.1 Boy with *bağlama* (photograph by author)

(Dance of the Forty Saints) and the *Turnalar Semahı* (Dance of the Cranes). The slow-moving Dance of the Forty Saints commemorates the *miraç* (the nocturnal ascent of the Prophet Muhammad to heaven) where the Prophet encountered forty saints. In the Alevi tradition, 'the gathering of the 40 saints refers to the moment after the Prophet's ascension, when he beheld the manifestation of Divine Reality in Ali' (Erol 2010: 379). The Dance of the Cranes, in which dancers imitate the actions of birds, is believed to derive from Turkish shamanic practices and is widely interpreted to symbolise both the ascending soul of Imam Ali and the transformation of the shaman into a bird.[9] While there are differing interpretations of the dances, many Alevis believe that each gesture and movement (*yürütme*) performed in the context of the various ritual dances expresses the inter-relationship of the members of the trilogy of God (God, Muhammad and Ali), the universe and humanity, and that the whirling movements of the dance symbolise the fact that nothing remains the same but the universe is always changing (Erol 2010: 378–80).[10] One can now view recordings of public Alevi ceremonies (the *semah* is traditionally held in private, though that has changed over time, as will be discussed below). One video from the Hacı Bektaşı Veli Cultural Foundation Semah Troupe from Çorum[11] features young Alevi dancers performing a *semah* to a traditional Alevi song, '*Hü Diyelim Döne Döne*' ('Let's Turn/Dance while Saying "Hü"' – *Hü* or *Huwa* ('he') is a name for God in Islamic mystical traditions). A large audience watches and sometimes sings along, and on the wall behind the dancers pictures of Ali, Hacı Bektaşi Veli and Atatürk are hanging from left to right. The first stanzas of the song are as follows:

> *Yarabbi aşkın ver bana efendim*
> *Hu diyeyim Allah Allah döne döne*
> *Aşkın ile yana yana efendim*
> *Hu diyeyim Allah Allah döne döne*
>
> *Cahe düştüm Yusuf gibi efendim*
> *Derde düştüm Allah Allah Eyyub gibi*
> *Ağlayayım Yakub gibi efendim*
> *Hu diyeyim Allah Allah döne döne*

> O Lord, give me your love, my effendi
> I say 'Huwa Allah Allah' while dancing
> With your love to your side, my effendi
> Dancing, dancing, I say 'Huwa Allah Allah'

> Like Joseph I fell into a well, my effendi
> Like Job, I suffered trials, Allah Allah
> Let me cry like Joseph, my effendi
> Dancing, dancing, I say 'Huwa Allah Allah'

The Alevi musical repertoire is vast, and many songs, whether upbeat or plaintive, have become popular in Turkey and beyond. The *bağlama* is a central instrument in Turkish folk music, and its significance in Alevi music has often meant Alevi bards and other musicians have come to represent Turkey's distinctive musical heritage.

The rituals of the *cem* can last several hours and can be performed as frequently as participants wish. There are, however, seasonal restrictions on *cem* performances. The *cem* cannot be performed in the time period between the celebration of *Hidrellez* on 6 May and the annual performance of the *görgü* in preparation for winter plowing that occurs in the autumn. *Hidrellez* is a spring festival celebrated on the day when two especially righteous Prophets, Hızır (Khidr) and Ilyas (Elijah), were believed to have met on earth ('*Hidrellez*' is a combination of the two names).[12] This is a popular festival for peoples throughout Eastern Europe, Central Asia and parts of the former Ottoman Empire, but for Alevis it has particular religious significance. The *görgü* is a complex set of rituals whose overall focus is the mediation of conflicts that exist in the community, emphasising the restoration of peaceful relationships among community members (see Shankland 2003: 121–31). In many ways, the peace-making aspect of the *görgü* sets the stage for the *cem* rituals to come, since the rituals cannot be performed when there is conflict in the community. Both the *görgü* and the *cem* are processes by which purification of the heart and purification of the soul takes place. Just as one must purify the body before the rituals through the performance of ablutions so must the heart and mind be purified in preparation for communion with the divine.

Migration and Alevi dynamism

Alevis have tended to absorb appealing ideas and practices from the various peoples and traditions they have encountered, and as the historical-cultural landscape has changed, so have strands of Alevism. One of the most dramatic transformations that has taken place in Turkey is the gradual emptying out of the countryside as people migrated to the cities looking for work and educational opportunities. Before the Second World War, 75 per cent of the population was rural and only 25 per cent was urban. Beginning in the 1950s, however, more and more Turks from the countryside moved into the cities, mostly to larger cities such as Istanbul, Ankara and Izmir. The population shift was so large that by the end of the twentieth century, 65 per cent of the Turkish population lived in urban centres, almost completely reversing the rural/urban population ratio. This made Turkey one of the fastest urbanising countries in the world (Delibas 2015: 108–9).

There was a variety of factors that spurred this influx of rural migrants into cities. Development was very uneven in Turkey, and migration tended to follow strong development and the unskilled labour opportunities that went with it. In the cities, the incomes were higher – the average per capita income in the cities was often four times higher than that in the villages. Furthermore, the cities offered more consistent and higher-quality services than villages, including education, healthcare, electricity, water and transport. Migrants streamed into cities, and sometimes most or all of the population of a village would migrate en masse. Because the migrants were often poor, they would build their own make-shift houses, known as *gecekondus* (meaning 'built at night') that ringed the major cities well into the twenty-first century. Indeed, some *gecekondu* communities are still in evidence in the second decade of the century, though there have been concerted efforts to replace the *gecekondus* with modern apartment buildings – often to the disadvantage of the *gecekondu* dwellers (Erman 2011).

Figure 3.2 A *gecekondu* neighbourhood outside Izmir, 1998 (photograph by author)

This migratory trend has had important religious and political effects. In terms of religious identity, when villagers migrate to the cities, the notions of 'proper' religious practice, as well as personal identity, become unsettled and conflicted, and many migrants find themselves disorientated and somewhat alienated from the lifestyle and worldview they had taken for granted. Newly arrived migrants often have to search for who they will be, since the framework within which their own identities were formed has disappeared, at least in part. As the migrants adjust to new and different ways of living and thinking, they also often become aware that there are discrepancies and varieties in religious view and practice. Suddenly, they have to actively choose how they are going to be Muslim – or perhaps whether they want to practise Islam at all.

How the migration experience affected some Sunni communities will be discussed in future chapters. For Alevis, migration into cities led to changes in Alevi ritual and social organisation. For instance, *dede*s lost some of their authority both in urban and in rural settings. As they moved away or died, their numbers dwindled in the villages, as did the numbers of followers who were traditionally devoted to them, so much so that *cem* rituals led by an effective *dede* have become less common in villages. For those who moved to the cities, *dede*s and *dede* lineages were not always settled in proximity to their follower lineages, so that the hereditary social networks that centred around the *dede*s became fragmented and dispersed, weakening the Alevi sense of social solidarity. Eventually, movement into cities also necessitated the construction of buildings dedicated to Alevi ritual. In villages, the *cems* were held in a room in a private home, but in the cities, Alevis built *cemevis* (*cem* houses) to host the *cems* and other activities associated with the local Alevi population. The *cemevis* were usually larger than anything found in the villages, and some were large enough to serve several hundred people (Shankland 2003: 146).

At a more fundamental level, the very concept of Alevism shifted with migration. Living in close contact with Sunnis compelled many urban Alevis to conceptualise 'Alevism' as a distinct identity, not only as a religion. That is, Alevis felt themselves more keenly to be 'different' from Turkish Sunni society than when they lived in the villages. In the 1960s and 1970s, this sense of distinction compelled many urban Alevis to become involved in leftist political organisations that stood in opposition to the various nationalist right-wing groups (such as Turkish ultranationalist or Sunni Islamist groups) that emerged at the same time. Alevis – as well as Kurds – largely supported leftist and communist parties in part because the universalistic worldviews of socialism and Marxism downplayed religious and ethnic difference, which promised a way for Alevis and Kurds to escape some of the prejudices they faced as religious and ethnic minorities. In this context, politically involved Alevis did not emphasise their religious identity as much as their political affiliations since they saw leftist politics as presenting hope for a fairer and more just future (Dressler 2008).

Nevertheless, Turkish ultranationalists targeted Alevis not just because of their political difference but also because of their religious and supposed ethnic differ-ence. Right-wing groups spread propaganda, such as by using the slogan *Kürt, Kızılbaş, Komünist* ('Kurd, Kızılbaş, Communist) that equated Alevis with Kurds, rebels and communists, all perceived to be threats to the Sunni Turkish nation (Tambar 2014: 86–7). To be sure, the three groups specified in the slogan are not totally identical but they do overlap. About 20 per cent of Alevis are Kurds, but most Kurds are actually Sunni. Many Alevis and Kurds identified with com-munist groups in the 1970s, but not all did. The reference to *Kızılbaş* harkened back to the violent rebellious movements that arose in the eastern borderlands of the Ottoman Empire, and linking the Alevis with those movements was meant to denote supposed Alevi treachery and impiety (Shankland 2003: 19).

As the 1970s progressed, the many rival political groups took their battles more and more to the streets and to public institutions. The various weak coalition governments of the time were unable to curb the violence or provide any sort of political stability. This civil conflict affected Turkish life at almost every level, in schools, universities and workplaces, as well as in public venues. Jenny White vividly describes the complexity and extent of the violent rivalries between leftists and right-wing groups (2013: 34):

Everyone, even school children, was forced to choose a side, or risk being attacked by those on the 'other' side. This was no easy choice, since 'left versus right' did not do justice to the many splinter groups that formed. The left was split into socialists, Che Guevaraists, Maoists, and other ideological persuasions. These groups would attack each other for their lack of ideological purity; extremists of all stripes battled with guns, bombs, knives, and whatever else came to hand . . . On the 'right', fundamentalist and secular nationalist youth groups fought for control of the streets, campuses and neighborhoods. The ultranationalist Gray Wolves acted as the shock troop for the far-right Nationalist Action Party, a party that was represented in parliament while shielding its radical members. The Gray Wolves carried out drive-by shootings of leftists and Alevis, who were associated with the left, sometimes choosing their victims simply by the style of their mustache. (Leftists liked to sport a Fu Manchu mustache that drooped at the sides of the mouth.) The violence and ideological extremism were inescapable, whether one lived in a village, shantytown, or middle-class housing.

Ultranationalist violence against Alevis and Kurds intensified into bloody massacres in several Anatolian cities, such as Malatya (1978), Sivas (1978), Kahramanmaraş (1978) and Çorum (1980). These acts of violence increased Alevis' sense that the Turkish state had abandoned them, since many believed that the state had done nothing to stop the violence and may have even supported the perpetrators (Mutluer 2016: 147).

One central objective of the military coup of 12 September 1980 – discussed in the last chapter – was to bring the civil violence to an end, and through martial law and incarceration the rival groups were pacified, at least temporarily. But it quickly became clear that the military government, with its Sunni Turkish nationalist outlook, punished and suppressed the leftists to a much greater extent than they did right-wing interests. This anti-left bias makes sense in the context of the Cold War and Turkey's position in NATO as a bulwark against the spread of communism. Turkey shared a direct border with the USSR in Turkey's north-east and was the only Western-bloc country on the Black Sea, controlling the crucial shipping lanes through the Bosporus Strait and the Dardanelles. The Turkish military government, which was allied with the countries of the North Atlantic, viewed itself as defender of Western capitalist interests around the world, and thus viewed leftists sympathetic to communism as an existential threat to Turkey and to the international military alliance to which it belonged. The suppression of the left in the wake of the 1980 coup especially affected the Alevi population. Many Alevis were jailed, and the military and state institutions and politicians continued to view Alevis with suspicion – a situation that continues to this day.

Beginnings of the 'Alevi Revival'

The period after the 1980 coup found Alevis at a loss. Their sources of political identity in the 1960s and 1970s – the left-wing organisations – were widely suppressed, if not completely wiped out. Furthermore, the state's project of the Turkish-Islamic Synthesis included increasing pressure on Alevis to assimilate to Sunni Islam. For example, after the 1980 coup the religious education classes became mandatory for all students from the 4th grade on, and these courses promulgated Sunni Muslim religion while ignoring Alevi beliefs and practices. Alevi students were not even allowed to skip the classes, but were forced to take them along with their Sunni classmates. During the 1980s the Diyanet also oversaw an acceleration in the building of mosques in Alevi villages and neighbourhoods, staffing the mosques with imams and preachers to inculcate Sunnism into the surrounding communities. This was also done against the will of the community inhabitants (Dressler 2008: 286; Göner 2005: 116–17).

In reaction to the imposition of the Turkish-Islamic Synthesis and to the loss of leftist political activism, many Alevis started to assign more importance to their identity as Alevis rather than as socialists or communists. This is the beginning of what many have called the 'Alevi Revival', in which members of the community emphasised the religious principles and history of Alevism. But because of the process of rural-to-urban migration and the weakening of traditional Alevi social networks revolving around the *dede* lineages, the Alevi revival was not a simple renewal of old practices but a reimagining of Alevism as a broad religious tradition. The regional variations and the flexibility of traditional Alevism gave way to attempts at creating a common universal identity. Alevis began to establish foundations (*vakıflar*) and associations (*dernekler*) geared towards reviving and supporting the heritage of the Alevis – these organisations were most often responsible for the construction of *cemevis*. They also acted as political and social support for the Alevi community, especially vis-à-vis the national and local governments (Mutluer 2016: 148–9). With the support of the Alevi foundations, Alevis began publishing books and creating radio, TV and (later) internet programmes designed to spell out the basic principles of *Alevilik* (Alevism). The *semah* dances from the *cem* rituals, which had always been done in secret, were now performed in public for non-Alevi audiences, thus becoming an 'artifact' of Alevi Turkish folk culture. Not just Alevis themselves, but scholars, journalists and other observers became more interested in Alevism and produced both academic and popular works about the Alevis. The proliferation of publications and programmes – which accelerated in the 1990s and 2000s – contributed to 'the increased presence and visibility of Alevi subjects in the Turkish public sphere, and the Alevi subjects' growing conviction that Alevism should be the main site of political, social, and cultural mobilization' (Erdemir 2005: 939–40; see also Massicard 2013: 96–103).

The role of the *dede* continued to change during the revival too. In the traditional villages, a *dede* had mediated disputes, guided the rituals and instructed the community on religious principles believed to come down to him through sacred lineages. In the urban context after 1980, *dede*s no longer practised mediation and were not always the centre of an Alevi community. They were still regarded as necessary to conduct rituals, including the *cem*, and larger *cemevi*s usually had a least one *dede* available for ritual purposes. But over time the *dede*s competed for authority with non-*dede* Alevis who were well educated and active in their own communities, in the broader public sphere and in local politics. Many of these leaders were the central authority figures in Alevi organisations while *dede*s played only marginal roles. The education and middle-class status of the non-*dede* leaders often meant that they could speak about Alevism to a wider audience and represent Alevi interests to the government. On the surface, the Alevi revival seems like an optimistic turn of events, where Alevis were able to solidify their community and whose principles could be articulated in the public sphere. But even as Alevism evolved over time, the Alevis continued to face opposition and oppression from the Turkish state and other Sunni groups, as will be examined in later chapters.

Notes

1. The Arabic-speaking Alevi communities that live in southern Turkey near the Syrian and Iraqi borders are actually more closely associated with the Alawites (also known as the Nusayris or Tahtacıs), which have a different history from the Alevis of modern Turkey (Van Bruinessen 1996: 7).
2. Not all Shi'a accept that there were twelve imams, though 'Twelver' Shi'ism has been dominant in Iran/Persia since the sixteenth century. Some Shi'a, for example, hold that there are only seven imams. They are called Sevener Shi'a or Isma'ili Shi'a, because they believe that the last imam was Isma'il ibn Jafar. There is also a small group who believe that there were only five imams. Twelver Shi'ism is the most widely practised form of Shi'ism.
3. Sufi orders in Turkey in general will be discussed in greater detail in Chapter 4.
4. John Kingsley Birge thoroughly described Bektaşi doctrines and beliefs in his book *The Bektashi Order of Dervishes* (2015). Though Birge's book was first published in 1937, scholars still view it as one of the best comprehensive works on the Bektaşi order.
5. There are some Alevis who accept the idea that Alevism is not a form of Islam, but most Alevis do identify as Muslim.
6. This contrasts with the Sunni ideal (though not necessarily the reality) in which God supposedly has an equal relationship with all believers, and no human can mediate between the believer and God.
7. The nature of Sufi ritual will be discussed in greater depth in the next chapter.
8. In fact, Alevis tend not to practise strict gender segregation in everyday life either – again, unlike Sunnis – though traditional gender roles typify Alevi social organisation.
9. See the following video for an illustration of the Dance of the Cranes: https://www.youtube.com/watch?v=CDF8X-e2LaI&list=RDe2zsCoNnfg8&index=2
10. While the Alevi *semah*s have similarities to the dances of the Mevlana *semah*, they have very different histories and meanings.

11. https://www.youtube.com/watch?v=YGwv8we3p38&list=RDe2zsCoNnfg8&index=5
12. Ilyas is listed as one of the most righteous Prophets in the Qur'an in Surah Al-Anaam 6: 85–7. Hızır (Khidr) is not mentioned by name in the Qur'an, but according to Qur'anic commentary it is Hızır who Musa (Moses) encountered in the Surah al-Kahf (18: 62–80). Hızır is supposed to be a loyal follower of God and source of divine wisdom who has transcended human limitation, and Musa seeks him out to gain further divine insight (Kreinath 2014).

CHAPTER 4

Practising piety: popular religious organisations

Attending Ramadan services at the Golden Generation Compound of Fethullah Gülen

In 2015, I was studying the works of Bediüzzaman Said Nursi, an influential twentieth-century theologian from Turkey. Given the complexity of the texts and the old Turkish they were written in, I depended on the expertise of my friend, Meral, who was a follower of Fethullah Gülen, a contemporary Turkish preacher heavily inspired by Said Nursi. Meral had long studied Nursi's writing and was familiar with his texts, and so could provide much-needed guidance as we worked through the material. On one occasion when we met, during Ramadan in 2015, I was delighted when Meral invited me to a Ramadan service at the Golden Generation Compound where Fethullah Gülen lived, in eastern Pennsylvania. There he instructed his students in Qur'an interpretation and gave sermons to the Turkish community living nearby. During the thirty-day period of Ramadan, it is customary to read one-thirtieth of the Qur'an every day – the Qur'an is divided into thirty parts, each called a *cuz* (Arabic: *juz'*). We would be attending the last day of Ramadan to listen to the reading of the final *cuz*.

Meral and her family drove me to the Golden Generation Compound, which comprised a number of buildings. We entered the main building where the *mescit* and congregational rooms were. Meral's husband and sons went to the men's section, while Meral and I entered the women's section of the large room where the service would take place. The women's section was much smaller than the men's section, which was big and airy, with lots of divans around the rim of the room. Many older men sat on the divans, while younger men sat on the floor. On the floor in front of the couch where Gülen would sit were arranged his students with their Qur'ans and Qur'an stands. Most of them sat on the floor though some sat on chairs. All the men had on prayer caps, and the students wore long navy coats. There was a large computer screen with the Qur'an text placed in front of Gülen's spot. The women's section was separated from the men's section by a wooden screen. This screen made it possible for the women to watch the men, but the men were unable to see the women very well, because there was no light on in the women's section. There were some chairs and stools but clearly not enough for everyone in the women's section, so as the room filled up, many women ended up sitting on the floor from which they would have no view of the main room.

Figure 4.1 Students of Fethullah Gülen studying at the Golden Generation Compound in Saylorsburg, PA, 2015 (photograph given to author by one of Gülen's students)

Hocaefendi ('honoured teacher', as Gülen is called by his followers) entered and walked solemnly to his spot on the sofa, which was not far from where I was sitting. He was unsmiling (and indeed never smiled the whole time, from what I could see), and people did not stand up when he entered. Meral said that he does not allow people to stand up in respect. He sat, and said a few words as people quietened down. Soon, a reciter began the last *cuz* of the Qur'an, starting at Surah 78, *An-Naba'* ('The Tidings'). After each *surah*, a student would read the Turkish translation. Hocaefendi would comment on the Qur'an recitation but most of his commentary was about the various translations; he would sometimes stop the student to suggest a better translation for a concept or a term. At other times he asked another student to look at an alternative translation to see if it was better. After one of the *surahs*, Hocaefendi asked everyone to do a *secde* (the kneeling part of the customary prayer), and the whole community did so as best they could. In the women's section, there was barely enough room.

People chanted customary prayers after the final three *surahs*, and Surah 112, *Al-Ikhlas* ('Sincerity') was repeated three times. *Al-Ikhlas* is one of the most often recited and memorised *surahs*. Its text emphasises the Divine Oneness of God: 'Say, "He, God, is One, God, the Eternally Sufficient unto Himself. He begets not; nor was He begotten. And none is like unto Him"'. After pausing to meditate on *Al-Ikhlas*, the last two *surahs* were read and translated, and a student read a long prayer of praise, during which the congregation said *amin* (amen) after each praise. The older lady sitting next to me was deeply emotional during this prayer, saying *amin* with a lot of feeling, and had begun to cry. This lady was accompanied by some young women, who seemed to hold her in deep respect. After the prayer, some people left, but others stayed behind, and Hocaefendi asked that we do fifty repetitions of *Al-Ikhlas*. We sat and whispered the *surah*, many people using their *tespih* (a string of beads like a rosary that helps the worshipper to keep track of repetitions of prayers).

Hocaefendi was still with his followers and students when Meral and I left to go to *iftar* at a friend's house. Meral also told me that Hocaefendi and his students had spent the previous five years going through the whole Qur'an, and for each verse, they had read from many different *tefsirs* (interpretations) – as many as twenty at a time. Some of the *tefsirs* come from the earliest times in Islamic history, while others are more recent. The most recent is the *Hak Dini Kur'an Dili* by Elmalılı Muhammed Hamdi Yazır, a Turkish theologian who wrote his *tefsir* at the time of the early Republic. Hocaefendi would also provide his own commentary, clarifying or adding to *tefsirs*.

Spiritual seeking on the Sufi path

There are many ways a devout Muslim can seek spiritual enlightenment – the experience that I describe where followers look to an esteemed master for spiritual guidance is just one such path. Probably one of the most common ways to approach religious learning is through study of the Qur'an, *hadith* and the various Islamic sciences, such as *tefsir*, *kalam* (theology), *fikh* (Islamic jurisprudence) and *siyer* (study of the life of the Prophet). But this course of study is often intense and difficult, since it requires the student to become proficient in Qur'anic Arabic[1] and spend considerable time mastering difficult subjects. Turkish students of the Islamic sciences study under teachers who are known for their mastery of the material. These teachers may be products of the education provided by the Diyanet or of the divinity faculties in universities, or they may be individuals who have gained knowledge through religious communities or Sufi orders operating outside of the state institutions. Fethullah Gülen, for example, served as a Diyanet-appointed imam in Edirne and later in Izmir, but he had received most of his religious education from his family and from informal teachers in his home town of Erzurum. Eventually, Gülen separated from the institutions of state religion to cultivate a *cemaat* (religious organisation) based on his own principles and charisma (the Gülen *cemaat* will be discussed below).

Many devout Muslims may also seek spiritual enlightenment by participating in Sufi communities. Sufi orders (*Tarikats*) were once widespread throughout the Ottoman Empire, and Sufi religious movements have remained popular and influential in the modern Turkish Republic. Turkey is currently

> home to many tarikats and their branches: *Kadiri, Nakşbendi, Mevlevi, Rifai, Halveti, Galibi, Cerrahi, Uşşaki, Melami, Haznevi, Menzilci, İsmailağa* group, *Işıkçı, Erenköy*

group, and so forth. The overall picture is complicated by inter-group divisions and overlaps. Each has a special outlook on politics, on the aspects of modern life such as finance, education and customs, as well as a distinguishable symbolism and terminology, and finally a sense of higher objectives. They appeal to different social strata in terms of wealth, education and occupation: where they do not, they compete with one another. (Kaya 2018: 40)

We have already encountered the Bektaşis, which was one Sufi order that was important in Turkish history. As we saw in the last chapter, the Bektaşi Sufi order was abolished in the nineteenth century because of its political involvement with the Janissaries, who were themselves eliminated in 1826, yet Bektaşism has endured in part in certain communities of Alevis. Many other Sufi communities have flourished in modern Turkey, despite the early republican prohibition against Sufi orders. This chapter examines the processes of transformation and adaptation of Turkish Sufi movements that have persisted into the republican era, concentrating on some orders that have had deep impacts on Turkish society and politics in the twentieth and twenty-first centuries.

Sufism: problems of definition

Sufism (*tasavvuf*; Arabic: *tasawwuf*) is most often translated into English as 'Islamic mysticism', but such a term does not capture the complexity of Sufi beliefs and practices. In the Christian context, 'mysticism' indicates the striving of the believer to directly encounter the divine through the abolition of the ego. Such experiences are understood to be intensely personal, where one transcends the confines of the material and social world. The prescribed rituals and rules of religion are often downplayed or discarded as the mystic draws closer to God. But in general, Christian mystics operate as individuals, sometimes in seclusion, to transform the self in its relationship with the divine.

While some Sufi practitioners have incorporated such personal, otherworldly practices, most Sufis are embedded in communities where social relationships and religious law are not diversions from spiritual striving but the main channels of spiritual enlightenment. Traditionally, a Sufi community depended on the guidance of a Sufi master – a friend (*vali*; Arabic: *wali*) of God – who inherited his religious authority and powers to bestow divine blessings (*baraka*) through a sacred bloodline. The *dede*s of Alevism described in Chapter 3 are an example of this type of sacred authority. Followers of the Sufi masters practise a set of disciplinary techniques – ways in which the followers seek to put aside their own desires – in order to help them cultivate deeper devotion to God and develop ethical Muslim selfhood and ways of thinking. Coupled with the idea of self-cultivation is the common Sufi belief that spiritual awakening involves understanding the true nature of reality and of the Qur'an. In Sufi thought, there is an outer, superficial appearance of the world and of the Qur'an. In the case of the

Qur'an, superficial comprehension would be to take all of the words and verses at face value without looking for deeper significances. But Sufis argue that the Qur'an and all reality have 'true' inner meanings that can only be discovered through the 'eyes of the heart', not of the mind. Relying on a master-guide, the Sufi disciple strives to uncover the esoteric reality embedded within superficial materiality. To be clear, this is not necessarily a rejection of the material world but an appreciation that the material world links to a transcendent reality that can be encountered and comprehended by the Sufi practitioners (Abenante and Vicini 2017; Yavuz 2003: 134–5). The different Sufi orders offer a variety of techniques to aid disciples in their journey towards self-mastery and comprehension of ultimate reality.

In the early days of Islam, Sufism developed along various currents, with influential religious leaders promoting diverse beliefs and practices. Sufism was then largely unstructured, where

> instruction took the form of a shaykh [sheikh] imparting Sufi wisdom in a conversation or in a lecture to a single aspirant (*mürid*) to Sufism or to a whole circle of aspirants and other interested listeners in random or regular meetings held in the shaykh's house, or more typically, in a mosque. (Karamustafa 2007: 116)

Some of these Sufi masters did encourage an otherworldly devotion to God that rejected attachments to social roles, and they were even sometimes critical of the developing religious law (*Shari'ah*) for being too focused on affairs of this world. But most promoted some degree of worldly involvement and social obligations, seeing participation in the material world and devotion to God as complementary aspects of religious life (Karamustafa 2007: 87–108).

By the eleventh century, formal Sufi orders with established rules and membership requirements became the norm, and this formal structure seemed to contribute to the orders' lasting power. These were based around a 'spiritual lineage' in which a founding master, the *vali*, would teach a particular set of beliefs and practices – a 'path' (*Tarikat*) – to his group of followers. The master would most often give his name to the order, and would be succeeded by an elected disciple, who would likewise be followed by one of his disciples and so on. This type of spiritual genealogy, known as a *silsile* (Arabic: *silsila*), has been the organisational core for most Sufi orders.

The master-disciple relationship has always been an essential feature of Sufism, where the disciple makes a complete and exclusive spiritual bond (*rabıta*) to a teacher or master (*mürşid*). The master would oversee the details of the disciples' lives, traditionally in the context of a community living in a Sufi lodge (*tekke, dergah* or *zaviye* in Turkish). During Ottoman times, these lodges were funded by foundations that would provide support to the members, and the orders were largely left alone to manage their affairs and select their leaders (Silverstein 2011: 66–7). Membership in orders was solemnised through rituals, such as the recitation of an oath of allegiance and the wearing of distinctive clothing, and over time a follower could advance along the path of divine wisdom by passing through stages of spiritual attainment (*seyr-i süluk*) (Karamustafa 2007: 170; Özal 1999).

The orders served as places where the adherents could enhance their spirituality by performing rituals such as the *zikir* (Arabic: *dhikr*), a collective recitation of prayer formulas by which the participants attempt spiritually to draw closer to God. In some orders, the *zikir* is performed aloud (*sessli* or *cehri*), sometimes with rhythmic dancing, as the participants attempt to reach an ecstatic state of communion with God.[2] In other orders, the *zikir* is performed silently (*sessiz* or *hafi*), though with some of the same goals. The repeated recitation of Surah 112 described in the introductory vignette for this chapter would be an example of a silent *zikir*. *Zikir*s might include the recitation of the 99 Beautiful Names of God or repetitions of one of the names of God. Commonly, they consist of short phrases, such as *La ilaha illallah* (the first part of the Shahada, meaning 'There is no God but God'), *Subhanallah* ('Glory be to God'), *Allahu ekbar* ('God is Great') and *Alhamdulillah* ('All Praise to God'). It is very common to see individuals handling a *tespih*, a string of beads like a rosary used to keep count of prayers or for reciting phrases as an act of *zikir*. These rituals are meant to help the participant to focus on God, thereby cultivating a closer or even a direct relationship to God. The *zikir* does not necessarily require extensive learning of Arabic or Islamic law in order for the followers to take part, though some Sufi masters have encouraged study of the Islamic sciences. Furthermore, many Sufi orders have been non-discriminating in terms of membership, guided by the philosophy that all believers should seek experience of the divine. And beyond spiritual guidance, many *Tarikat*s offered essential social services, such as education, healthcare and informal adjudication of local problems in the provinces that were relatively remote from Istanbul and other centres of power.

Sufi orders in a changing political reality

In the Ottoman Empire, the *Tarikat*s had been so popular that by 1920, just before the Kemalist revolution, there were 305 Sufi lodges in Istanbul alone (Yavuz 2003: 138–9). Some Sufi orders, as we saw with the Bektaşis, were heavily involved in politics or rebelled against reform efforts, which was one of the reasons that Atatürk and the nationalists eventually banned the orders after the foundation of the Turkish Republic. More generally, though, Atatürk and his supporters came to see the brotherhoods as arenas in which unauthorised forms of Islam could flourish and as impediments to the secularisation and Westernisation of the new nation. The abolition of the Sufi orders entailed the closure of many Sufi lodges, the elimination of Sufi offices and titles, such as *şeyh*, *pir*, *dede*, *mürşid*, *çelebi* and *derviş*, and the abolition of the distinctive clothing and headgear of the orders. Only religious officials of the state were permitted to wear religious clothing while conducting state functions. The Turkish state closed the shrines (*türbe*) of Sufi saints, which had been the focus of much popular piety, though some remained open or reopened later. Even calligraphy and Sufi musical traditions were subject to bans. And, as discussed in Chapter 1, the 1938 Law of Associations made illegal the formation of independent societies, especially those based on religion, sect and *Tarikat*, as well as societies formed for the purposes of religious prayer and practice. The Turkish constitution in its various versions has barred religious communities from being involved in politics, such as by forming a political party, nor are political parties permitted to be formed in order to represent any religious belief.

There were some devout citizens of the Republic, especially those attached to the new bureaucratic system, who welcomed the end of the orders, some of which were seen as corrupt and filled with charlatans and false prophets (Silverstein 2011: 86–91). But given that Sufi practices had been so popular and widespread, they were not so easily expunged from Turkish society. During the period of the one-party Republican rule (1923–46), most *Tarikats* went underground and continued their activities in modified forms while maintaining followers among the populace. However, the introduction of multi-party democracy in 1946 and the expansion of civil liberties in the 1961 constitution meant that gradually the religious communities based around the Sufi orders could operate more openly, even though the ban on their activities was never formally lifted. Furthermore, the rapid urbanisation that began in earnest in Turkey in the 1960s and continued to the 1980s meant that the rural-to-urban migrants who were uprooted from their traditional environment had to adjust to new and different ways of living and thinking. In so doing, they often became aware of the wide varieties in religious view and, suddenly, they had to choose actively how they were to be Muslim, that is, what sorts of beliefs and practices were necessary to be a good Muslim. One effect of this trend, as economist and journalist Mehmet Altan has argued (2010), was that the Sufi orders and religious communities provided a major means by which the rural-to-urban migrants could find identity and some sense of continuity after the disruption associated with uprooting oneself from one's ancestral home to take up life in an alien and alienating urban environment. The Sufi communities have thus been especially attractive to Turkey's many migrants.

Moreover, the Turkish-Islamic Synthesis that developed after the 1980 coup led the government to recognise that the *cemaats* could also serve as a bulwark against the much-feared encroachment of communism. The utility of religion and the religious orders for maintaining public unity against communism led to policy changes regarding religious activities in the last decades of the twentieth century. For example, the state eased restrictions on Islamic publishing and allowed some *cemaats* to establish radio and television stations that provided religious programming.[3] These changes allowed for the Sufi communities to expand and become more socially and politically visible, a process that accelerated in the twenty-first century.

Mevlevis – domestication and exemplary status

Probably the most famous of all Turkish Sufi orders are the Mevlevis[4] of Whirling Dervish fame. The founding master of the order was the now world-famous Jalal al-din Muhammad Balkhi Rumi (1207–73), known as 'Mevlana' ('our master'). The Mevlevis have been able to maintain a visible presence in Turkey, even during the early days of the Republic when anti-Sufi sentiment was at its height in the Kemalist government. Acceptance of the Mevlevis stemmed partly from the fact that important intellectuals in early Turkish history reinterpreted the order – and especially the figure of Rumi himself – to fit their vision of the Turkish state. A common assumption in Kemalist circles was that the Ottoman Empire, especially in its later years, obscured and corrupted the authentic mystical aspects of Turkish Islam. An intellectual and cultural task for the founders of the modern state was to reclaim the genuine Sufis of the imagined 'pure' Turkish past, and Rumi was a prime candidate for this 'rehabilitation', given his international reputation as a great thinker and the fact that he was author of such widely regarded works as the *Mesnevi* (Persian: *Mathnawi*). Mustafa Kemal Atatürk himself 'called Mevlana a "reformist" who accommodated Islam, which is a "tolerant" and "modern" religion, into "the spirit of Turks"' (Sağlam 2017: 419). The fact that Rumi actually came from Balkh in Central Asia and wrote in Persian did not deter this reinterpretation of Mevlana as a source of genuine Turkish Islam, since the Kemalist reformers viewed Central Asia itself as a source of Turkish ethnicity and identity.

This embrace of Rumi as a spiritual source of pure, 'moderate' Turkish Islam did not mean that the Mevlevi order simply carried on as it had before the Turkish revolution. Instead, the central lodge in Konya, which houses Rumi's tomb and the tombs of early members of the Mevlevi *silsile*, was converted in 1926 from an active *tekke* into the Konya Museum of Historical Works. In 1954 the structure was renovated and renamed the Mevlana Museum. There visitors can view the ornate tombs of the Mevlevis and peruse the displays of old books and traditional clothing of the Mevlevi order.

Because Sufi orders are still illegal in Turkey, the Mevlevi *Tarikat* itself does not technically exist. Instead, the hereditary leader (*Makam-i Çelebi*) of the Mevlevis, Faruk Hemdem Çelebi (a twenty-second-generation descendant of the bloodline of Rumi) is President of an organisation in Istanbul and Konya called the International Mevlana Foundation (*Uluslararası Mevlânâ Vakfı*). This foundation is not registered as a religious community since that would be a violation of the 1938 Law of Associations. Rather, it is registered as a cultural

Figure 4.2 The *türbe* complex for Jalal al-din Rumi in Konya, Turkey (photograph by author)

and educational foundation that provides a context in which Mevlevis continue to study the classical works of Rumi and the many commentaries generated over the centuries on those works.

The Mevlevis also continue to practise the ritual centrepiece of the community, the *zikir* that culminates in the famous 'dance' (*sema*) of the Whirling Dervishes. This ritual includes recitations of prayers and poetry from Rumi's *Mesnevi*, and the whirling, meditative *sema* is accompanied by music played on classical Turkish instruments and sung by a small chorus (Markoff 1995: 157–8). The dervishes wear clothes that symbolise death to this world: a white gown that represents a shroud, a black cloak that represents the grave and a tall brown felt hat that symbolises a tombstone (Harmanşah et al. 2015: 359). The *sema* signifies the mystical journey of the soul from spiritual unconsciousness to ecstatic experience of the divine. The spinning or 'whirling' of the dervishes facilitates the ecstatic experience, as the dervishes spin in imitation of the spinning of the great heavenly bodies and the smallest atom, that is, they harmonise themselves with all creation.[5] Rumi was a prolific writer and poet, and while his writings cover many different topics, his poetry often alludes to the believer's search for the divine in the self and in the world. Here is just one example:

> There is a life in you, search that life,
> Search the secret jewel in the mountain of your body,
> Hey you, the passing away friend, look for with all your strength,
> *Whatever you are looking for, look in yourself not around.*[6]

In classical Sufi fashion, this poem admonishes the spiritual seeker to concentrate not on finding God out in the world but on developing self-knowledge as the best path to encountering the divine. God is always near and available to those who seek Him. This drawing close to God is reinforced in Qur'anic recitations that close the Mevlevi *sema*, which almost always include a reading of verse 115 from Surah 2, *Baraka*: 'To God belong the East and the West. Wheresoever you turn, there is the Face of God. He is All-Encompassing, Knowing.'

Traditionally, the Mevlevi *sema* would be conducted in a closed setting in which disciples would dance under the direction of the master. But the *sema* of the Whirling Dervishes has become a popular tourist attraction in Turkey, and visitors can visit the Mevlevi Lodge in Galata, Istanbul, or attend the Mevlana Rumi Festival in Konya to watch a Mevlevi *sema*. Mevlevis have even taken Whirling Dervish performances on international tours, and in 2005, UNESCO declared that the Mevlevi Sema Ceremony is one of the 'Masterpieces of the Oral and Intangible Heritage of Humanity'. This public display of such an essential Sufi ritual makes clear the full 'domestication' of the Mevlevis. Rather than being a threat to Turkey's secular order, the Mevlevis have become a source of national pride as their ritual displays advertise Turkey's beautiful, tolerant cultural heritage.

Religious communities in the modern Republic

The transformation of the Mevlevi *Tarikat* into a cultural foundation that preaches a tolerant Turkish Islam acceptable to the secularist order provides one model by which traditional Sufism has adapted to the Turkey's secularising reforms. Some Sufi communities are, like the Mevlevis, organised around a *silsile* and include regular performance of *zikir* by which participants attempt to achieve a direct experience of the divine. In the past these groups largely escaped state censure as long as they remained outside of party politics.

Other Sufi communities adapted to the political realities of the Turkish Republic in different ways. Many transformed into more informal groups called *cemaats* or *meclis* (assembly). Unlike *Tarikats*, modern *cemaats* generally do not have initiation rituals or membership requirements, nor do they always maintain formal organisational structures, such as the master-disciple relationship, thus the boundaries of the *cemaats* are often diffuse and vague. Some *cemaats* are more directly associated with the institutionalised, hierarchically organised Sufi orders that include ecstatic rituals emphasising direct contact with God (Raudvere 2002). Others focus more on developing 'proper' religious belief and moral behaviour with a strong social justice component. These *cemaat*s are sometimes referred to as 'neo-Sufi' in that they share many of the beliefs and philosophy of traditional Sufi orders, but forgo the formal hierarchy of the *Tarikat*s. Some *cemaat*s have appealed to the growing rural-to-urban migrants in the cities, since the *cemaat*s provided migrants with a message of social justice and moral integrity that was in line with the values of the countryside and in opposition to an urban environment that migrants often perceived as immoral and hostile (Yavuz 2003: 83–9). Many *cemaat*s have also provided institutions of religious education available to those who sought greater religious knowledge than that provided by the religious education mandated in the public schools or available through the Diyanet.

Nakşibendis

Among the many *Tarikat*s that have been influential in Ottoman and modern Turkish history, one of the most prominent has been the Nakşibendi[7] *Tarikat*. The order was named after Baha al-din Nakshband (1318–89), the Central Asian religious leader whose disciples spread the order to many parts of the Muslim world, including into the emerging Ottoman Empire. One especially influential Nakşibendi leader, Khalid al-Baghdadi (1776–1825), founded a branch of Nakşibendi Sufism, the Khalidi branch, that established a strong presence in the Ottoman Empire. Khalidis have traditionally held the view that the moral righteousness of a society depends on the piety and obedience to *Shari'ah* exhibited by the Sultan-leader. Thus the Khalidis resisted any reforms – such as the nineteenth-century 'Tanzimat' reforms – that would reduce the centrality and power of the Ottoman Sultan (Silverstein 2011: 68–9). Their resistance to the reforms was occasionally violent, but later Khalidi leaders, such as Ziyaeddin Gümüşhanevi (d. 1893) spearheaded a more subtle resistance. He formed a Khalidi branch in Istanbul, known as the Gümüşhanevi Nakşibendi-Khalidi order, centred around the İskenderpaşa mosque. This organisation had broad reach and provided religious and community services in parallel to, rather than directly against, Ottoman reformist developments. After the founding of the Turkish Republic, the Nakşibendis continued to make their community services available – sometimes clandestinely – to followers in both rural and urban settings, even as Nakşibendis participated in anti-reform rebellions that led to the execution of some Nakşibendi sheikhs and the suppression of the order.

Over time, aspects of the Nakşibendi-Khalidi philosophy helped the Sufi community adapt to the political realities of the Turkish Republic. For example,

Sheik Khalid's particular interpretation of zikr [zikir] and rabıta did not require any outward, institutionalised religious rituals. At the level of popular religion, many people replaced outward manifestations of faith with inner expressions as spirituality was restructured within the confines of the neighbourhood and family. (Yavuz 2003: 140)

The Nakşibendis preached a type of personal and private religious devotion that could easily co-exist with a regime that maintained that the public sphere should remain secular. The *cemaat* was able to take advantage of the mosque system created by the Diyanet. Many Nakşibendis sought religious education through the Diyanet, which meant that they could serve as state-appointed imams assigned to mosques around the country. While serving as civil servants from the Diyanet, these religious leaders continued Nakşibendi practices within the mosque settings, such that some of these mosques became de facto Nakşibendi lodges.

Mehmed Zahid Kotku and the Gümüşhanevi Nakşbendis

When the grip of secularist policies began to loosen in the 1950s, a number of Nakşibendi leaders contributed to the development of a more public Islamic intellectual discourse. One of the most influential of these thinkers was the charismatic sheikh Mehmed Zahid Kotku (1897–1980). Like many other Nakşibendi leaders, Kotku was appointed by the Diyanet to serve as imam at various important mosques, first in Bursa and later in Istanbul, even as he continued his involvement in the Nakşibendi order. He was actually the Diyanet's imam to the famous İskenderpaşa mosque in Istanbul from 1958 until his death in 1980, while he served as the leader of the Gümüşhanevi Nakşibendi order[8] (Mardin 1994: 133). There he served as a spiritual advisor to many important politicians who emerged in the 1960s and 1970s, such as the current President of Turkey, Recep Tayyip Erdoğan, and former prime ministers Turgut Özal and Necmettin Erbakan. Kotku preached gradualism in transforming Turkey into a more Islamically moral society. He rejected efforts to overthrow the secular order to establish an Islamic state in favour of changing society organically from within. He emphasised economic development and industrialisation, believing that growing a pious middle class would create the conditions for the easing of Kemalist restrictions on religion. To that end, Kotku's movement developed lively community centres and schools in the large cities and organised popular public activities. This ability to operate both in tandem with and parallel to the state allowed for the Nakşibendi order to develop into one of the broadest and most important religious organisations in Turkey today.

After the death of Kotku, leadership passed to his son-in-law, Esad Coşan (1938–2001), who attracted younger followers and intensified the order's development of community, political and economic projects. Coşan encouraged education of all members – boys and girls – and stressed that members should use the latest technology, learn foreign languages (including Western languages) and travel to foreign countries. As part of the effort to encourage education, the Nakşibendis built hostels for college students and developed stand-alone 'schools' in which religion could be taught in a more independent way than what was provided by the state in its religious education courses and religious secondary schools (see Chapter 6). In his later publications, Coşan placed special emphasis on business and trade as a mechanism by which to create an ethical society as long as those who engaged in these activities maintained proper morals and focus on God. The community also published magazines and journals and set up radio and television stations by which they could spread their ideas and promote a generation of Nakşibendi intellectuals. Like the Mevlevis, the Nakşibendis got around the old restrictions on public and publishing activities of religious associations by operating through foundations that were formally cultural or educational in nature.

Clearly, the Nakşibendis have not been world-denying, but see involvement in the world as a necessary part of religious life. The basic Nakşibendi idea is that with proper discipline and training, one can concentrate on or maintain a connection to God, even as one is engaged in the noisy world (Silverstein 2011: 102–5; Yavuz 2003: 143). Nakşibendi practice centres around self-discipline and restraint of material desires (*nefs*) through concentration on God and experience of the divine in one's heart. Under Kotku and Coşan, the *cemaat* developed techniques to discipline the *nefs* even in the midst of daily life, looking especially to the *Sunnah* (the sayings and deeds of the Prophet) for guidance. Anthropologist Brian Silverstein (2011) gives many examples of how members of the Nakşibendi *cemaat* at the İskenderpaşa and Süleymaniye mosques in Istanbul attempted to cultivate a properly religious disposition. For example, Nakşibendi members tried to maintain a state of physical purity as much as possible (that is, they performed ablutions at other times than before formal prayer) so that they could worship God at any time and place. Another idea important among Nakşibendis was that everyday work can be a form of worship, if one maintains a properly worshipful disposition. The division between sacred (religious) and profane (non-religious) realms of existence break down under these circumstances – the ordinary life may have transcendent significance. This helps to explain the Nakşibendis' comfort with being involved in business, politics, media and other 'worldly' pursuits.

In her book *Living Islam: Women, Religion and the Politicization of Culture in Turkey* (2002), sociologist Ayşe Saktanber provides an interesting portrait of the female members of a Kotku Nakşibendi community in Istanbul in the early 1990s. This community consisted of people who viewed the secularism of Turkish society as an impediment to proper Islamic practice. As a response, a group of families bought and shared an apartment complex (*site*) where they created a devout environment for Muslim families with a common Islamic worldview.

This arrangement allowed residents to 'live Islam' as conscious Muslims, that is, where the individual's entire life could be led 'in accordance with Islamic precepts', including observance of the Five Pillars of Islam and the domestic requirements of *Shari'ah* (Saktanber 2002: 164). For example, the community prohibited drinking alcohol, dancing and gambling, women always wore the Muslim headscarf in public and they rejected the modern holidays spread from the Western world, such as New Year celebrations. The community organised worship and activities in communal spaces associated with the complex, including a building devoted to Qur'an courses, dormitories for male and female university and secondary school students, a nursery school and a mosque. Relatives of Esan Coşan lived in the complex, and so on occasion Coşan would give sermons at their mosque, attracting large crowds. Community members followed the precepts of Islam closely and concentrated on cultivating family life considered ideal, where women's primary (and Godly) roles were defined by duties to the family and to the faith. Indeed, for many of the women Saktanber encountered, fulfilling traditional roles of wife and mother were simultaneously ways of fulfilling religious obligations – that is, everyday life has transcendent significance. What this portrait shows is that these *cemaats* can create a sense of community and shared belief for many devout Muslims while also opening space for members to lead religious lives in ways that they see most satisfactory and genuine.

The Nakşibendis have continued to be very important in Turkish public and political affairs and, if anything, the *cemaat* has grown more powerful over time as Islamist political parties have increased in power and come to dominate the Turkish government over the last three decades. These developments will be discussed in greater detail in later chapters.

Bediüzzaman Said Nursi and the Nur movements

One of the most distinctive and influential religious thinkers in modern Turkey is the great theologian Said Nursi (1877–1960), known as Bediüzzaman ('wonder of the age'). Nursi came from remote eastern Anatolia and was of Kurdish origin. The Nakşibendi-Khalidis had proselytised and established unofficial seminaries in eastern Anatolia, and Nursi was deeply influenced by the great Nakşibendi thinkers, such as Khalid and especially Ahmad Fauqi Al-Sirhindi (1563–1624) (Mardin 1989: 54–60). Nursi had limited formal education, but at a young age he became renowned among members of the Ottoman *ulema* as a master interpreter of the Qur'an and the *hadith*, and was invited to speak in important religious centres such as Damascus and Istanbul. He moved to Istanbul in 1907, but his criticism of the late Ottoman government and its secularising trends made him an object of harassment, and he was jailed on several occasions. After the founding of the Republic, he was subject to repeated incarceration and house arrest, most famously in Isparta in Western Anatolia. These periods of house arrest did not impede Nursi's development.

Nursi did not consider himself a Sufi – he was not a sheikh and did not have formal disciples as was typical of Sufi orders. In fact, Nursi argued with the coming of the Turkish Republic; the *Tarikat* ('way') based on the master-disciple relationship was a thing of the past. Now was the 'way' of *tasavvuf* pure and simple – Sufism without the *Tarikat* structure – and his philosophy incorporated and expounded upon many Sufi concepts. It was during his confinement that he produced his best-known works, collectively called *Risale-i Nur* (*Epistles of Light;* often shortened to *Risale*). It was a volume of the *Risale* that I was studying with Meral in the vignette that opened this chapter. The state prohibited the printing and distribution of these texts, but Nursi's students copied them out by hand and circulated them, enough so that Nursi gained a significant underground following. When Nursi died in 1960, the military kidnapped his body and buried it in an undisclosed location in order to prevent his grave from becoming a saint's tomb (*türbe*) that would attract pilgrims. Some believe he is buried in Şanlıurfa where he actually died – there is a *türbe* for him there (Figure 4.3), but more recent evidence suggests that he was buried in a secret grave near Isparta. His

Figure 4.3 The *türbe* of Bediüzzaman Said Nursi, Şanlıurfa, 2012 (photograph by author)

followers regularly visit his *türbe* in Şanlıurfa, and the location of his final resting place is a subject of dramatic speculation.

Nursi's *Risale* is a 'collection of collections' of Nursi's sermons in which he interprets the Qur'an and the *Sunnah*. Nursi's writings and sermons are gathered into various volumes with titles such as *Lem'alar* (*Flashes of Light*), *Mektubat* (*The Letters*), *Şualar* (*The Rays*) and *Sözler* (*The Words*). These collections are not systematically organised, but contain Nursi's meditations on various concepts and practices that aim to deepen the individual's devotion and attention to God. In his foundational biography of Said Nursi, Şerif Mardin (1989: 160–1) demonstrates the 'helter-skelter' nature of Nursi's writings by giving a sample list of topics found in *Flashes of Light*:

> Jonah, the meaning of his tribulations; the affliction of Job . . .; an interpretation of the *Qur'anic* verse of Man's attachment to the transitory as summarized in a *Nakşibendi* axiom; commentary on a verse of the *Qur'an* concerning the leadership of the Muslim community . . .; an interpretation of *Sura* 48 ('Victory') on the moral strength instilled by Islam even in times when this religion appears to have lost its moral authority; God's way of warning humans; following the path of the Prophet Muhammad at a time when unauthorized innovations (*bid'at*) are rife; an answer to Re'fet Bey's two questions concerning God's control of one's deserts (*rizk*) and the seven layers of heaven and earth.

Clearly, it would be difficult to derive any sort of systematic theology or ethical code from such a set of unrelated topics. Nursi instead seems to be addressing important concerns of the Muslim community, especially as the place of religion in Turkish society changed so drastically with the founding of the secular republic.

Rather than attempt to summarise Nursi's many topics, I will instead highlight important themes that emerged from his writings with an eye on illuminating why his teachings have found such resonance among pious Turks. Nursi provided a path forward for devout Muslims as the traditional institutions of religious authority, such as the *ulema*, broke down and the state did not fill the gap – the expansion of the Diyanet occurred very late in Nursi's life and he died before the refinement of the Diyanet organisation in 1965. To address the lack of religious authority, Nursi emphasised a more personal, psychological approach to religious devotion and practice. To this end, Nursi reimagined Sufi concepts in a quietist way in which the believer cultivates a fear of God (*takva*), remembrance of God (*zikir*) and love of God (*muhabbet*) through the study of texts and shared acts of devotion (Walton 2017: 29). Nursi pointed the way towards creating an enhanced religious consciousness in the individual believer.

In response, Nurcus (those who follow Nursi) strive to develop deeper faith in their own lives not only through individual study, but also through participation in discussion groups with like-minded people. These groups, or 'textual communities' (Yavuz 2003: 164), meet regularly, usually weekly (men and women generally meet separately) to study the *Risale*. They may gather in a *dershane*, a dedicated apartment or room for a Nur congregation to meet in order to study and discuss the *Risale*. In these meetings, there is usually an authority who reads from the *Risale* and helps the participants understand the text, and gives a talk (*sohbet*) on its subjects. This is especially important because Nursi wrote in Ottoman Turkish and used many Arabic and Persian words and phrases, so it is difficult for even native Turkish speakers to read Nursi's works without training. The participants may chime in with questions or thoughts and may connect the text to events in their own lives or in society at large (Yavuz 2013: 100–6).

The *Risale* certainly lends itself to intensive study and consideration, given the complexity and density of the text. In it, Nursi demonstrated that the believer must approach the Qur'an not as a text for mere recitation but as one that must be interpreted according to the individual's context. He presented the Qur'an as a living text that could be read in many ways; no one could claim that a particular interpretation excludes all other potential interpretations. Here, he drew on a traditional technique in Qur'anic interpretation in which the meaning of each text can be approached in two ways, called *zahiri* (superficial, literal interpretation) and *batini* (search for deeper meanings). The *Risale* is not only an example of engaging in *batini* interpretations of the Qur'an, but provides a path by which the readers-believers can incorporate the meaning of the Qur'an into their daily lives.

I give an example from my own experiences of the way in which a Nurcu approaches the *Risale* from one of the *sohbet*s I attended with Turkish Nurcus in the United States. Meral, who I introduced at the beginning of the chapter, acted as *hoca* and helped me and others to read and understand a volume of the *Risale* entitled *The Words*. In the seventh *Word*, Nursi uses allegories and parables to illustrate the nature of patience (*sabır*), an important Sufi concept. For Nursi, cultivating patience is a component of the surrender to God's will that is essential to Islamic piety – 'Islam' means 'submission', after all. But patience is also a way to deal with life's challenges, such that when one is tested by difficult events, one submits to God for strength and help. As Nursi puts it (2010: 45),

> What is there to fear when, realizing our helplessness, we rely upon the Owner of the command, *Be, and it is* (36:82)? Even when confronted with a most frightening situation and a great calamity, he says: *Surely, to God do we belong, and to Him is our return* (2:156), and places his trust in his All-Compassionate Lord with utmost serenity. Those who have true knowledge of God are content to realize their helplessness before God and put their hope in His judgment. There is pleasure in the fear of God.

In reflecting on this text, Meral paired the cultivation of patience in the face of calamity with the need for thankfulness (*şükür*) in response to bounty and happiness. She argued that all good things God gives should be met with thankfulness, while hardships should be met with patience in the knowledge that God is testing believers for their own good. Either way, God is benevolent. Acknowledging that benevolence – whether with patience or with thankfulness – is essential to maintaining a properly pious disposition. The believer can manifest these interior states through prayer and other acts of devotion such as giving *zekat* to the needy.

Another important theme that Nursi presents in his writings is his conception of the material world as a reflection of the divine – the world as a mirror of God is a recurring image in the *Risale*. Some strains of Islam have been 'otherworldly', treating the material world as a potential snare that diverts believers' attention away from God. Conversely, Nursi felt that the splendour of nature and of the universe mirrors the divine, just as the Qur'an itself is a manifestation of God's word on earth. Learning about the world is an act of worship in that it is a way to gain knowledge of God's power and majesty. This positive conception of the phenomenal world led Nursi to support the development of modern forms of scientific education over and against the traditional education promoted by the *ulema* in the *medrese* system with its focus on rote learning and imitation. Nursi saw science and religion as not only compatible but reflections of one another. This view has been an important feature of all the Nur communities in that they have all stressed education and worldly involvement as essential components of a Godly life.

The Gülen movement

A number of Nurcu groups emerged in the last half of the twentieth century, but none has been as influential as the Gülen movement, a *cemaat* based on the teachings of Fethullah Gülen. Though originally from Erzurum, Gülen served as a government-appointed imam in several western Turkish cities. In Izmir he used the Kestanepazarı Qur'an School to educate and cultivate male students in order to establish an exclusive religious community. This community was especially well known for its boys' summer camps, in which Gülen instilled in the attendees a commitment to faith-based activism in which Muslims can work towards a more perfect society through civic engagement, interfaith dialogue and education (Yavuz 2013: 8). This 'activist pietism' would be a hallmark of the Gülen movement.

Gülen's religious viewpoints were influenced by several theologians from Turkey, but two stand out. Muhammed Lütfi Efendi (known as Alvarlı Efe, 1868–1956) was a Nakşibendi sheikh and poet from Gülen's home province of Erzurum. Lütfi Efendi was a charismatic preacher who encouraged his followers to develop both intellectual and emotional virtuosity as a way to deepen their religious experience. Gülen was able to deploy this virtuosity in his preaching, delivering sermons that were both inspiring and emotional. The second influence was Bediüzzaman Said Nursi. As Gülen himself became a popular preacher in the 1970s and 1980s, he drew on Nursi's teachings, recognising the role of reason in both interpreting the Qur'an and engaging in scientific research. Gülen developed his own form of Islamic thought and practice that included a message of respect for the secular state. His moderate message appealed to the Turkish secular elites, and some politicians, such as Turgut Özal, facilitated the reach of Fethullah Gülen's message as a counter to more extremist Islamist groups after the 1980 coup – Gülen supported the 1980 coup as a way to tamp down communist influences in Turkey (Kuru 2003).

Like Said Nursi, Gülen preached that involvement in and transformation of this world is an essential part of Muslim piety. He viewed the state itself as an appropriate vehicle for the development of an ideal Muslim society, and stated that it was important that observant Muslims be strategically involved in all levels of government in order to create a society modelled on the 'golden generation' (*altın nesil*) of the Prophet Muhammad, his family and companions. Gülen encouraged his followers to pursue education to the highest level possible not so much in religious studies, but in socially impactful areas such as engineering, medicine, law and business. To this end, the Gülen movement founded a whole array of high-quality private schools and universities in Turkey, as well as in countries around the world. These schools featured a secular, science-orientated curriculum, and no special religious education was provided in the schools' curricula besides the Religious Culture and Ethics courses required by the state. The religious influence occurred in extracurricular spaces, especially in the Gülen-affiliated dormitories or the *ışıkevler* (lighthouses), which were single-sex residences where young students stayed while they pursued their education. In such residences students were closely supervised by upright dorm leaders who not only enforced moral codes but also encouraged regular prayer and religious study, and cultivated the residents' piety and ethical sensibilities (Hendrick 2013: 107–15; Vicini 2013, 2014).

The Gülen movement also developed Nurcu-style study groups or study centres composed of interested people who met to study the Qur'an and *hadith* and to read the works of Said Nursi and Fethullah Gülen – Gülen's followers call this 'the four-text method'. The Gülen *dershane*s could be found in villages and neighbourhoods all over Turkey and in other countries that host a Turkish diaspora. The study groups not only provided an environment in which religious knowledge was contemplated and transmitted, but, in keeping with the movement's focus on education in Turkey, they were also places in which educated followers tutored younger students in academic subjects, such as maths and science, in preparation for the high-stakes secondary school and university exams crucial to a student's educational success. Some observers have noted that these *dershane*s served as channels by which the movement identified particularly talented youth who they then attempt to cultivate – through educational and social support – into pious social, economic and political leaders.

These schools gained a good reputation not only in Turkey, but also in many of the countries where they were established, especially in areas of the world where educational opportunity has been spotty, such as Central Asia and Africa. Though many critics of the Gülen movement have assumed that the Gülen schools in various countries are established primarily in order to 'spread religion', most inside observers have noted that the schools seemed just as orientated towards enhancing and exporting Turkish nationalism as towards creating Muslim identity. As M. Ali Kılıçbay observed of the schools he visited in Russia and Kazakhstan (2005: 68), the mission of the Gülen school teachers 'is to spread a kind of Turkish-Islamic synthesis that has been affected by the views of Fethullah Gülen, but of this Turkish-Islamic synthesis, I think the heavy emphasis is on Turkishness' (my translation). Turkish language and history were taught in the schools and, at least initially, almost all teachers were Turks educated in the Turkish educational system, though indigenous teachers later joined the faculty, if they were so qualified. To some extent, a mission of the schools has been to create a global familiarity with and friendliness towards Turkey.

Gülen drew on the teachings of Said Nursi to proclaim that the best way to deal with the most serious problems of the world – ignorance, strife and poverty – is through providing education (to combat ignorance), hence the establishment of schools and universities. The movement has also promoted interfaith dialogue (to combat strife) and initiated many charitable projects (to combat poverty). In terms of interfaith dialogue, Gülen espoused the idea that building bridges of understanding between faith communities not only leads to a more peaceful world, but is a way in which the individual may cultivate a more profound understanding of the world and nurture genuine tolerance. As Gülen put it (2006: 33–4),

> Tolerance, a term which we sometimes use in place of the words respect, mercy, generosity, or forbearance, is the most essential element of moral systems; it is a very important source of spiritual discipline and a celestial virtue of perfected people. Under the lens of tolerance, the merits of believers attain new depths and extend to infinity; mistakes and faults become insignificant and wither away until they are so small that they can be placed into a thimble.

For Gülen, tolerance in this sense is partaking of God's mercy. One of God's most cherished qualities is His mercy, and when the believer reaches out to a religious or cultural 'other', one is participating in that mercy (Yavuz 2013: 181–91).

Gülen and his followers have also developed the notion of *hizmet* (service) to society as essential to religious devotion – the movement is known as the Hizmet movement. Much of the movement's civic engagement has been to develop non-governmental institutions to deal with the problems of poverty both within and outside Turkey. For example, participants in the movement have contributed

to the development of hospitals, medical missions, well-digging in poor communities and an international aid association (*Kimse Yok Mu*) that helped people
in crisis in many parts of the world. These various projects were supported by
the donations of money and time by the movement's many members, and especially by Gülen-affiliated networks of Turkish businesspeople. The Gülen movement established broadcasting companies and ran a popular television channel,
Samanyolu, and also produced a number of popular and academic periodicals.
Most notably, Gülen's organisation bought out the daily newspaper, *Zaman*, in the
1980s. Appearing in both Turkish and English, *Zaman* would eventually become
one of the most widely distributed newspapers in Turkey and abroad before it
was closed in the 2010s. The movement also established publishing houses that
issued Gülen's many books and sermon collections in multiple languages, as well
as the works of Said Nursi and other texts relating to religion and Turkish history
and culture. More publishing ventures related to the movement appeared in
countries where there was a significant Turkish migrant community.

As with the Nakşibendi movement under Esad Coşan, the scope of the movement's ventures clearly indicates that one cannot easily characterise the *cemaat* as
a purely religious organisation. As long-time Gülen observer, M. Hakan Yavuz,
has pointed out (2013: 200),

> [The Gülen movement] is an amalgamation of diverse socio-religio-political
> ideas and interests which defy traditional categorizations ... It is essentially
> a religious movement with its own agenda for shaping the public sphere by
> introducing ideas and promoting programs informed by Islamic values in order
> to transform society and the state. In other words, a sharply delineated boundary
> between what is religious or what is profane may not be very helpful in categoriz-
> ing the movement, since it transgresses these arbitrary boundaries of secular
> and religious, social and political, national and transnational, and private and
> public.

Also like the Nakşibendi movement, Gülen and his followers took advantage of
modern forms of communication in order to broaden their message. The Gülen
movement established broadcasting companies and ran a television channel,
Samanyolu, and also produced a number of academic periodicals.

Religious communities and their discontents

As the Gülen movement and the Nakşibendis became more and more sophisticated, their influence on Islam in modern Turkey would increase greatly well
into the twenty-first century. Not surprisingly, many Kemalists were critical of
the influence of the Sufi orders and *cemaats*, seeing their activities as a violation
of Turkey's secularist principles – the effects of this criticism will be discussed in
later chapters. But it is also noteworthy that some pious Turks also sometimes
expressed reservations about the nature or organisation of the *cemaats* and

*Tarikat*s. One of the most controversial issues about the religious organisations is the potentially dominating or even overwhelming role a *hoca* or sheikh could take within a community. There have been cases where a sheik has seemed to want to act as a divine intermediary, claiming that he and his message are indispensable for followers to gain access to the divine. Such an expression is deeply troubling to many pious Muslims in Turkey because it contradicts essential beliefs of Sunni Islam. That is, Sunni Islam – with its emphasis on faith, the unity of God (*tawhid*) and the one-to-one relationship between the individual believer and God – demands, at least ideally, that religious leaders should only assist the individual in cultivating faith in God and in maintaining a lifestyle that adheres most closely to the will of God. But these same leaders should not insert themselves between the individual and God. This is not to say that there is no role for religious authority, since clearly the individual may need assistance in cultivating a proper type of faith and behaviour (see Fernando 2010; Mahmood 2005). Ultimately, though, it is up to a believer to submit to God appropriately. By placing a sheikh or some other authority as a go-between in this relationship is a violation of the principle of *tawhid*. Some of the pious Turks I worked with felt that some *cemaat* leaders – those who made unreasonable and overbearing demands on the followers – violated this fundamental principle of Muslim thought. Similarly, Silverstein (2011: 120–1) noted that the relationship between sheikh and devotee (*rabıta*) created some controversy in the Nakşibendi *cemaat* he studied, enough to cause some participants to leave the *cemaat*. Those who left were alienated by 'the practice of concentrating one's attention and affection so enthusiastically on the sheikh that it became confounded with one's devotions, which should naturally be reserved for God alone.'

These questions about the nature of appropriate religious authority point to a much deeper philosophical debate that has existed in Islam throughout its history: is the path to authentic religious knowledge best pursued through reasoned interpretations of texts or through the other, extratextual religious experiences made possible by non-scriptural practices, such as *zikir* and *rabıta*?[9] This debate has waxed and waned over time, but it has recently intensified as the result of the worldwide Islamic revivalist movement that began in the late 1970s. This revivalist movement has encouraged a return to the study of scriptures (the Qur'an, the *hadith* and other sources of recognised religious authority) and a purging of those traditional practices that have no basis in the scriptures. According to such 'scripturalists', it is the individual's responsibility to cultivate an understanding of the scriptures through careful study and discipline and to apply scriptural principles to daily life without referring to traditional (non-scriptural) interpretations. Any 'addition' or unfounded elaboration on scripture is *bid'a* (improper innovation), which is a grave sin.

Scripturalists have criticised those 'traditionalists' (a term used by John

Bowen (1993)) who accept religious practices and ideas not articulated in the scriptures. Where scripturalists insist that the texts are assessable to all who seek their wisdom, traditionalists are more likely to see scripture as fundamentally ambiguous, and therefore they support turning to tradition and other authorities to understand the nature of belief. Following the ritual or lifestyle prescriptions of a respected sheikh or other religious leader – whether these prescriptions can be found in the scripture or not – is acceptable as long as the proper intent (*niyet*) is maintained and the instructions further the cause of genuine Islam and the development of a pious society. Such a view allows for some degree of flexibility and for the incorporation of rituals and beliefs that cannot be traced to foundational texts. For example, voiced *zikir* and the veneration of saints or sultans become acceptable to traditionalist practitioners as long as the believer has the proper intent and orientation towards God and as long as these practices enhance the religious orientation of society as a whole.

While scripturalists may criticise aspects of traditionalism, they do not necessarily reject human authority per se, since one can only adequately gain knowledge of the texts with the assistance of a teacher who has acquired significant expertise. Beloved authorities, such as Kotku, Coşan, Nursi and Gülen, were valued for their enlightened approach to scripture and their abilities to convey vivid and inspiring interpretations of texts to their followers. But it is also easy to see how the believer's devotion to a beloved *cemaat* leader or sheikh might divert the believer from proper attention to God – hence the discomfort expressed by Silverstein's friends.

Another tension in Muslim evaluation of Sufi orders or *cemaat*s is the ways in which emotion is used as a pathway to religious understanding. In some *cemaat*s, the emotional aspect of *zikir* can be so powerful that participants have ecstatic or mind-altering experiences of the divine in a way that more scripturalist Muslims might find suspicious. The type of *zikir* in which an individual simply concentrates on God through the repetition of prayers or words is not so problematic since it is really a form of prayer that draws one's heart and mind closer to God. But the more ecstatic *zikir*s practised in certain *Tarikat*s, such as the Kalendari or the Halveti *zikir* described by Raudevere (2002), verge on blasphemy for some. In these *Tarikat*s, participants seek an altered state of consciousness brought on by the repetitive ritual that allows the believer to experience the divine more directly. Indeed, the overt goal of some *Tarikat*s is the annihilation of the self (*fanā*) by folding the self into the divine (see Raudvere 2002: 196–229; Schimmel 1975: 167–86). Thus, *zikir* participants in the throes of mystical ecstasy may claim to see manifestations of God, perhaps His 'eye' or His 'hand'. Others may experience a more diffuse 'overwhelming presence' or 'warmth' that is associated with the approach of the divine. For more scripturalist Muslims, these types of experiences are questionable in terms of authenticity and may reflect only the wishes and ignorance of the participant.

Figure 4.4 Praying at the *türbe* of Molla Yahya Efendi (1494–1570), Istanbul, 2014 (photograph by author)

The contemporary Turkish *cemaat*s I have discussed in this chapter – the Khalidi-Nakşibendi branch of Kotku and Coşan, the Nurcus and the Gülen movement – have tended toward the more scripturalist approach to Islam. This is not to say that emotional experience does not inform their practices in essential ways. Experiences of emotional intensity are welcomed as a way to comprehend and draw closer to God – Fethullah Gülen in particular is renowned for his ability to stir up the emotions of his congregants during his sermons, as he himself frequently cries as he speaks. But these large, influential

religious organisations have all encouraged followers to develop refined understandings of religious texts through study and discussion, while they have also
embraced modern forms of secular education, communication and technology
as a means of serving God and his community.

Notes

1. Qur'anic Arabic is very different from Modern Standard Arabic, in terms of both vocabulary
   and grammar. Native speakers of modern Arabic also require study in order to understand
   the Arabic of the Qur'an.
2. For a description of the voiced *zikir*, see Raudvere 2002. There are many video recordings of
   the voiced *zikir* available on YouTube and other video streaming sites. For an example of a
   Helveti *zikir*, see https://www.youtube.com/watch?v=iSTh0ybvSLk
3. The Islamic media were also able to get around the older printing and broadcasting restrictions by operating through foundations that were secular in nature, at least on the surface.
4. The order is known as the Mawlawiyya in Persian and Arabic.
5. The website of the International Mevlana Foundation describes each step of the *sema* in detail,
   and includes a video of a *sema* at the Mevlevi Lodge in Galata, Istanbul. See http://mevlana.
   net/sema.html
6. The poem is published without attribution on the English-language website of the International
   Mevlana Foundation. See http://mevlanafoundation.com/mevlana_works_en.htm
7. By using the title 'Nakşibendi' I am following the Turkish spelling of the *Tarikat*. However,
   readers may encounter different spellings, such as Naqshbandiyya or Naqshband, based on
   transliterations of Arabic or Persian versions of the name.
8. There are other Nakşibendi-Khalidi branches besides the Gümüşhanevi, but the
   Gümüşhanevis are the wealthiest and most influential. The group of rural-to-urban migrant
   families I studied in my anthropological fieldwork in the 1990s were mostly former members
   (some were still current) of a very conservative Nakşibendi branch, the İsmailağa *cemaati*
   centred in the Fatih district of Istanbul.
9. Other religions, such as Christianity and Judaism, have historically had similar tensions.
   In the case of Islam, Western orientalist scholars have tended to interpret the conflict to
   be between the 'rational' *ulema* and the 'irrational' or 'emotional' Sufis. Many more recent
   scholars have pointed out that study of Islamic science and involvement in Sufi orders are not
   necessarily opposed, but may actually go hand in hand (Abenante and Vicini 2017; Green
   2012).

CHAPTER 5

Islamic political parties

Political rally in support of the Virtue Party, December 1998, in Ankara

I attended a political rally in support of the Islamic-oriented Virtue Party (VP) staged at the Atatürk Sport Stadium near Ankara's main train station. I went in the company of Meryem (introduced at the beginning of Chapter 2) and her family, who were religious conservatives living in Sincan, a suburb of Ankara. When we arrived, there were long lines of people waiting to get in at the door. We got in immediately through a side entrance, thanks to Ali – Meryem's brother – who worked at HEDEF, the radio station that was co-sponsoring the event. There were guards at the gate who searched our bags, and female police officers padded us down. The hall itself was like a basketball stadium and the rally reminded me of a sporting event, with people talking in the audience so that there was always a dull roar, children running around and vendors selling things like sunflower seeds and other goodies. The stadium was filled, and almost all the women were wearing the *tesettür* – the Muslim headscarf typical of religious women in Turkey in the 1990s. There was a roped-off section with nice chairs reserved for attending VIPs, which included a number of VP representatives and party affiliates.

Around the stadium were large signs, banners, wreaths and a very large Turkish flag. The banners mostly displayed slogans supporting the VP, and there was no picture of Atatürk – unusual at a political event. Some of the banner slogans expressed a degree of grievance and supported religious freedom. For example:

'Çoğulcu ve katılımcı demokrasiye evet; Azınlık diktasına hayır'
'Düşünce ve inanç özgürlüğüne evet; Baskı ve dayatmaya hayır'
'Haber alma ve verme özgürlüğüne evet; İftira ve yalana hayır'
'Hukukun üstünlüğüne evet; Gücün hukukuna hayır'

'Yes to majority and participatory democracy; no to minority dictatorship'
'Yes to freedom of thought and belief; no to oppression and coercion '
'Yes to the free exchange of information; no to slander and lies'
'Yes to the rule of law; no to the law of power'

early as the 1950s, the movement of the Turkish population picked up in the 1980s. Between 1980 and 1997, as many as 10 million people migrated into the *gecekondu* (squatter) neighbourhoods surrounding the big cities, such that the populations of cities such as Istanbul and Ankara swelled so rapidly that urban infrastructure, public services and employment prospects could not meet the pace of growth, leading to soaring rates of unemployment and urban poverty (Delibas 2015: 123).

The precarious position of the migrants was made worse by the liberalisation of the economy, beginning in the 1980s. Economic liberalisation refers to the process by which private interests take over public services and roles, subjecting them to economic calculation (profit maximisation) rather than evaluating success by improvement in the human condition. The liberalising impulse was a global phenomenon, but in the case of Turkey, powerful business interest groups, such as the Organisation of Turkish Industrialists and Businessmen (TÜSİAD),[1] pushed for drastic economic reforms, which were supported by the post 1980-coup military government and, later, by the prime ministry of Turgut Özal. The reforms – a so-called 'structural adjustment programme' – led to the privatisation of many state-owned industries, the shrinkage of public-sector jobs, the reduction of the welfare state and restrictions on labour-friendly policies, such as the right to unionise. These policies had a devastating effect on the urban poor, as the share of public-sector jobs – these jobs had served as an important gateway to the middle class – were eliminated in favour of private-sector jobs that proved to be much less stable. The decrease in welfare spending robbed many of the poorest of an important source of material support.

Furthermore, the poorer *gecekondu* dwellers also faced an attitude of condescension and disdain from the middle-class citizens of many Turkish cities. To many middle-class urban Turks, these low-wage-earning migrants became known as the inhabitants of the so-called *varoş*, the proverbial immigrant suburb, usually consisting of *gecekondu*s. According to Jenny White (2002a: 59), middle-class Kemalist Turks saw these communities as 'the urban location of a set of characteristics – poverty, rural origin, Muslim lifestyle, veiling, patriarchy'. These characteristics stood in contrast to the dominant Turkish notions of modernity, 'characterized by middle-class, urban values and lifestyles, secular clothing and the autonomous individual'. The *varoş* 'infect' the modern city, in Kemalist eyes, with a cultural pollution of backwardness.

The combination of the growing urban poor population, the increased visibility of income inequality, the condescension of the middle classes and the alienation many migrants experienced primed the large migrant population for a new political message. The WP situated itself especially well to articulate the frustrations of the migrants and to offer potential solutions to their problems. It promised to build an *Adil Düzen* ('Just Order'), that would bring about greater economic equality and create a clean, uncorrupted government that would listen to the needs of the poor. The WP spread its message through a widespread grassroots network in municipalities – including poor municipalities – in the major cities. In Istanbul, for example, the WP networks centred around the municipal offices, which were staffed by party leaders and Islamist activists well versed in the religious and cultural idioms of the residents they served. These WP activists could appeal to the Qur'an, the *hadith* and the life of the Prophet Muhammad in their community outreach activities and interactions with local citizens. WP activists included Islamist women who wore the *tesettür*, the target of denigration by secularist Turks since its inception in the 1980s. These activists successfully mobilised poor and working-class women to support the WP, not just through exhortation but by sustaining face-to-face relationships in which they identified themselves with the women while helping them deal with the economic and social stresses of urban life.[2] Representatives from the centre-left secularist parties failed to sustain such an interaction and largely came off as distant and elitist (White 2002a: 256–60). In sum, the WP was successful in coupling its message of economic justice with Islamist language and actions that appealed to the migrants and other pious citizens who felt alienated from the secularist demands of the Kemalist state. By the 1990s the WP had emerged as the '"one guardian" of the exploited, poverty-stricken urban masses. With its promise of a "Just Order", the WP . . . appealed to the *gecekondu* dwellers more strongly than any other party' (Delibas 2015: 128). In the 1994 local elections the WP managed to secure twenty-eight out of seventy-six mayoral seats in the provincial capitals, including in Istanbul and Ankara, going on to dominate in the national elections of 1995 to head a coalition government.

Reworking public symbolism

Beyond its political gains, the WP was able to turn Islam in to a 'storehouse of images' (Yavuz 2003: 224) by which it could remake public spaces to conform to a new concept of Turkish modernity and national identity, one in which Islam and Ottoman history played more substantial roles than they had under Kemalist governments. For example, Erbakan and WP officials used Islamist messaging that disparaged the Christian West and opposed Turkey's bid – beginning in 1987 – for membership of the European Union (Dağı 2006: 92). Welfare officials would openly neglect and even belittle Republican-day festivities, which were replete with Atatürk imagery and secularist symbolism and often included official visits to Atatürk's mausoleum, the Anıtkabir, in Ankara (Figure 5.2). Furthermore, WP mayors of various cities attempted to close or limit restaurants and nightclubs that served alcohol, and many had nude statues removed from public parks. Some party supporters even promoted a plan to build a mosque in Istanbul's Taksim Square, home to the massive Atatürk Cultural Centre and dominated by a monument commemorating Atatürk and the founding of the modern Republic (Figure 5.3) (Çınar 2005: 114–18; White 2002a: 116–18).

Figure 5.2 Atatürk's mausoleum in downtown Ankara: the mausoleum was built in a neo-Hittite style that harkens back to pre-Islamic Anatolian history (photograph by author)

Though the Taksim Square mosque plan was not realised until 2017, WP officials – including then-Istanbul mayor Recep Tayyip Erdoğan – were able to transform another previously secular space in Istanbul: Çamlıca Park and restaurant. Çamlıca was (and still is) a popular attraction on the Asian side of the Bosporus. It is situated high on a hill overlooking the Bosporus Strait, the Bosporus Bridge and the Topkapı Palace on the Sarayburnu cape. There had previously been an expensive patisserie and a coffee house and tea garden in the park. These concessions had been run by a private firm, but during Erdoğan's tenure as Istanbul's mayor, the city took over management of the site and reno-vated the whole area to create restaurants and gardens that evoked nostalgia for Ottoman times. The new Çamlıca restaurant and its attached Ottoman Coffee House featured calligraphy, furniture and dishes meant to create an Ottoman experience for both domestic and foreign visitors. The restaurant served no alcohol and even went so far as to ban carbonated beverages because they were supposedly foreign to 'authentic' Turkish culture. Instead, *şerbet* (fruit juices), Turkish coffee and tea, and traditional pastries were featured (though instant coffee – not a Turkish tradition but popular nonetheless – stayed on the menu) (Çınar 2005: 127–34).

Another arena in which the WP could deliver its message of prosperity and piety was in the various media outlets that multiplied from the late 1980s

Figure 5.3 Republic Monument in Taksim Square, Istanbul
(photograph by Deniz Ertaş)

onwards. All kinds of new TV and radio outlets appeared in Turkey's media landscape, and Islamic programming and publications increased too. Islamic television shows, as well as Islamic newspapers and magazines, included discussions of topics large and small, attracting significant audiences. The proliferation of media also provided platforms for a new kind of intellectual: the Muslim intellectual. These were people (usually but not always men) who were well educated

Figure 5.4 Ottoman-style teahouse at Çamlica Park in Istanbul
(photograph by author)

in the secular education system but came from pious backgrounds and identified
as practising Muslims. Unlike most other Turkish intellectuals of the time, the
Muslim intellectuals critiqued the Kemalist system and various Western influences, and called for a re-Islamisation of Turkish society. They argued their
points in newspaper columns and books, on TV programmes, and in political
panel discussions (Meeker 1991).

All these transformations – of the media, the economy, public symbols and
so on – proved to be popular with the WP's electoral base. But even with these
developments, the nature of governance in Turkey did not significantly change
in the WP's era. Previously, Atatürk and his governing partners had issued top-
down directives aimed at transforming Turkish society to match their conceptions of a modern society based on a particular understanding of history and
plan for the future. Likewise, the WP attempted to implement a paternalistic,
top-down transformation of public spaces and symbols to create a particular type
of society – a *fazilet toplumu* (a virtuous society) that emphasised the expression
of 'Islamic identity in the public domain and the construction of a community
marked by Islamic morals and virtues (*ahlak ve fazilet*)' (Yavuz 2003: 238). Both the
Kemalist and the Islamic national projects gave advantages to certain portions

of the population while neglecting or even discriminating against other groups. Atatürk's Turkish secularist, nationalist venture highlighted Turkish ethnicity and language over and against other languages and identities, while also suppressing Islamic practices that did not conform to the needs of the secularist state. Using the same style of governing, the WP government favoured its pious Sunni Muslim populations by giving them a voice in governance and appealing to their religious sensibilities, while neglecting and even disparaging other social groups.

Continued Alevi exclusion

The WP's emphasis on Sunni Islamic identity led to the increasing vulnerability and political isolation of the Alevi population. The Alevi revival discussed in Chapter 3 was in fact a response to the Sunni nationalism promoted by the state through the Turkish-Islamic Synthesis. The Alevi revival attempted to counteract Sunni nationalism by underscoring the rich distinctiveness of Alevi traditions and by increasing the number of Alevi associations and cultural festivals that celebrated aspects of Alevi history and culture. Nevertheless, the Alevi community suffered from acts of often brutal violence in the 1990s, and the various governments of that time seemed unable or unwilling to protect them.

The most notorious of these acts of violence was the July 1993 massacre of Alevis in the central Anatolian city of Sivas. In this case, Alevi writers, artists and intellectuals had gathered for an annual multi-day festival organised by the Pir Sultan Abdal Culture Organisation – Pir Sultan Abdal was a sixteenth-century dissident Alevi poet who had been executed by the Ottoman state (Soileau 2017). This organisation and its corresponding festival were devoted to discussing social and political issues of concern to Alevis (Mutluer 2016: 148–9). In the 1993 meeting, the controversial Turkish writer Aziz Nesin (1915–95) participated in the discussions. Nesin was not Alevi, but he was a well-known leftist intellectual who supported civic freedom in Turkey, including the rights of the Alevis. As part of Nesin's commitment to freedom of expression, he had just published a portion of Salman Rushdie's highly controversial novel *The Satanic Verses* in a newspaper.[3] In response Sunni religious conservatives disparaged Nesin in various media outlets, calling for a war on the 'friends of Satan'. His presence at the Pir Sultan Abdal festival attracted the attention of Sunni residents of Sivas, and a large hostile crowd gathered in the city centre around the Madımak Hotel, where many festival guests, including Nesin, were staying. At some point, the crowd set the hotel on fire and prevented many of the occupants from escaping while also blocking the fire brigades who came to put out the fire. The fire was not extinguished for many hours, the police did little to help and the municipal governor (a WP party representative) seemed to egg on the violence. In the end thirty-seven people were killed, almost all of them Alevis. Aziz Nesin was injured but survived. The Sivas massacre shocked the secularist establishment. Throughout the violence, the Sunni Islamist had not only protested against the Alevis, but had shouted anti-Atatürk slogans and destroyed a statue of Atatürk.

Alevis, of course, were horrified. They came to realise that the greatest threat to their community was the Islamist forces at work in Turkish society, and the state would not protect them. This sense of vulnerability was reinforced when another violent attack against Alevis occurred in the Gazi neighbourhood in Istanbul in March 1995. In this case an unidentified person strafed an Alevi coffee house with machine-gun fire, killing one Alevi man and wounding fifteen others. There was a police station nearby but the police were very slow to respond to the situation, leading many Alevis to believe that the police were involved in the shooting. When Alevis gathered to protest, sometimes violently, the police responded with force, which spurred even further protest and violence in other parts of Istanbul and in Ankara. In the end twenty-four people died, many of them from police gunshots.[4]

Other forms of anti-Alevi action further alienated the Alevi population. The WP municipal head of Sivas was implicated in the Sivas massacre, and further, lawyers associated with the WP were part of the legal counsel defending the Sunni attackers for their involvement in the Sivas event. As mayor of Istanbul, Erdoğan attempted to demolish an important *cemevei* in the city in 1995. His plan did not come to fruition, but only because of strong protests from the Alevi community. This degree of hostility caused Alevis to advance causes and practices designed to defend the community. The number of Alevi books, magazines and radio stations (and later websites) promoting Alevi culture increased rapidly, as did the organisation of Alevi festivals and celebrations at traditional Alevi religious sites (Göner 2005: 119–20). Young Alevis felt motivated to openly declare themselves to be Alevis, sometimes by wearing a necklace with a double-tipped golden sword, indicating the sword of Imam Ali called the *Zülfkar*, or by tattooing the sword on their arms (Sökefeld 2008: 69–70). Alevis of different backgrounds and persuasions redoubled their efforts to form new associations in order to organise activities reflecting Alevis interests and to advocate for their positions in Turkish society.

The Cem Foundation is the largest and most influential of these Alevi non-governmental organisations (NGOs), founded by the Alevi intellectual İzzetin Doğan in 1995. The philosophy of the foundation is that Alevism combines aspects of Twelver Shi'ism and Central Asian mysticism to form a coherent religious tradition on an equal standing with Sunnism. What the Cem Foundation seeks to do is 'orthodoxise' Alevism by trying to create a distinctive definition of Alevi religious practice. A goal of this effort is to legitimise Alevism in the eyes of the Turkish state, in that Alevism would have the coherence and systematisation of the Sunnism promulgated by the Diyanet (Massicard 2013: 96–7; Walton 2017: 81–4).

Other Alevi NGOs took different stances vis-à-vis the Turkish state. The Haci Bektaş Veli Anatolian Culture Foundation (HBVV), for example, is not concerned with creating a coherent definition of Alevism and is accepting of the variations in Alevi practice and belief that have always prevailed. It does not want to try to mould itself to Turkey's form of secularism, where the state (through the Diyanet) controls many aspects of public religious practice. Instead, it advocates for a transformation of governance to 'passive secularism', where the state separates itself as much as possible from religious affairs. As one member of the HBVV told anthropologist Jeremy F. Walton (2017: 84–5):

> We don't want anything to do with the DIB [Diyanet]. We'd prefer that it not exist. And that's the basic difference between us and the Cem Foundation. They claim that the state should support both Sunnis and Alevis. In our opinion, the state should support neither Sunnis nor Alevis. Each community should attend to its own needs, separate from the state. This is the true meaning of secularism.

Other Alevi NGOs support the HBVV position, while some follow the Cem Foundation's philosophy. Some NGOs hold that Alevism is not part of Islam at all, while others claim that there is no substantial difference between Sunnism and Alevism. In a word, there is a plurality of civil society organisations that reflect the variety of types of Alevism that exist in modern Turkey. But what most Alevis could agree on was that they needed to bolster their collective identity in the face of the untrustworthy and potentially dangerous state and Sunni-dominated society.

A 'post-modern' coup

The WP's promotion of Sunni Islamist policies and practices not only disaffected Alevis, but often proved to be unacceptable to Turkey's secularist powers, such as the military and judicial leadership. WP representatives in both municipal and national governments not only encouraged the development of Islamic symbols, spaces and practices, as described above, but also wilfully neglected and even disparaged traditional nationalist ceremonies, such as the annual commemoration of Atatürk's death on 10 November. In 1997, after less than two years of rule, the military forced the ousting of the WP government because of its supposed violation of Turkey's secularist principles. This military action was triggered in part by an Islamist rally held in a religiously conservative urban centre. In February 1997, in the Sincan neighbourhood of Ankara, the town mayor (and ally of Erbakan) held a *Kudüs Günü* (Jerusalem Day) rally to protest the Israeli occupation of Jerusalem. Jerusalem Day was actually a holiday celebrated in Iran that had been introduced by the Islamic revolutionary leader Ayatollah Khomeini. The Iranian ambassador to Turkey, Mohammed Reza Bagheri, took part in the Sincan rally and, in a well-received speech, he condemned Israel and called for the return of *Shari'ah* in Turkey. Participants held up flags supporting Hamas and Hezbollah,[5] and the rally included skits portraying Islam's projected victory in the coming (imagined) jihad. Ambassador Bagheri proclaimed: 'Do not be afraid to call yourselves fundamentalists! Fundamentalists are those who follow the words and actions of the Prophet. God has promised them the final victory!' (Kinzer 2001: 74–5). The Jerusalem Day rally, as well as Erbakan's leadership style, brought the already heightened concern about the rise of Islamic fundamentalism and the spectre of an Iranian-style revolution to a tipping point. After this rally, the military forced the WP-led government to arrest the mayor of Sincan and expel the Iranian ambassador. The military also sent tanks rolling through the streets of Sincan, bringing the city to a standstill as the citizens were too frightened of the tanks to leave their homes.

Soon after, the military issued warnings to the WP-led coalition government, culminating in the so-called 'process' of 28 February 1997. The NSC issued eighteen directives (NSC decision no. 406) to the WP government, and the ruling party had to accept these recommendations or face violent consequences. The directives instructed the WP government to enforce the principles of secularism and to curtail independent Islamic organisations (such as religious facilities and foundations, media groups and *cemaat*s) and activities like the Jerusalem Day rally in Sincan.[6] In the end, the military pressured the Constitutional Court to shut down the WP, which it did in January 1998. Both Erbakan and Erdoğan were penalised for overly 'religious' activity. Erbakan was removed from office and banned from politics, and Erdoğan was later jailed briefly for 'inciting religious hatred' when he recited an allegedly Islamist poem at a speech in Diyarbakır in 1997 (Introvigne 2006: 37–9).[7]

This process – the NSC directives and the removal of the WP – is known as a 'soft' or 'post-modern' military coup. Normally, a military coup is a violent overthrow of a government, but in this case, the NSC only threatened violence if its demands were not met, hence a 'soft' rather than violent coup. Given Turkey's history of military coups, it is not surprising that Erbakan and the WP chose to step down rather than face the potential consequences of resistance.

The Virtue Party

After the closure of the WP, its members regrouped and formed the VP in December 1997. Although Erbakan was formally barred from political activity, he nevertheless tried to manage the new party behind the scenes while formal control of the party passed to an older member, Recai Kutan. It was during this period that a younger cadre of Islamist politicians gained ascendancy, including Istanbul mayor Erdoğan and his colleague, Abdullah Gül. Erdoğan in particular seemed able to bridge the gap between the more traditional religious conservatives and the up-and-coming young pious middle-class professionals who were looking for new ideas and opportunities. Erdoğan led a group within the VP called the *Değişimler* – the ones who change things (sometimes called the 'Young Ones') – and many viewed him as someone who could identify with regular people in a way the older politicians of any political party could not (White 2002a: 137–8). These 'Young Ones' were able to make good use of the face-to-face activist networks laid down during the WP era to galvanise their base.

The VP had learned from the experiences of the WP and tried to moderate the party's message. Rather than rejecting secularism per se, as Erbakan had, VP party members favoured establishing an American-style 'passive' secularism, rather than the laicism that prevailed in Turkey. Erdoğan, for example, felt that American-style secularism would give people religious freedom, which would mean allowing women to wear the headscarf when and where they wanted. He also asserted that he had no interest in changing Turkish law to conform to the requirements of *Shari'ah*, as some more radical Islamists had demanded. Rather, he said he wanted a more just system (*Adil Düzen*) which could be achieved if Turkish law were fairly enforced (White 2002a: 139). Many sceptics have questioned the sincerity of Erdoğan's and the VP's claims of moderation, but it is nevertheless significant that the party chose to adhere more closely to the traditional Kemalist philosophy as a way to remain politically viable. And the party was relatively popular, supported by rallies such as the one described at the beginning of the chapter. In the end, however, the party received only 16 per cent of the vote in the national elections of 1999, mostly because many of the voters who had supported the WP were reluctant to support a party that might be closed down as Welfare had been. Also in 1999, Turkish nationalism increased in the face of dramatic developments in the long-standing battle with Kurdish separatists, so many religiously conservative voters switched their allegiance to the Turkish nationalist party, the Nationalist Action Party. Even with its weak showing, the VP and its successors emerged as a viable political force that actively engaged in some important cultural and political debates in the 1990s and 2000s.

The headscarf question

Probably one of the most visible struggles that intensified in the era of the Welfare and Virtue Parties was the debate about the acceptability of the Islamic headscarf in public spaces and institutions. The expectation that Muslim women cover their hair and dress modestly while in the presence of men they are not related to has a long history in Islamic societies, even though what counts as 'modest' has been subject to dispute and change. In the late Ottoman Empire, for example, clothing in general was subject to regulation, and women – especially upper-class women – were enjoined to wear head coverings and body-concealing clothing in public places (Norton 1997; Şeni 1995). As discussed in Chapter 1, Atatürk and his supporters had discouraged women's Islamic clothing practices, including the headscarf, and, for the most part, educated women and those affiliated with Kemalist institutions no longer veiled except when necessary.[8] Yet many women continued to wear headscarves and modest clothing, especially those women of lower socio-economic status engaged in agriculture or manual labour. Even now, many such women wear distinctive clothing styles that include hand-embroidered scarves and loose shirts and trousers or long skirts (Figure 5.4). They have been socially and often geographically distant from the centres of Kemalist power and have thus been seen as benign and even quaint.

But a new form of veiling called the *tesettür* or *türban* (Figure 5.5) appeared in Turkey beginning in the 1980s.[9] The new style emphasised stricter types

Figure 5.5 Village women selling handiwork to tourists, Cappadocia, 1992 (photograph by author)

of veiling and clothing that more thoroughly covered the body. The *tesettür* was inspired by the international Islamic revivalist movement with its focus on establishing proper Islamic ethical conduct, including clothing practices. Many women who adopted the *tesettür* justified their clothing choice by arguing that that the old 'village' style of veiling did not really conform to the requirements of Islam, and women who dressed that way were 'ignorant' of proper Islam. In their opinion, the *tesettür* more closely followed the women's clothing requirements specified in the Qur'an and the *hadith* in which the shape of a woman's body should be completely concealed in public. The extent to which a woman's face should be covered was (and still is) a matter of dispute among those who wear the *tesettür* – most veiled Turkish women do not cover their faces. In fact, many different styles of Muslim women's dress have appeared over the decades since the 1980s, becoming a significant sector of Turkey's fashion industry (see Chapter 7).

From its first appearance, the visibility of the *tesettür* in urban spaces posed a threat to many members of the Kemalist establishment, who feared that this clothing style associated with Islamic revivalism indicated emerging dangerous anti-modern trends in Turkish society. In response, the state administration established policies that limited the access of veiled women to certain public institutions, such as political offices, civic institutions and jobs, and universities. Even politicians and military officers who had wives or daughters who wore the *tesettür* were held in suspicion by Kemalists, who saw them as potential members of a dangerous anti-secularist movement at work in Turkish institutions of power. One criticism Kemalists lodged against representatives from the Welfare and Virtue Parties – and later the JDP – was the fact that the politicians' wives wore the *tesettür*, thus indicating the supposed anti-Kemalist sentiments of the politicians themselves.

In all the debates around the 'headscarf question' (*başörtüsü sorunu*), the issue that dominated public discourse and the media was the presence of veiled students at universities. There was no law requiring female college students to refrain from wearing Islamic head coverings, though uniform requirements in the primary and secondary schools included prohibitions on headscarves. But the Council of Higher Education (CHE) of Turkey – established in the wake of the 1980 coup – formally banned the Islamic headscarf from all state university campuses in 1982 (at that time, all universities were state-controlled). The vigilance with which university officials enforced the headscarf prohibition waxed and waned, often in correspondence to larger political trends in Turkey. One period when enforcement of the headscarf ban was particularly intense was around the time of the closure of the WP in 1998. Indeed, when I first began field research in the summer of 1997, I heard little about the 'headscarf question', but by late 1997 and early 1998, the issue had regained intensity and was again being hotly debated on campuses and in the media. Women students

Figure 5.6 Women wearing *tesettür* (photograph by author)

who refused to uncover their heads at Istanbul University, for example, were barred from classes and exams, or were not allowed to register without a photo ID in which they were pictured bareheaded. In return, these women and their supporters would stage protests of various sorts: marches, sit-ins, hunger strikes, petition campaigns and so on.

External observers of Turkey were often baffled by the fixation on – even fetishisation of – the veil in Turkish political discourse. I heard more than one foreigner call the headscarf debate 'silly' or 'strange'. How could keeping veiled women out of universities protect Turkey from Islamist fundamentalism? Why did women in the *tesettür* seem to pose an existential threat to Kemalists?

One answer to these questions requires us to reflect on the fact that the original Kemalist reforms were not only aimed at changing institutions but were also directed at the daily practices of ordinary citizens, including the clothing practices of both sexes. For many Kemalists, the appearance of the *tesettür* in Turkish society, especially in traditionally secularist institutions, suggested that the Westernisation and secularisation projects of the Kemalist Republic were in danger of failing. In response, secularist authorities, such as university presidents, academics, politicians and news commentators, claimed that the *tesettür* itself is a most visible sign of radical Islam, and that the women who don the *tesettür* do so for purely political reasons – to demonstrate their opposition to Atatürk and Kemalist principles and to indicate their allegiance to anti-secularist movements committed to creating a theocracy based on Islamic law. For example, a former president of Istanbul University, Bülent Berkarda, declared that the *tesettür* is a first step on the road to an Iranian-style revolution that would bring down the secular government (Cumhuriyet 1998). Another prominent academic likened the Muslim headscarf to the Nazi swastika (Abadan-Unat 1998). This type of reaction to the veil was part of the Kemalists' persistent concern that 'the inclusion of signs and symbols associated with Islamic cultural tradition means Islamisation of society par excellence' rather than being about creating a democratic society that honours freedom of choice and conscience (Saktanber 2006: 24).

In general, though, women's appearance and roles often play an outsized role in how a nation thinks of itself, not just in Turkey but around the world. Scholars of colonialism and nationalism have long observed that women may symbolise the collectivity in significant ways. Nira Yuval-Davis (1997: 45–6) argued that 'women in their "proper" behaviour, their "proper" clothing, embody the line which signifies the collectivity's boundaries'. In the case of Turkey, women's appearance serves as a particularly potent symbol of the nature of the state. Women 'stand for' the nation, so that their actions and appearance reflect directly on the character of the nation as expressed in public discourse. When a nation struggles with issues of identity and feels itself threatened – as the secularist Turkish establishment did under the threat of Islamic fundamentalism – the reaction is often to articulate and re-articulate acceptable roles and appearances for women. As such, the controversy about the appropriateness of covered women vs uncovered women (that is, women in Western-style clothing) was at base a debate about the nature of Turkey, whether it was Islamic and Middle Eastern or secular and European. Women's bodies acted as a supreme symbolic field in the intense contest over Turkish national identity (Delaney 1991).

Atatürk imagery

The *tesettür* was not the only symbol that was wielded in the public battle over Turkish national identity. New and traditional images of Mustafa Kemal Atatürk multiplied in Turkish public spaces in the 1990s too. Certainly, images of Atatürk had long been popular in Turkey. Every classroom, community centre, civil service office and public square traditionally displayed at least one picture, bust or statue of Atatürk, but the images proliferated in the wake of the 28 February process. In a fascinating study, anthropologist Esra Özyürek (2006, 2007; see also Navaro-Yashin 2002b) discussed some of the reasons for this proliferation and explored the new types of images that appeared in the late 1990s. More common images of Atatürk in the past had typically displayed him as a soldier and a statesman, but new images also portrayed him as a man at home with family, doing leisure activities such as sports and dancing. Kemalists would often display these pictures in households and would insist that public images meet a certain standard of aesthetics and respect. Özyürek argued that Kemalists drew on these particular images of Atatürk to portray an idealised era of Turkish history, when supposedly 'perfect harmony and unity existed between the state and its citizens' especially in terms of strides made in the direction of modernisation and secularisation. That is, Kemalists were nostalgic for a time when their version of secular 'modernity' was being realised, even if that time never really existed in the way they imagined (Özyürek 2006: 154).

When I was doing my field research in Turkey during the late 1990s, I certainly remember being impressed and was made not a little nervous by the countless images of Atatürk gazing down upon me from buildings, from walls in homes, schools, theatres and so on. I remember feeling that we – the Turkish people and I – were being watched by a rather stern father figure for any untoward, 'un-Turkish' behaviour. In 1999 in Ankara I came across a startling set of billboard-size images of Atatürk in Kızılay Square in the city centre. In these images, Atatürk was shown engaged in modern activities using modern technology. One portrayed Atatürk talking on a mobile phone while standing in front of the Atatürk Dam on the Euphrates River in eastern Turkey. Another was of Atatürk running a race (ahead of his competitors, of course), while, in a third, Atatürk was a surgeon, gowned up to perform surgery. In yet another (Figure 5.7) Atatürk is helping a young girl with a computer (girls' education was important to him). The computer screen displays the words '*Harf devrimi*' (Alphabet revolution), referring to the Latinisation of Turkish orthography, a 'revolution' spearheaded by Atatürk himself. These images seemed to suggest that Atatürk had not really died – or at least his principles and revolutions (*ilke ve inkilap*) had not died – and he was still guiding Turkish society into a promising and technologically advanced future.

A number of my Turkish friends – at least the ones who were a little cynical – would joke about the seeming omniscience of Atatürk, as if he were judgmentally searching everyone's soul for appropriately Turkish sentiments. A prominent novelist commented to me that the ubiquity of these pictures suggested that the Kemalists thought that if they shouted 'Atatürk' loud enough, the fundamental-

Figure 5.7 Atatürk helps a young girl working at a computer, 1999 (photograph by author)

ists would go away. But, ultimately, the omnipresence of Atatürk was not about Atatürk himself. Rather, the battle was always about Kemalist nostalgia for what Turkey had supposedly once been and fantasies about what it would be: a truly laicist state where Islam was properly controlled.

The VP leaders also seized on public imagery of Atatürk, but they displayed a different set of images of Atatürk and the early Republic, ones that emphasised the religious origins of the Turkish state and its continuity with the Ottoman Empire. Some of these images included photographs of Atatürk praying, accepting sacrifices of sheep, visiting the tombs of religious leaders, walking with his veiled first wife Latife Hanım or kissing the hand of his veiled mother. Some religiously conservative commentators and newspapers juxtaposed these images with ones of headscarved women being barred from university. They would also repeat Atatürk's speeches in favour of Islam, veiling and the caliphate he had made in the 1920s (before taking a harder line against public religious expression) (Özyürek 2006: 156–7). Religious conservatives claimed that the Kemalists had wilfully erased that aspect of Atatürk's past to promote their own narrow goals. In sum, both sides of this polarised debate about the meanings of Atatürk's images used a 'nostalgic representation of the past as a blueprint to transform the present, representation of the past became a battleground for a struggle over political legitimacy and domination' (Özyürek 2007: 117).

The end of the VP

The debate about Kemalism and the role of Atatürk in Turkish history would, like the headscarf question, persist well into the twenty-first century, long after the shuttering of the VP. As in the case of the WP, the VP pushed the envelope too far for the Kemalist establishment. Secularists in the judiciary in particular argued that the VP was just a continuation of the WP, which had been outlawed, and they worked to close the VP as well. An event that gave ammunition to the case against the VP occurred just after the 1999 elections when a veiled VP representative from Istanbul, Merve Kavakçı, was elected to parliament and attempted to be sworn in while wearing the *tesettür*. The reaction to her presence in parliament was so explosive that she was never able to take the oath, left the parliament and had her citizenship stripped on a technicality (Shively 2005). Soon after, Supreme Court justice Vural Savaş opened a case against the VP, which resulted in the closure of the party in 2001 for anti-secular activities.

The party that worked: the rise of the Justice and Development Party

After the closure of the VP, the political differences between the 'Young Ones' and older members of the party played out when the two contingents regrouped to form two different parties. Older, traditional politicians formed the Felicity Party while the younger *Değişimler*, led by Recep Tayyip Erdoğan and Abdullah Gül, formed the JDP in 2001. The Felicity Party did not attract many votes, never enough to enter parliament. But the JDP became popular and eventually very powerful. Indeed, almost all of Turkey's political history in the twenty-first century so far is defined by JDP dominance.

In the early 2000s, the JDP represented something new and promising for those who were completely disillusioned by the existing political parties. The reasons for the disillusionment were many. The 1990s had been a turbulent period in Turkish history. Political parties had risen and fallen with startling regularity – not just the Islamic parties but many others as well. The decades-long conflict between the state and the Kurdish separatist PKK continued, political scandals revealed the depths of corruption in the military and political parties, and the strident secularism that alienated so many ordinary Turks created a sense of a failed state. The coalition government established after the 1999 national elections revealed its weakness and incompetence when it failed to adequately respond to the massive July 1999 earthquake that killed over 17,000 people. Finally, there was a devastating financial crisis in 2001 that led to the collapse of many businesses and the loss of savings for individual households. The financial turmoil was the last straw for many: the government needed to change. Any party or leader that could offer some degree of competence and some promise of change was bound to attract electoral attention. Erdoğan and members of the Welfare and Virtue Parties had served very effective terms as mayors of major cities, such as Istanbul and Ankara. As these leaders formed the basis of the JDP, many in the electorate were attracted by their appearance of capability and vigour, while the JDP attracted the religious vote because of the party members' devoutness. The JDP won by a landslide in the 2002 national elections, gaining two-thirds of the national parliamentary seats.

The emergence of the JDP as a dominant political force was one of the most profound and welcome events for many pious Turkish citizens. The JDP's electoral wins seemed to represent positive pay-off from all that they had endured as the result of the 28 February 1997 process, and provided a chance to imagine the development of a country that fitted their own aspirations and values. For example, the fact that Erdoğan had been jailed for 'inciting religious hatred' only increased the party's appeal to many observant Turks. They were often outraged at the limits placed on religious practices and thereby viewed Erdoğan's jail time as unrighteous persecution from which he had emerged triumphant. For them, Erdoğan was *mazlum* (oppressed) (Yavuz 2009: 119), just as they themselves were *mazlum* too.

The JDP was careful to appeal to religiously observant citizens, who were the party's electoral base. Just as Erdoğan had limited the sale of alcohol in certain parks when he was mayor of Istanbul, the JDP extended anti-alcohol policies to all of Turkey by suppressing alcohol sales through increasing taxation and licensing requirements. Furthermore, the JDP politicians followed pious lifestyles themselves. They prayed five times a day, fasted during Ramadan and refrained from alcohol, and many of the representatives' wives wore headscarves – a point that garnered much criticism from the Kemalist opposition. In a word, the JDP seemed to both talk the talk and walk the walk of Muslim piety.

Another important way in which the JDP courted the devout population of voters was by openly supporting the right of women to veil at universities. In 2007, for example, the JDP proposed changes to the constitution that would allow women in headscarves to attend universities, and in 2008 the JDP-dominated parliament voted in favour of lifting the ban, though the Constitutional Court annulled the parliament's decision. The JDP's gestures towards loosening restrictions on Islamic head coverings were especially important in light of legal developments around veiling in Europe. In 1998, a medical student at Istanbul University, Leyla Şahin, brought a case to the European Court of Human Rights (ECHR) contesting the university's decision to bar her from campus because she wore a headscarf. But in 2005, the ECHR issued a ruling upholding Turkey's policy of barring veiled women from university campuses, claiming that the ban was necessary to maintain social order and prevent showing any preference for a particular religion. Even though the JDP's 2007 attempts to lift the ban were not effective at first, the situation changed in the long run. In 2013, when the JDP had gained concentrated political domination,

Erdoğan unilaterally lifted the prohibition on headscarves in universities, and veiled women could freely attend public universities. While parliamentarians and civil servants were still officially prohibited from wearing the *tesettür* in office, that prohibition was also quietly removed. Now veiled female representatives, especially from the JDP, regularly serve in parliament with little backlash.

Besides pious Turks, another constituency that was drawn to the JDP, at least in the early 2000s, was the urban and rural poor who wanted a political party that would provide real services and opportunities in contrast to the parties of the 1990s.[10] A number of my Kemalist friends chided the JDP for 'bribing' the poor with free handouts of food and heating coal – what many secularists saw as empty populism and vote-buying. But these secularists also tended to underestimate the complete alienation experienced by so many of the poor, who felt that the dominant political parties demanded loyalty and but gave very little in return in terms of economic security and access to essential services. In contrast, the JDP maintained a reputation for good stewardship and provision of service, and it dealt effectively with some of the many economic issues – inflation, joblessness and bank instability – in ways that inspired confidence among business owners and consumers alike.

Even though the JDP members were initially careful not to overplay the religion card, secularists were nonetheless dismayed by the turn of events in the 2000s. There was concern that the JDP was implementing a policy to slowly and stealthily Islamise the Turkish government by hiring only pious officials and bureaucrats into governmental positions while purging secularists from those same positions. The fact that the JDP government attempted in 2007 to lift the ban on headscarves in the university was evidence to many secularists that the religious aspirations of the JDP were more intense than its secularist rhetoric suggested. More controversially, in 2007 the JDP-dominated parliament also elected Abdullah Gül, a co-founder and prominent member of the JDP, to the presidency to replace the secularist President Ahmet Necdet Sezer, whose term had expired. The prospect of Islamic-leaning politicians in the positions of both president and prime minister – along with the possibility of veiled women being permitted on university campuses – drove massive crowds of secularist protestors into the streets of the major cities. The military also issued a statement on their website threatening a coup if the JDP deviated too far from Turkey's secularist principles, and the Constitutional Court opened up an action to shut down the party for violating Turkey's laicist principles. Erdoğan called early elections in response. But the opposition was poorly organised, and the 2007 elections strengthened the JDP's position as it gained 46 per cent of the vote, more than any single party in two decades. The JDP continued its mandate and in the elections of 2011, managed to get almost 50 per cent of the vote. The military's threat of a coup came to nothing while the Constitutional Court's case to close the party was struck down in 2008.

With its continuing domination, the JDP was able to accomplish something new in the history of modern Turkey: it was able to maintain a strong state system while separating it from traditional Kemalism. That is, rather than identifying state power with Kemalist assumptions about the role of Islam in public life, the JDP government was able to meld together state power and Islamic populism. Yet while the JDP era has provided some relaxation on Islamic expression in public spaces, the JDP government of the 2000s did not attempt to turn Turkey into a state based only on Islamic principles, nor did it attempt to resurrect *Shari'ah*. Rather, the JDP configured itself as a conservative democratic party that promoted Muslim nationalism, which emphasised Islamic brotherhood rather than ethnic nationalism (White 2013: 9). The reality was that religiously observant Turks, including the JDP itself, long absorbed and naturalised some of the assumptions of secularism and liberal individualism (such as freedom of belief and expression) that played such central roles in Turkish thought. They were not prepared to eject the secular state entirely but sought to transform it to be more accommodating of Islamic practices.

In his study of Sultanbeyli, a religiously conservative squatter district in Istanbul, sociologist Cihan Tuğal (2009) describes the process by which the residents came to absorb assumptions of liberalism while remaining religiously observant. When Tuğal began his research in the 1990s, the district's residents tended to be not only deeply conservative, but even radical in their approach to religion and politics. Some expressed disdain for the WP and the VP, seeing them as too compromised by Kemalism and Turkish nationalism to serve the interests of 'true' Islam. There were groups in the district that were so radical that they refused to engage in the mosques and religious services provided by the Diyanet. Some also disparaged the moderate Islam associated with *cemaats* such as the Gülen movement and other Nurcus. They saw these *cemaats* as pro-Western, Turkish nationalist and embedded in capitalism, rather than devoted to creating a global Islamic unity that would stand in opposition to the Christian West and to the capitalist structures controlled by Western countries.

As the JDP rose in power and the economic transformations accelerated during the early 2000s (see Chapter 7), the attitudes of many of Tuğal's acquaintances softened. The rapidly expanding economy that characterised Turkey in the 2000s meant that the job prospects and material conditions of life in Sultanbeyli improved considerably. The increasing number of Islamic civic organisations provided platforms for pious residents to enact their social-religious goals outside the direct control of the state. These factors and the JDP leaders' discourse of piety – as well as their discourse of grievance against the old Kemalist order – attracted many of the once cynical radicals of the Sultanbeyli district. The religious conservatives experienced simultaneous social, political and economic changes that eventually persuaded them to buy into the entire system in its transformed (that is, friendlier to religion) condition rather than go through the risky and potentially fatal process of trying to overthrow the secular state.

Tuğal calls this process a 'passive revolution', in which the organs of power manage to win over a potentially revolutionary movement and incorporate it into an already existing system.[11] A passive revolution worked in this case because the Turkish state of the 2000s was able to reproduce a discourse and set of practices that both accommodated in 'bits and pieces' the desires of the residents of Sultanbeyli and similar conservative districts throughout Turkey, thus facilitating interactions between ordinary believers, the secular state and Islamism. 'These interactions create a political field in which the traditional and the modern, the religious and the secular, mutate in unexpected ways and produce hybrid positions' (Tuğal 2006: 246). For example, in the 1990s Sultanbeyli residents saw the Diyanet as enthralled to the Kemalist order, but by the 2000s, they had started to seek out its services more and expressed respect for its efforts. People who had once been scathingly critical of Fethullah Gülen in the 1990s now referred to him as Hocaefendi and regularly read his material and listened to his sermons (Tuğal 2009: 198–204). Tuğal argued that the boundaries of conservative Islam and those of liberal democracy are porous, and under the right conditions, the two domains of human experience could adapt themselves to each other to create a relatively stable social reality.

Transformed society

Just as the 1980 coup brought on a period of rapid transformation in the relationship between Islam and politics in Turkey, so did the post-modern coup of 1997 spell some significant changes for the practice of Islam in modern Turkey. In terms of Islamic politics, the forced closure of the WP and the VP brought to a head long-term tensions within the old NOM, the network of the Islam-sympathetic politicians that had been functioning in Turkey since the 1960s. The old guard represented by Necmettin Erbakan was giving way to a younger, more dynamic group of politicians, represented by Abdullah Gül and Erdoğan. These 'Young Ones' embraced relatively progressive social and economic positions while recognising the importance of religious practice to the larger Turkish population. The JDP was formed out of this younger, progressive cohort and represented something new and promising for those who were disillusioned by the existing political parties.

At least in the 2000s, some of the rhetoric of the JDP extolled the virtues of a democratic and secular society, though the party sought to redefine the concept of secularism to make it less restrictive. In a 2006 speech Erdoğan argued that while secularism required that the state should not be structured according to religious laws, it also required that 'the state should be neutral and keep an equal distance from all religious beliefs and should be the guarantor of individuals' freedom of religion and belief' (in Yavuz 2009: 159). Even though Erdoğan's position became much less accommodating in later years, the stance he articulated in his 2006 speech was quite distinct from the old dominant Kemalist-style laicism, a policy by which religion is subordinated to the state. For the traditional Kemalists these changes were, of course, profoundly threatening to the secularist order that they saw as the heart of modern Turkey. But for pious Turks, the JDP represented an opportunity for economic advancement, political accountability and religious freedom – at least for Sunni Muslims – in a rapidly developing society.

Notes

1. TÜSİAD describes itself on its English-language website (https://tusiad.org/en/tusiad/about) as 'a voluntary, independent, non-governmental organisation dedicated to promote welfare through private enterprise . . . TÜSİAD's activities are aimed at creating a social cohesion based on the competitive market economy, sustainable development and participatory democracy'.
2. Works by Jenny White (2002a) and Yeşim Arat (2005) describe in detail the nature of WP grassroots activism.
3. In his 1988 novel, *The Satanic Verses*, Salman Rushdie draws on a traditional story about the Prophet Muhammad to make the Prophet seem fallible. The portrayal of Muhammad led some Muslim groups to make death threats against Rushdie. Most dramatically, the Ayatollah Ruhollah Khomeini, the Supreme Leader of Iran, issued a *fatwa* calling for his assassination. The British government had to put Rushdie, a British citizen, under police protection.
4. There are many accounts of the Sivas and Gazi massacres. Here I was relying on the descriptions provided by Martin Sökefeld (2008).
5. Hamas is a Palestinian political and activist organisation that has fought especially intense battles against the Israeli state – indeed, has called for its destruction. Hezbollah is a religious organisation that also has a starkly anti-Israel platform.
6. A list of the directives can be found in several places, for example in the appendix to Yavuz (2003: 275–6).
7. The State Security Court convicted Erdoğan of 'inciting religious hatred' and calling for the 'overthrow of the government' when he read a poem out loud at a 1997 rally in Siirt. The poem that offended the secularist authorities read in part:

    The mosques are our barracks
    The domes our helmets
    The minarets our bayonets
    And the faithful our soldiers

    Erdoğan was sentenced to ten months in jail, removed as mayor of Istanbul and barred from standing for elected office. Interestingly, this poem, written by the liberal Ziya Gökalp, had appeared in a state-published book, and had been recommended to teachers by the Ministry of Education.
8. Women are required to cover their heads when entering a mosque and reading the Qur'an, and most women, even those who are secularist, comply with these expectations.
9. The Arabic terms for these new forms of clothing include *hijab* and *niquab*. The Turkish

words are different and do not really correspond exactly to clothing practices in Arabic-speaking countries, though there are clearly mutual influences and shared marketing strategies. See Lewis (2015) and Tarlo (2010).

10. Of course, the pious population and the poor population of Turkey are not mutually exclusive but overlap substantially.

11. Tuğal adopted the concept of 'passive revolution' from the work of Italian philosopher Antonio Gramsci.

CHAPTER 6

Religious education: institutions and popular practices

Visiting the Ankara Beşevler imam-hatip secondary school, 1999

I made a visit to the *imam-hatip* school in Beşevler in Ankara, guided by my friend's daughter, Sevil, who had been a student there. The school was quite large, consisting of a number of buildings and a roomy central courtyard. Boys and girls were taught in separate buildings at the time I visited, though the classrooms had been co-educational prior to 1990. There was also one building for what was left of the middle school. Since *imam-hatip* education at the middle school level was eliminated by the state in 1997, the final middle-school grades were just finishing up that year (that is, the ones who entered two years previously), and it would close the next year. When we arrived in the girls' building, all the female students were milling in the halls. Some wore plain school uniforms while others wore a *pardesü* (a long, form-concealing coat) over their uniforms, and all wore the school's white headscarves. The students seemed to be very interested in me and would stare at me, often smiling.

The school director, Ismail Bey, wanted to meet me beforehand to make sure I wasn't a journalist or someone with hostile intentions. When we entered his office, there was a female teacher talking with him, and this teacher wore no headscarf at all. It turned out that she was an English teacher and she conversed with me in English a little. Ismail Bey talked to me for a long time, practically giving me a sermon on the greatness of Islam, emphasising that everyone who studies Islam eventually converts to it. Over the course of our long conversation, he made some repeated suggestions that I convert to Islam, that it was the final religion, and there was a sense that since it was the last, it was also the most perfected.

After the meeting with Ismail Bey, Sevil suggested that I observe a class, to which Ismail Bey replied that I could sit in a 9th-grade Qur'an class that he would be teaching. When we entered the class, Ismail Bey told the students that I was a foreign guest in the class, and I could sit wherever I wanted. Immediately, the girls started to invite me to sit next to them – everyone wanted me to sit next to them, it seemed. There was an empty seat, though, and Ismail Bey suggest I sit in it. The girls stared at me with curiosity, and even throughout the course, they kept taking peeks at me. The day's class consisted of girls reciting passages from the Qur'an by heart. The students would volunteer to do a passage, and Ismail Bey would correct the students as they recited and would give them marks in a book when they completed their passages. While one girl would recite, I could hear others practising under their breaths. Ismail Bey would also write troublesome phrases or syllables on the board.

After the class was over, the girls crowded around me to talk, asking me questions such as 'What do you think of Islam?', 'Do you know who Leonardo DiCaprio is?', 'Where do you come from?' and 'Why are you here?', 'Do you want to become a Muslim?'. They were a rather enthusiastic and nice bunch of girls and they told me that I should definitely convert to Islam since it was the best religion. One girl asked what I thought about the headscarf issue, and said that everyone should do what they want, and the state should leave the headscarf alone. One girl also gave me a book. At first I thought she was just lending it to me but she wrote in it that she was giving it to me as a present. I was rather surprised and a little confused by this – it was a very nice book, *Islam Ilmihali* (the Islamic catechism). But I didn't feel I thanked the girl properly (and made sure she really wanted to give me the book), mostly because I didn't realise right away that she was giving it to me. The girls also told me that after their next class, physics, they had *siyer* course (a course on the life of the Prophet), and they invited me to come. I agreed to return and went to sit in Ismail Bey's office while the girls had their physics class. Then I returned for the *siyer* course, and again the girls showered me with questions. The teacher eventually showed up and was quite welcoming to me. Both he and Ismail Bey talked about how important it is to be friends with foreigners and try to understand each other's religions. Over the course of the class, the teacher gave some basic information about Muhammad: he was born in 571 CE and died in 632, but he was actually sixty-three when he died, since there was a change in the European calendar during his lifetime. He became a prophet when he was forty years old. The teacher liked to compare Muhammad and Isa (Jesus) for my sake, saying that Isa died when he was thirty-three and became a prophet when he was thirty. After finishing the work at hand, the teacher wanted me to tell the class about what Christians believe about Isa. I told the class that pious Christians believe that Isa is not just a prophet but is the son of God and an expression of God. I also said that most Christians also believe in Judgement Day and heaven and hell, and so on. The teacher seemed to know a lot about Christianity, and asked some good questions. Again the girls talked to me after the class and a couple of the girls offered to bring me books to read. One book was about a Christian woman who converted to Islam. The other was *The Prophet's Letters of Invitation to Islam (Rasulullah'ın Islam'a Davet Mektupları)*, which would be a very meaningful gift. I left with a promise to return in a few days.

Religious education takes many forms in Turkey. In keeping with the principles of laicism, in which the Turkish state has authority over religious policy and institutions, the state itself is responsible for providing Sunni Islamic religious education to the majority of Turkish citizens.[1] In Chapter 2 I described the Religious Culture and Ethics courses required of all Turkish students from the 4th to the 12th grades. These courses have traditionally provided an important site in which Turkish authorities have been able to lay out their understanding of official Islam, which promotes personal piety and allegiance to Turkey as a secular nation. These courses have not been without conflict – some devout Sunni Muslims find them too bland to be useful, and many Alevis object to being forced to submit to Sunni Islamic education that does not reflect Alevi beliefs and practices. But the Religious Culture and Ethics courses are just one form of religious education available in Turkey. There are many other religious educational platforms by which different types and ranges of Islamic knowledge are transmitted. The state itself provides a great deal of more intensive religious education, both within the public school system and within the context of the Directorate of Religious Affairs (Diyanet). Beyond these are a wide range of formal and informal religious educational establishments and traditions that operate outside – and sometimes against – those state institutions. This chapter will examine state-controlled religious education practices and describe some of the non-state arenas that deliver different forms of religious instruction to people with a range of interests and beliefs.

State religious education: *imam-hatip* schools

The public educational institutions most heavily involved with religious education in general and the training of religious officials in particular have been the *imam-hatip* schools. These schools were established in the early days of the Turkish Republic to train the imams (prayer leaders) and *hatip*s (preachers) serving the state mosques, but the *imam-hatip* schools had a rocky beginning. The 1924 Law of Unification of Educational Instruction (*Tevhid-i Tedrisat*) replaced the old Ottoman *medrese* and sectarian schools with a national school system administered by a new Ministry of Education, and in the new system, the *imam-hatip* schools were opened to serve as vocational schools, similar to those that taught technical trades. Because of low enrolment, however, the *imam-hatip* schools were completely shut down in 1930. But the problem of enrolment was due not to lack of interest but to lack of state support. Many students of the early *imam-hatip* schools had sought secure careers as civil servants in the Diyanet and state-run mosques, but in 1926, the state determined that religious staff were no longer civil servants and thus could not be paid. With the career incentives eliminated, enrolment naturally dropped until the 1930 closures. After that, the only means of 'official' religious education were Qur'an courses provided by the Diyanet, but these courses only covered the reading and memorisation of the Qur'an and provided no credentials (Çağlar 2013: 34–5). As discussed earlier, the lack of religious education meant that there were not enough professionals available to carry out essential religious roles.

Not only was there a lack of religious officials, but members of the government were also concerned that without properly educated religious leaders, people would learn 'incorrect' forms of Islam, turn to superstitious beliefs or come under the sway of false religious leaders or village *molla*s educated in the old *medrese* system that existed before the founding of the Republic. Thus the government of the Republican People's Party (Atatürk's party that reigned during Turkey's period of single-party rule) bowed to pressure from rival political parties and in the 1940s allowed the establishment of some training centres where *imam-hatip* courses were offered. But the quality of religious instruction in these courses was notoriously poor, leading Ahmet Hamdi Akseki, the president of the Diyanet at the time, to complain that these courses were still inadequate and provided only 'a pseudo-consolation' to the problem of too few imams and *hatip*s (Çağlar 2013: 37–8). After the Democrat Party came into power in 1950, it closed the *imam-hatip* courses and replaced them a year later with more formal *imam-hatip* schools for middle- and secondary-school students in various cities to begin to address the shortage of credentialled religious personnel.

The *imam-hatip* schools had to follow the guidelines stipulated by the Ministry of Education under advisement from the Diyanet, so that the type of Islam taught in these schools remained in line with official religious ideology. Ultimately, the schools came under the management of a special Directorate of Religious Education within the Ministry of Education where they had the status of a 'vocational school'.[2] Students received instruction in vocation-specific topics, such as Qur'an, *hadith*, Arabic and Islamic law, as well as general education subjects (such as maths, sciences, history, Western languages, and civics). Instructors for the vocational classes in the *imam-hatip* schools of the 1950s and 1960s were largely former imams, *hatip*s and muftis, some of whom had been trained in the old *medrese* system. As such, they had much religious knowledge, but had never been trained as teachers, so their ability to convey knowledge was not always optimal (Ozgur 2012: 43–4).

As was typical of graduates from any type of vocational schools, *imam-hatip* graduates were not permitted to enter the universities, not even the faculties of divinity that began to develop in the 1950s and 1960s. Graduates could only expect to get civil service jobs as religious officials (all formal religious roles in Turkey are now part of the civil service), which would come with relatively low salaries. But in modern Turkey, citizens have long seen civil service as a path to financial security and stability, since though salaries may be low, they are steady and civil servants receive guaranteed benefits. Until the 1970s, most *imam-hatip* enrollees came from the poor or lower middle classes, and for them, working as a civil servant would guarantee an economically secure, lifelong career. As such, the *imam-hatip* schools proved to be so popular that the number of schools increased from seven to nineteen by the end of the 1950s and to seventy-two by 1971 (Ozgur 2012).

Yet the fortunes of the *imam-hatip* schools have always been subject to the vicissitudes of Turkish politics. Strongly Kemalist governments have tended to take actions to suppress the *imam-hatip* schools, by making them less available or by curtailing the future prospects of *imam-hatip* graduates. Governments more sympathetic to the religious concerns of the Turkish population have allowed *imam-hatip* schools to expand and flourish. For example, a military coup in 1971 brought the expansion of the schools to a temporary halt, since the military government of the time stipulated the formation of a government based on Kemalist principles, and part of this effort included shutting down the middle-school section of the *imam-hatip* schools, thus eliminating three years of *imam-hatip* education.[3] But after the initial downsizing, the *imam-hatip* schools continued to increase in number, and their mission broadened. In 1973, for example, the government enacted the Basic Law on National Education, which stipulated that *imam-hatip* graduates were not limited to being religious functionaries but could go on to study in the university, though they were only permitted to enter programmes in the humanities or social sciences. This attracted religious students who aspired to higher education but would have avoided the *imam-hatip* schools before because they were a barrier to university education.

Another change in *imam-hatip* schools that made them more popular was the acceptance of female students beginning in 1976. Women could not serve as religious functionaries until the 2000s (see Chapter 8), so educating girls in religious subjects could not be for vocational purposes but for general education. In many ways, this was a boon to girls' education in Turkey. Many families – especially poorer families – were reluctant to extend girls' education beyond the required 5th-grade education (if even that far). There were many reasons for this reluctance. Traditional gender roles confined women to largely domestic duties where advanced education would not be needed, while boys could use vocational education in middle and secondary schools to attain a civil service or other job. For many pious families, sending daughters of middle-school age (that is, pubescent) to a general co-educational school where girls were not permitted to veil was unacceptable. In *imam-hatip* schools, however, girls were usually permitted to wear the headscarf, and boys and girls were sometimes educated separately.

More generally, the education of girls became ever more acceptable in Turkey over time, but especially for rural-to-urban migrants who saw their children's education not only as a means of economic advancement but also as a form of social capital. That is, middle-class status is not only about a level of economic attainment, but also about partaking in the practices and aspirations of the middle class. In Turkey, as in most countries, the modern middle class values the education of children, both sons and daughters. As education becomes a means of upward mobility, families of all economic statuses sought it out, with the result that as time went on, the rates of advanced education of both boys and girls improved, leading to an increased number of secondary schools, including private schools, in all urban centres (Rutz and Balkan 2010: 5).

Imam-hatip schools and the Turkish-Islamic synthesis

The *imam-hatip* schools were affected by the vast institutional and ideological transformations introduced after the 1980 coup. The Turkish-Islamic Synthesis opened up an enhanced role for the *imam-hatip* schools, which could serve as venues where Sunni Islam and Turkish ethnic pride could be promoted. The post-coup government loosened restrictions on the job prospects of *imam-hatip* graduates by permitting them to enter any university department – not just humanities and social science departments – so long as the student received sufficient points on the university entrance exams.[4] By this time the teachers in the *imam-hatip* schools who were teaching the vocational (Islamic studies) courses were themselves graduates of university or higher education programmes designed specifically to produce teachers in religious education. Thus instruction became more sophisticated and systematic, and students from the *imam-hatip* schools were competitive in the university exams and earned places in the universities. These changes, coupled with the growing prominence of the WP in the 1980s and 1990s, led to a surge in the number of *imam-hatip* schools. By the time of the soft coup of 28 February 1997, there were 601 *imam-hatip* schools in Turkey, enrolling more than half a million students (Ozgur 2012: 50).

In theory, these schools were committed to furthering students' religious knowledge and were designed to produce a particular type of Muslim, one who was both virtuous and patriotic, committed to the Kemalist agenda in which religion is moderate, politically neutral and largely confined to the private sphere (à la the Turkish-Islamic Synthesis) (Pak 2004a). But as Soon-Yong Pak, who conducted research at an *imam-hatip* school in Mamak in Ankara province, observed, the reality did not always conform to the ideal, in that many *imam-hatip* schools did not always follow the Kemalist philosophy. The teachers were supposed to follow the curriculum issued by the Ministry of Education, but they had a fair degree of latitude in how to present and teach subjects. Some teachers followed the state-approved curriculum closely, but others added material or topics of their own choosing, or even ignored the state curriculum altogether. Some teachers justified this 'deviation' by arguing that the state-provided textbooks were weak and superficial, so they would introduce supplementary material as a way to enhance students' understanding of Islam. Some teachers went so far as to promote the restoration of *Shari'ah* in Turkey or introduce the teachings of Islamic radical thinkers, such as Sayyid Qutb[5] or the Ayatollah Khomeini[6] and many others – practices anathema to the Kemalist project (Ozgur 2012: 98–9). A colleague of mine who attended the *imam-hatip* schools in the late 1980s told me that almost all his teachers of Islamic studies (and sometimes teachers of other subjects) were *Shari'ah* minded. Teachers were generally affiliated with *cemaat*s and *Tarikat*s, and everyone would propagate their own ideology. Many of them supported the WP and would harshly criticise the Kemalist regime.

While teachers in the *imam-hatip* schools promoted course content that conformed to the teachers' political and educational agendas, the schools would also have what Ozgur (2012: 82–97) calls an informal or 'hidden' curriculum. A hidden curriculum is a collection of experiences and practices that impart implicit knowledge, values and expectations to students. For example, common practices in *imam-hatip* schools, such as gender segregation and veiling, instil in students a sense of Islamically correct gender relations. (Of course rules of gender segregation do not stop boys and girls from secretly meeting and exchanging letters, as one former student told me.) Some physical features of the schools encourage students to pray regularly – schools would have prayer rooms or sinks for ablutions, which would never be found in general education schools. Furthermore, *imam-hatip* students are surrounded by both teachers and other students who share many views on social and political issues. Even though the *imam-hatip* schools include the usual accoutrements of Turkish national secular identity – pictures of Atatürk, flags, posters with Atatürk's speeches and sayings – students and staff may be more critical of Turkey's laicist policies and practices than anything one would encounter in general schools. Through the curriculum and its variations, as well as the hidden curriculum, the *imam-hatip* schools impart a particular type of discipline and knowledge to create pious, socially engaged citizens. Of course, all schools in Turkey (and everywhere else) are institutions designed to discipline students into particular behaviours and attitudes – all schools have a hidden curriculum. What is interesting about the *imam-hatip* schools is that their original raison d'être was to create a safe or 'tame' form of Islam that would not challenge Turkey's secularist priorities. But Islam is not so easily controlled. The *imam-hatip* schools have been one arena in which the desires of the Kemalist state and the desires of pious citizens have diverged, sometimes radically.

The effects of the 28 February process
This 'divergence' has repeatedly brought the *imam-hatip* schools under the scrutiny of secularist authorities. In the context of the 28 February 1997 soft coup, *imam-hatip* schools faced several strictures designed to curb their influence and independence. One of eighteen 'recommendations' presented by the NSC to WP Prime Minister Necmettin Erbakan was that the government increase the state education requirement so that all students must complete the 8th grade, rather than only the 5th grade. On the surface such a stipulation does not appear like an attack on the *imam-hatip* schools, since many government officials were concerned that a 5th-grade education was not enough to prepare Turkish children for the challenges of the modern economy and vocational environment. But the effect was to close down all middle-grade *imam-hatip* schools, since

an *imam-hatip* education could not fulfil the state educational requirement. The NSC was in fact clear that the new middle-school recommendation was a way to curb the religious schools since it also required that all Qur'an instruction available to children had to be under the control of the Ministry of Education. In the end, the 8th-grade educational requirement was implemented abruptly, before the infrastructure and personnel were in place to meet the requirement. This led to vastly overcrowded schools and unprepared teachers, problems that persisted for years.

The shuttering of the *imam-hatip* middle schools was a shock for many pious families. Significantly more students attended the middle-school (lower secondary) sections than the higher secondary sections of the *imam-hatip* schools. But more critically, many devout Muslims considered the middle-school age (6th, 7th and 8th grades) a crucial time in which to introduce Islamic knowledge and train children into proper Islamic practice (Pak 2004b). It was thought to be the ideal time to introduce the study of Arabic, which is critical to Islamic worship and prayer. With the new education law, students would not be able to take Arabic in school until 9th grade, which many considered to be very late. Similarly, pious parents openly worried that female students graduating from 8th grade would be well into puberty by the time they were allowed to veil in school. In *imam-hatip* middle schools, girls were allowed to veil from 6th grade onwards, right when most girls were beginning puberty. Headscarves were not in fact 'officially' permitted in these schools but most *imam-hatip* schools escaped the headscarf ban. Thus the closing of the *imam-hatip* middle schools – as well as the whole 28 February process – galvanised intense protests on the part of religiously observant Muslims. But the show of unity and force among those the government considered to be part of the great 'Islamist threat' only strengthened the NSC's resolve to carry out its plans, and the *imam-hatip* middle schools stopped accepting new students in 1997 (Pak 2004b: 323–4).

This notion that the middle-school years (for students aged 11 to 14) is a particularly important time in a child's intellectual development also played a role in the NSC's decision to close the *imam-hatip* middle schools. The NSC, and its Kemalist supporters, argued in the media that if children of middle-school age attended the *imam-hatip* schools, such children could be subject to 'brainwashing' (*beyin yıkama*) by the anti-Kemalist religious forces present in the *imam-hatip* schools. A middle-grade education in the general schools would ensure that children of this vulnerable age would be 'protected' from the indoctrination of the *imam-hatip* schools. Such a concern over the brainwashing of children by improper religious education fits Turkey's Ministry of Education's philosophy of learning: that children are passive learners of school content and that if they are exposed to certain ideas, they will automatically adopt those beliefs. There has been little recognition that children are 'active appropriators' who receive and integrate education in various ways depending on many factors, such as conditions and expectations in the students' social milieu (Ozgur 2012: 104–6).

Another way in which the NSC attempted to control the influence of the *imam-hatip* schools in the wake of the 28 February process was again to make it harder for *imam-hatip* graduates to attend university. After the 1980 coup *imam-hatip* graduates were afforded the opportunity to enter the university in any discipline they chose, given that they had qualified. But in 1999, the NSC 'recommended' that the CHE change university entrance rules so that *imam-hatip* students would be penalised on the university entrance exams (that is, given an automatic point deficit). This made it much more difficult for students to place well in the university system. Sometimes, *imam-hatip* students who scored very highly on the entrance exams still could not attend college because their status as an *imam-hatip* graduate reduced their scores enough to disqualify them from entry. Both of these steps – the elimination of the middle school option and the university exam penalty – resulted in a dramatic drop in enrollment in *imam-hatip* schools, from over half a million in 1996–7 to less than 100,000 in the 2001–2 school year.

Imam-hatip schools under the Justice and Development Party

The political dominance of the JDP resulted in positive changes for the *imam-hatip* school system. Fully one-third of the JDP deputies in parliament in 2007, including Prime Minister Recep Tayyip Erdoğan, were graduates of *imam-hatip* schools. These politicians publicly extolled their educational experiences and directed funds to the schools, which pleased the religiously conservative voting population (Çağlar 2013: 48–9). The JDP government also took steps to make the *imam-hatip* schools a viable option for more people by eliminating the point penalty on the university exams in 2009 so that *imam-hatip* students could once again compete equally for positions in the universities. In order to deflect some of the criticism from secularists that this move instigated, Erdoğan argued that the point penalty was removed for all vocational school students, not just those in the *imam-hatip* schools. But based on attitudes and statements the JDP supporters had made, most secularists remained convinced that this policy was aimed especially at *imam-hatip* students[7] (Ozgur 2012: 137–9). Furthermore, as part of a large-scale educational reform bill passed in 2012, the JDP allowed the middle-school sections of the *imam-hatip* system to re-open. What the 2012 bill actually did was to make twelve years of education compulsory, and allowed all types of middle-school vocational schools to open. Again, secularist observers saw the opening of the middle-school vocational schools as a politically motivated action to allow for the re-opening of the middle-school division of the *imam-hatip* schools in particular. These changes introduced in the JDP era, and especially after the 2012 reforms, led to a surge in the *imam-hatip* school enrolment to over 1 million students, or about 10 per cent of the student population, by 2017.

While many *imam-hatip* graduates with higher-education aspirations choose to study in faculties of divinity in the universities, the most popular fields the graduates applied to have been law, medicine and business. People who had been through the *imam-hatip* education system often told me that the memorisation skills and focus on history and Islamic legal traditions typical of the *imam-hatip* education prepared students well for the rigours of courses of study in law or medicine. Whether or not this is true, *imam-hatip* graduates won respectable positions in the universities, especially after the university exam point penalty was abolished.

University theological departments and higher Islamic institutes

Religious education at the university level has, like that in the *imam-hatip* schools, been vulnerable to the vicissitudes of Turkish politics. Early in the history of the Turkish Republic, advanced schools of theological education that had operated during much of the history of the Ottoman Empire were gradually eliminated. To replace these schools, Atatürk and the nationalist government included in the 1923 Unification of Education Law a provision directing the establishment of a Faculty of Divinity (*İlahiyat Fakültesi*) at the *Dārü'l-Fünūn*, an institution of higher learning founded in Istanbul in 1846. When the *Dārü'l-Fünūn* was reorganised into Istanbul University in 1933, however, the government withdrew support for the Faculty of Divinity, and it closed down. From 1933 until the multi-party period – the period coinciding with the closure of the *imam-hatip* schools – no Turkish universities offered education in religious subjects. This too contributed to the lack of trained religious personnel that drew complaints from Turkish citizens, as noted above. And just as the governments of the multi-party era reopened the *imam-hatip* schools in response to the complaints, they also established a Faculty of Divinity at Ankara University in 1949. The four-year curriculum in the new university faculty included some studies in traditional Islamic sciences and in 'secular' disciplines, such as logic, sociology and Western languages.

For a ten-year period, this was the only institution of higher religious education in Turkey and, not surprisingly, this single department was inadequate for the provision of religious services. Furthermore, as the number of *imam-hatip* schools increased over the course of the 1950s, there were not enough teachers for the vocational/religious courses to staff these schools. The Ministry of Education dealt with this situation by establishing a Higher Islamic Institute (*Yüksek İslam Enstitüsü*) in Istanbul in 1959. As the number of *imam-hatip* schools increased over the 1960s, so did the number of the Higher Islamic Institutes. These Institutes were not known for innovation or advanced learning, as their curriculum was essentially an extension of the subjects learned in the upper secondary sections of the *imam-hatip* schools. But at least they provided graduates with the credentials necessary to teach in the *imam-hatip* schools or to serve some functions in the Diyanet. For university students who wished to study more specialised or advanced topics in religious knowledge, the Faculty of Divinity at Ankara was really the only option. By 1972, the Ankara programme had differentiated itself from the Higher Islamic Institutes by enhancing its rigour: the programme increased from four to five years of study, so that students could spend the first three years studying basic Islamic Sciences before they would choose one of two academic tracks: Tefsir (Qur'an interpretation) and Hadith, or Theology and Islamic Philosophy. From the beginning, the Ankara faculty attracted both male and female students, most of whom were interested in advanced religious study for its own sake, or for preparation to teach in the *imam-hatip* or the general secondary schools (Pacaci and Aktay 1999: 401–2).

As with so much in the history of Islam in modern Turkey, the 1980 coup introduced drastic changes in higher religious education. The CHE, formed by the military government in 1982, initiated reforms in which the Higher Islamic Institutes were turned into faculties of divinity associated with universities. The CHE took steps to standardise the curriculum of the faculties, but the curriculum design went through many versions as different experts and government functionaries tried to reach a consensus on what religious knowledge would be best suited to the needs of the Turkish population. By the 1990s the faculties of divinity throughout Turkey offered a curriculum in three different divisions.

1. The Basic Islamic Sciences (Qur'anic Exegesis, Hadith, Islamic Jurisprudence, Kalam, History of Islamic Sects, Sufism, and Arabic Language and Rhetoric)
2. Philosophy and Religious Studies (History of Philosophy, Islamic Philosophy, Philosophy of Religion, Logic, History of Religions, Sociology of Religion, Psychology of Religion and Religious Education)
3. Islamic History and Arts (Islamic History, History of Turkish-Islamic Arts, Turkish-Islamic Literature and Turkish Religious Music)

Undergraduate students were required to take courses from every division, and specialisation would begin at master's level. These divisions remain in place as of this writing but after the 1997 soft coup, a fourth division was added: the Primary Education Religious Culture and Moral Knowledge Teacher Programme. This new division represented the state's attempt not only to increase the qualifications of the teachers of religious ethics courses but to guarantee that only properly trained teachers transmitted state-approved religious knowledge to Turkish students.

The number of faculties of divinity increased dramatically after the 1980s so that by 1992 – ten years after the beginning of the education reforms under the CHE – there were twenty-three faculties of divinity in Turkey. In fact, the increase in the number of these faculties is a reflection of the increase in the number of universities (public and private) in Turkey in general. Until 1986, Turkish universities were strictly state institutions, and there were not enough of them to accommodate the growing population of students seeking to pursue higher education. The high-stakes university exams were the only path to entrance into the few schools that did exist, such that only a fraction of university aspirants could enter each year. As part of the liberalisation process begun during the prime ministry of Turgut Özal, private universities were permitted to open. The first one, Bilkent University in Ankara, launched in 1986, while the CHE also oversaw the expansion of the public university system. This development accounts for much of the increase in the number of faculties of divinity in Turkey.

Some of the faculties conformed to the needs of the Kemalist state more than others did. From its beginning, Ankara Faculty of Divinity has always leaned towards the more reformist Islam promoted by the Turkish state, while some other faculties of divinity, such as that at Marmara University in Istanbul, had a more traditional curriculum of subjects relating to standard Islamic sciences. During the years of controversies preceding the 28 February soft coup, for example, the Ankara Faculty played a role in trying to combat so-called political Islamist tendencies expressed in Turkish society. In 1995 it published a book, *Islam Gerçeği (Reality of Islam)*, prepared by a group of well-known reformist scholars. The purpose of the book was to impress the state's policies upon religiously devout citizens and to 'enlighten' the nation about some debated subjects such as the headscarf, secularism and Islamic law.

As with the *imam-hatip* schools, the fortunes of the faculties of divinity improved under the auspices of the JDP governments. For example, prior to 2010 the state did not allow the private universities to establish divinity faculties, but in 2010, the JDP lifted that prohibition and private universities started to open religious studies programmes. In 2011, Fatih Sultan Mehmet University in Istanbul opened a department titled *İslami İlimler Fakültesi* (Faculty of Islamic Sciences) rather than *Ilahiyat Fakültesi* (Faculty of Divinity), claiming that such a title was more descriptive of the programme content than was 'Faculty of Divinity'. Some other universities adopted the new name while others kept the traditional title, but the curriculum is largely the same in both programmes. The end result of these changes was that by 2018, there were in Turkey at least eighty faculties of religious study, combining the departments of divinity and those of Islamic sciences. This surplus of divinity graduates could then easily find jobs in the Diyanet, which vastly expanded under the JDP or as teachers in the increasing numbers of *imam-hatip* schools or as professors in the divinity faculties. As we will see in Chapter 8, the education system and the Diyanet formed a symbiotic relationship to expand the official channels of religious practice and education in Turkish society.

Religious education through the Diyanet

Influence of the Süleymancı cemaat

Religious education is a lifelong pursuit for many, extending well beyond the age of formal schooling. For this reason, the Diyanet offers Qur'an and religion courses and seminars to the wider public, usually held in neighbourhood mosques. Such Qur'an courses have in fact been a feature of religious education since the founding of the Republic. At that time, the teaching of the Qur'an courses were largely under control of the Süleymancı *cemaat*, which was based on the teachings of the founder Süleyman Hilmi Tunahan (1888–1959). The Süleymancıs placed emphasis on the training of imams and *hatip*s, and on general Islamic education that is steeped in the so-called 'Sunni-Hanefi-Ottoman' interpretations of Islam free from the influences of secularism, political Islamism, Shi'a-Alevi or Wahhabi[8] interpretations of Islam (Yavuz 2003: 145). After the establishment of the secular school system in 1924, Tunahan and his followers opened 'seminaries' – including one in Tunahan's own house – to teach Qur'anic recitation. His schools were especially popular among those Turkish citizens who feared that the abolition of traditional religious institutions by the Kemalist regime would lead to social and moral decline (Çakır 1995: 127–30). As with other Sufi communities, Tunahan and his followers were able to take advantage of the relaxation of secularist limitations on religious expression during the multi-party years. When the government under the Democrat Party expanded the Diyanet, Tunahan's experience with Qur'anic education allowed him to take up a position where he could train preachers for the Diyanet. The *cemaat* formally institutionalised its network of Qur'an schools into the Association of the Qur'an Seminaries, and between 1949 and 1965, the 'graduates' of these seminaries had a virtual monopoly on positions in the hierarchy of the Diyanet. One way the Süleymancıs made themselves acceptable to the nationalist secularism of the state was 'by incorporating nationalism and some Republicanism into religious identity and adopting a religious position that was pro-state, nationalist, anticommunist, and anti-political Islam' (Yavuz 2003: 146).

Not surprisingly, this presence of the Süleymancı *cemaat* in a government ministry created a fair amount of unease in official Kemalist circles (Özdalga 1999: 430–1). In 1965, laws were passed that required all members of the Diyanet to have either a diploma from the increasingly numerous *imam-hatip* schools or a university degree from a faculty of theology. While this law was aimed at creating more educated Diyanet personnel, it also served as a way to weed out Süleymancıs and to decrease the popularity of the courses taught by the *cemaat* members. Finally, after the 1971 military coup all Qur'an courses and schools were to come under state control. While the Süleymancıs maintained some courses, the government seized a number of the *cemaat*'s Qur'an school buildings and put them under the jurisdiction of the Diyanet – a process that was repeated with vigour after the 1980 coup (Çakır 1995: 130–1). All authorised avenues to Qur'an education were put progressively under state control, and alternative modes of religious education became more and more suspect on grounds that they violated the 1924 Unity of Education law.

Diyanet Qur'an and Religious Ethics courses

Since the 1980s, official Qur'an and Religious Ethics courses outside of schools have been the exclusive purview of the Diyanet. Specially trained instructors offer the courses in mosques or Qur'an learning centres to adults – these tend to be especially popular with housewives who have the time and inclination to further their religious knowledge (Ata 2008: 306). There are also popular summer study programmes available for children beyond 5th-grade level. The curriculum of the Qur'an and religion courses offered by the Diyanet is ori-entated towards teaching the correct methods of reading the Qur'an, helping students to recite and perform prayers, and instructing the students in proper morals and the 'correct' religious knowledge. And according to Ulvi Ata, the head of the Diyanet's Religious Education Department in the 2000s, part of the purpose of the courses is to make sure that the religion learned by the 'masses' enhances Turkish-Islamic nationalism. As he puts it (2008: 305), the Qur'an courses 'contribute to attaining a sense of national Turkish unity, solidifying connections of love, respect, and friendship, distinguishing national values and developing consciousness of existence and responsibility'.

When I was doing my doctoral field research in Turkey in the late 1990s, I observed the nationalist orientation of the Qur'an course curriculum. At that time, a standard publication from the Diyanet, a text called *Basic Religious Information (Temel Dinî Bilgiler* (Yazıcı 1997)), was used in the Qur'an courses for adults – updated versions are still commonly used. Rather than going into any depth about the Qur'an or the history of Islam, the book emphasised issues of conduct such as establishing proper relationships with family, community and nation. It also provided an extensive life history of Atatürk, and there were long sections describing the appropriate attitudes and conduct incumbent upon every Turkish citizen, including how it is important to fight for one's country. That is, the text seemed to align with the general goals of the Turkish-Islamic Synthesis, in which Turkish identity and Sunni Muslim identity were intertwined. This combination of religious and ethnic nationalism is still a regular feature of the Diyanet Qur'an courses, and despite (or because of) the nationalist rhetoric, the courses have been quite popular and have provided a way for the state – through the Diyanet – to establish an extensive network of mosque schools in which Turkish Sunni Islam is promoted to the population.

Religious education associated with the *cemaat*s

There are some other educational options for religiously conscientious Turks, though these exist outside the official, 'authorised' realm of the Ministry of Education and the Diyanet. Many of the *cemaat*s provide more structured religious education for students who have completed their primary schooling – after 5th grade prior to 1997 and after 8th grade from 1997 onwards – or to provide extensive religious education while students are still in school. Most often, the *cemaat*s form a foundation (*vakıf*) or association (*dernek*) to support student dormitories (*yurt*) in which religion is taught according to the philosophy of a given *cemaat*. Usually, there are separate hostels for men and women, and the women learn home economics (cooking, sewing and so on) besides religious and secular subjects. These dormitories might be whole buildings dedicated to religious instruction, or they may simply be apartments that house a small group of students and an instructor. My friend Meryem, for example, had completed her required (5th-grade) education in the early 1990s and then entered a relatively rigorous two-year Qur'an study course in a small girls' dormitory offered by the conservative İsmailağa (Nakşibendi) *cemaat* her family had belonged to. There she studied Arabic and Persian, Qur'an recitation, *tefsir*, *kalam* and some religious history. Other young women from her extended family pursued religious education through the İsmailağa *cemaat* also.

The Süleymancı *cemaat* has been especially dedicated to providing traditional religious education. They run many residential programmes all over Turkey – mostly for boys – with 160 different dormitories in Istanbul alone by the mid-2010s. During the course of my research in Turkey, I got to know many men who had been through the Süleymancı educational programme. One such former student that I came to know well, Melih, grew up in the northern Istanbul neighbourhood of Beykoz in a family of Süleymancıs. Beykoz is home to a very large boys' Süleymancı dormitory, the *Beykoz Talebe Yurdu* (Beykoz Student Dormitory), that Melih had studied in during his secondary-school years. In 2014, Melih and his family took me to the dormitory where one of the leaders gave us a tour. The building was quite large and nicely appointed. There were rooms for reading, eating, sleeping, study, lessons and, of course, *sohbet*s (sermons). There was also a very fancy office for receiving special guests. Everything was very clean and nicely furnished – this contrasted sharply with Meryem's experience at the İsmailağa girls' hostel, which, as she described to me, was housed in an old building in which there was little furniture and the young women had to sleep on the floor. In any case, the Süleymancı hostel was designed to allow students to attend normal secondary school. The students came to the hostel in the evening after school, when they would study religious topics, do homework on their secular subjects and use the building as a dormitory. The dormitory created a whole atmosphere of piety and moral behaviour, while providing a place for secular and religious education.

Gülen schools and dormitories

The Fethullah Gülen movement has established an international network of prestigious schools available to students who qualify. As discussed in Chapter 4, the Gülen schools provided a secular, scientific education, and only offered the religious instruction required by the state, namely the Religious Culture and Ethics courses. The explicitly secular nature of the Gülen schools in part accounted for the fact that the Ministry of Education accommodated them, though the Kemalist state and its supporters were often suspicious of them. Even though the Gülen schools were secular, extra-curricular activities and associated institutions, such as dormitories, were venues that provided opportunity for religious instruction and influence. For example, Gülen schools emphasised the importance of mentoring relationships – from the very early grades, students were grouped and matched with mentors (often the teachers) who did things with them after school, at weekends and during the holidays. These mentoring activities included religious studies, but also involved typical after-school activities, such as sports, games (especially chess), visual arts and music. According to a principal I interviewed at a Gülen school in Konya, the mentors and teachers, most of whom had some affiliation with the Gülen movement, were supposed to serve as role models – they did not smoke or drink, for example. The mentors taught the students about morals and religion by representing idealised behaviour rather than spending a lot of time preaching about it (Agai 2007: 106; see also Özdalga 2003; Yavuz 2013: 109–11). The idea was not only to educate kids but to shape them and build their characters, and all teachers and mentors in the schools should have seen their roles not only as a job but as a holy duty (*kutsi vazife*) since they were cultivating the new 'golden generation' that would bring about the moral redemption of Turkey (Agai 2003: 58–9).

The philosophy of conveying religious knowledge and ethics by modelling appropriate behaviours also occurred in the Gülen dormitories and 'lighthouses' (*ışıkevleri*), which were single-sex residences where young students could stay while they pursued their education. In such residences, students were closely supervised by dorm leaders associated with the Gülen movement. These dorm leaders – *abiler* (big brothers) and *ablalar* (big sisters) – would not only enforce behavioural rules, such as curfews, but also model appropriate pious behaviour and try to cultivate the students' ethical sensibilities (Vicini 2013, 2014). In terms of more explicit instruction, the *abiler* and *ablalar* would encourage regular prayer, organise basic Qur'an study and lead discussions of texts by Said Nursi and Gülen (Yavuz 2013: 100–6). Like the schools, the lighthouses were supposed to be 'incubators for the Gülen Movement's "golden generation"'. Gülen himself argued that the lighthouses are sacred places where plans and projects are produced . . . and faithful persons are raised. Here these soldiers of spirituality and truth raised in lighthouses will pour the light God has given them for inspiration onto empty minds and help them flourish on the way to the conquest of the world in spirit and reality. (in Hendrick 2013: 108–9)

Many former students I knew who had lived in the lighthouses spoke fondly of their experiences and appreciated living in a community of like-minded individuals. One graduate of a Gülen secondary school in Samsun told me he was jealous of the fact that since he lived at home, he had not been exposed to the mentoring activities as had his friends in the boarding facilities. His friends could live in a situation where they spent much time in religious devotion and study, learning about Gülen's religious thought. But this does not mean that every student was happy with their experiences in the lighthouses. A follower of Gülen in the US told me about her experience as an *abla* (older sister) in a girls' lighthouse in the south-eastern Turkish city of Gaziantep. She complained that while there were many fine students, some were also uncooperative, refusing to follow the rules and ignoring curfews, and there was little she could do to change their behaviour. These were often students of secondary-school age whose parents had chosen the Gülen lighthouses as a safe, trustworthy housing option for their children, but of course not every teenager wants to submit to the wishes of their parents or of the broader community.

Gülen dershanes (tutoring centres)

Another arena in which the Gülen movement provided religious instruction to school-age children was through *dershanes* (tutoring centres). *Dershanes* are a common feature of the Turkish educational landscape. Turkey's entrance exams for secondary school and university are so competitive that students spend years preparing for them and often seek out extra help for the preparation process. Students from wealthier families may engage private tutors – these are often teachers from public or private schools who take on tutoring to earn extra money. But students may attend the many private *dershanes* operated by all kinds of organisations, businesses and interest groups, as well as by the Ministry of Education. As education opportunities grew from the 1980s onwards, so did the *dershanes* that would help students to gain entrance into these institutions of advanced learning. The Gülen movement operated several tutoring centre companies that had branches all over Turkey, and while these centres concentrated on preparing students for the exams, they also served as arenas in which religious behaviour and ethics were modelled for the students, in the same way as in the Gülen dormitories and lighthouses. That is, students would not be required to participate in religious activities, but both instructors and other students might exert significant pressure on students to conform.

Emine, the older sister of a student at a Gülen *dershane*, described what she viewed as excessive pressure on her brother to participate in religious activities. Emine's brother was not connected with the Gülen movement, but the staff and students at the *dershane* would invite him to participate in fun activities and make him feel part of a social group. But they were also pressuring him to follow a more pious path. For example, when everybody prayed, it was hard for the boy to not to go along with it, even if that was not his inclination. They also had more subtle forms of pressure, according to Emine. For example, the *dershane* invited all the students to a dinner on New Year's Eve (New Year celebrations are seen as a Western, Christian import and are opposed by many conservative Muslims). So the dinner took place early in the evening, and Emine's brother thought it would end by 9 p.m. and he could go home to celebrate with his family. But the dinner went on and on with more activities until after midnight, by which time the New Year celebration was over. Was this pressure to lead a more pious lifestyle? Emine thought it was, but also noted that the Gülen movement is good at pressuring young people to conform without forcing anyone to do anything in particular. Emine noted that the *cemaat* seems to target and cultivate people like her brother – he was very smart but also socially awkward. The movement both supported education and provided him with a social group.

I include this vignette in order to emphasise the idea that religious education (and, indeed, all education) goes beyond the imposition of particular types of knowledge or explicit instruction about particular types of activities. Religious education in many different arenas involves a 'hidden curriculum', to use Ozgur's terms (2012). This curriculum includes the implicit cultivation of dispositions, proclivities and even bodily habits to create a particular type of person – in this case, a well-educated and religiously conscientious individual committed to the acquisition of knowledge and service to God.

Informal religious instruction

Much religious education and training goes on outside of formal educational settings. Beginning in the 1980s, for example, Turkey experienced an increase in popular preaching in many different venues – in public squares, on the radio and television, and in private homes and institutions (Tütüncü 2010: 597). The burgeoning religious publication sector addressed some of the demands for knowledge by putting out books and cassettes by Turkish and foreign preachers and religious polemicists. Many charismatic and articulate individuals made names for themselves through preaching and leading study groups. This is the period when major *cemaat* leaders, such as Fethullah Gülen and Esan Coşan, could attract large audiences, but local leaders and preachers could also command a following by formulating messages in ways that appealed to the local community.

More traditionally, though, basic religious instruction came from family members, especially from older women. The most common experience, as I heard from many people, was for a grandmother or aunt to teach *namaz* (ritual prayer), *dua* (prayers) and verses from the Qur'an to young children. Or an older woman living in the neighbourhood would teach a children's Qur'an course to interested neighbours – Zehra Hanım (described at the beginning of Chapter 1) taught such a course in her neighbourhood in Safranbolu. On Sunday mornings in certain neighbourhoods in Ankara or Istanbul, it was not unusual to see groups of young girls wrapping their heads in scarves and hurrying down the street with a Qur'an in their arms, presumably on their way to their weekly Qur'an instruction at a neighbour's house. Friends and family often gathered to study the Qur'an in homes or community centres – indeed, my encounter with Maryam and her family began when I started to participate in one such study group (Figure 6.1) (Shively 2008, 2009).

But technically this type of instruction was not sanctioned by the state, in that it was not permitted for non-family members to teach others in the reading of the Qur'an in private (non-state) courses taught in homes. These laws were aimed at the activities of the *cemaat*s in the cities, whose members used Qur'an courses as a means of organising religiously orientated opposition groups. But

Figure 6.1 Women studying the Qur'an at a home in Sincan, Ankara, 1998 (photograph by author)

another reason for these laws that I often heard articulated in the media was that teaching Islam at home to children other than your own is forbidden since such teachings may brainwash children into anti-Kemalist thinking. Whatever the law, however, hardly anyone did anything about the informal Qur'an courses that existed all over Turkey, and this type of instruction has remained very popular throughout the country.

Conclusion

Even as the Turkish state developed forms of religious education that furthered its political and social goals, many educational options have been available for both children and adults interested in enhancing their own knowledge of Islam. Institutions associated with the *cemaat*s and the more informal 'classes' that quietly operate in neighbourhoods allow potential students to find teachers and courses that would provide instruction that more or less (often much less) conformed to the state's conception of Islam. Even within some of the formal institutions, such as the *imam-hatip* schools, Islamic studies curricula would follow the educational requirements of the Ministry of Education only to the extent that instructors or schools chose to follow those requirements.

In many ways, the diversification of religious education in Turkey – whether deliberate or not – corresponds to the broadening of the scope of many different institutions and opportunities, thanks to the country's accelerating economic liberalisation in the twenty-first century.

Notes

1. Non-Muslims are exempt from the religious education courses.
2. Turkey has different types of vocational schools, such as technical schools for boys, girls' vocational schools, schools for tourism studies or health studies and so on.
3. This had an immediate effect on the influence of the schools, since the majority of students enrolled in 1971 were in middle schools. Education was compulsory only up to 5th grade. Middle school and secondary school were considered extra schooling, and many students would attend middle school only if it was a requirement for attaining particular jobs.
4. Turkey has had nationally competitive entrance exams for both secondary schools and universities. The score a student receives on one of these exams determines which school they may attend, and in the case of universities, what department they may enter.
5. Sayyid Qutb (1906–66) was a member of Egypt's Muslim Brotherhood and the author of an extensive Qur'anic commentary and a number of influential works on Sunni political thought.
6. Ayatollah Ruhollah Khomeini (1902–89) was an Iranian cleric who led the Islamist faction of the 1979 Iranian revolution that overthrew the Shah of Iran. After the revolution, he became the Supreme Leader of Iran, a position he held until his death.
7. Due to challenges in the courts, the removal of the point penalty system did not take effect until 2012.

8. Wahhabism is named after the eighteenth-century Arabian reformist, Muhammad ibn Abd al-Wahhab, who promoted a stark purification of Islam by rejecting much traditional Islamic jurisprudence and by eradicating popular practices of piety, such as the cult of the saints. Wahhabism is the primary ideology of the Saudi state.

CHAPTER 7

Neoliberalism and the transformation of the 2000s

Visiting the Şakirin Mosque in Istanbul, 2010

Throughout the 2000s, mosque construction accelerated in Turkey, in the major cities as well as in smaller towns and villages. Turkish mosque architectural style, though, has tended to be relatively static, in that most mosques are built to mimic the Ottoman dome-topped mosque style (which the Ottomans borrowed from the Byzantines who came before them).[1] Efforts to build more modernist, non-traditional mosques have often been met with resistance. For example, the architects hired to design the Kocatepe mosque in Ankara in the 1960s (see Figure 2.1) originally envisaged a modernist mosque, and construction on the project even began. But in response to persistent complaints, the state abandoned the project and replaced it with a traditional mosque modelled after the sixteenth-century Şehzade Mosque in Istanbul (Batuman 2018: 271).

With the rise of the JDP and the expansion of the religiously devout bourgeois patrons, some new styles of mosque architecture began to emerge. One of the best known of these modern mosques is the Şakirin mosque in the Karacaahmet cemetery in the Üsküdar district in Istanbul. This unusual mosque was built in 2009 by the philanthropist Şakir family in memory of İbrahim and Semiha Şakir. The family had originally engaged a male architect, Hüsrev Tayla, who presented the family with a modernist design reminiscent of more traditional dome architecture. But because of a dispute over the interior design, he left the project, which was then taken over by Zeynep Fadıllıoğlu, the granddaughter of Semiha Şakir.

The result was an unusual exterior and an interior filled with thoughtful and illuminating ornament – the images I have included here do not do it justice. The exterior 'dome' is a concrete shell structure covered with fish-scale aluminium panels that reflect sunlight in interesting ways. The building itself has a double-layered façade; the outer layer is more opaque, but the interior layer that surrounds the prayer area is made of a 'glass curtain' wall, which is filled with semi-transparent script of the Qur'an. It is as if by looking at the mosque, the worshipper is reading the Qur'an itself. In the prayer hall, the *mihrap* (indicating the direction of prayer) and the *minber* (the steps from which the preacher delivers the sermon) are unique sculptural objects inspired by different features of

Figure 7.1 Şakirin mosque in Istanbul, 2010 (photograph by author)

the mosque interior. The central chandelier is also unusual, composed of a set of three circular frames at different angles, carrying Qur'anic verses, as well as glass 'drops' that refract and reflect the light. The overall visual effect was one of lightness and expanding space, even though the interior is rather small. One significant feature of this mosque is the fact that it allows women to be more centrally located in the worship space. Normally, women can only pray at the back of a mosque or on a balcony that lines the back and side walls – the tradition in Turkey is that the home is really the proper place for women to pray. But in the Şakirin mosque, the women's section is a balcony attached to the entrance façade and it is directly under the central dome of the mosque, so that women can share in the atmosphere of the prayer hall (Batuman 2018: 277).

This lightness and beauty of the mosque has attracted a lot of attention (not all of it positive) for the way in which it has melded the modern and the traditional. While some deplored what they saw as excessive ornamentation, others applauded the fact that it represented something new and different. I visited the mosque in 2010 and was struck by its freshness. I certainly admire traditional Ottoman-style mosques, but the Şakirin mosque was definitely innovative. When I visited, a funeral was starting outside in the mosque courtyard. A member of the funeral party told us that a prominent female lawyer had died,

Figure 7.2 Prayer room of the Şakirin mosque (photograph by author)

Figure 7.3 The *mihrap* of the Şakirin mosque (photograph by author)

and the service was going to start soon. I wondered if such high-status women were attracted to the Şakirin mosque because it was designed by a woman – one of the first, in fact, to be designed by a woman – and made so much effort to include women in the central space.

Neoliberalism

The Şakirin mosque was part of the remarkable transformation of religious life in Turkey made possible by the rise of the JDP party and the increasing effects of economic liberalisation in the twenty-first century. As discussed in Chapter 5, economic policies introduced in the 1980s and 1990s opened Turkey's previously protective, state-controlled markets to private enterprise, international trade and capital flows. These policies created a motivation for ambitious Turkish entre- preneurs from different socio-economic sectors to develop private businesses in order to exploit the new market opportunities, even as the public capital and labour sectors shrank. Private education at all levels expanded for those who could afford it. Publication and media offerings multiplied almost overnight, and technological and regulatory changes made it possible for Turkish citizens to gain access to international television and radio channels through satellite dishes. Average Turks were exposed to the world – and got a sense of their place in the world – in a way that had not been previously possible.

These types of economic change obviously have profound social and cul- tural effects, well beyond the marketplace – the willingness to allow for non- traditional mosque architecture, as found in the Şakirin mosque, could be seen as one of those effects. Social theorists have used the term 'neoliberalism' to talk about the broader social dynamic of which economic liberalisation is a part. Neoliberalism is a complex idea, but one of the more straightforward ways to think about it is as a process by which market principles and expec- tations are applied to many non-economic aspects of life.[2] The underlying philosophy of neoliberalism, according to David Harvey (2005: 2), is that human happiness and well-being can be maximised in the context of free market, free trade and strong private property rights. In this situation the individual is supposedly 'liberated' from state control, and so neoliberalism generally casts state intervention in institutional and economic life as poten- tially damaging to human happiness. The state's primary role is to put into place those institutions (military, police, legal apparatuses) that will guarantee private individual property rights and free markets, but, beyond that, the state should intervene as little as possible. Those who subscribe to the neoliberal philosophy believe that so-called public (not just individual) goods – such as the environment, education, healthcare and social security – should actually be handled through the markets and private enterprise, not through the state. Furthermore, neoliberalism values market exchange as 'an ethic in itself, capable of acting as a guide to all human action, and substituting for all previously held ethical beliefs,' it empha- sizes the significance of contractual relations in the marketplace. It holds that the social good will be maximized by maximizing the reach and frequency of market transactions, and it seeks to bring all human action into the domain of the market. (Harvey 2005: 3)

Neoliberalism came to dominate economic thought in the 1980s, and the col- lapse of the communist order in the Soviet Union in 1990 seemed to validate the theory. Now, neoliberalism is almost taken for granted; 'it has become incorpo- rated into the common-sense way many of us interpret, live in, and understand the world' (Harvey 2005: 3).

Neoliberal logic and practices have certainly been absorbed into Turkish society (Adaş 2006; Moudouros 2014; Walton 2013, 2017) and have affected the way in which people practise Islam. Just as the state retreated from its control of economic activity in Turkey, so did it cede some degree of control over the public sphere, including the expression of religion. An important consequence of these developments is the blossoming of civil society organisations – religious and non-religious – that provided some of the services and produced the kind of discourse that had once been largely in the purview of the state. But the retreat of the state from religious life was never fully realised. The Diyanet as purveyor of 'official' Islam remained as strong as ever, and in fact grew in size over the course of the 2000s to become one of the largest bureaucratic units in the Turkish state. This chapter will go on to explore these and other effects of neoliberalism in the twenty-first century.

The expanding economy and its effects on Islam in modern Turkey

One dramatic effect of the economic liberalisation that accelerated under the JDP was the enlargement of the middle class to include religiously devout citizens who had traditionally been excluded from Turkey's state-controlled markets that favoured families and businesses with Kemalist leanings (Gumuscu 2010; Öniş 2004). Now entrepreneurs originating from or based in the provinces – many of whom were devout and politically conservative – took advantage of the opening of markets to create enterprises that allowed for their own and their com- munities' enrichment. In 1990, for example, Islamic businessmen established the MÜSİAD (Association of Independent Industrialists and Businessmen), an organisation of like-minded entrepreneurs that played an important role in the propagation of Islamic work and business ethics. MÜSİAD also attracted some Islamic intellectuals and social theorists who in turn spread a normalising discourse emphasising the compatibility of religious piety and capitalist striving (Adaş 2006: 123–4). The Gülen movement also created networks of business leaders – TUSKON and ISHAD – that had substantial economic influence throughout Turkey and beyond. These networks and other newly enriched Muslim entrepreneurs created organisations that invested in education, health and the media outlets that favoured pious Muslims, many of whom had been negatively affected by the shrinkage of the welfare state and its various social services.

As pious Turks became more and more economically involved and began to attain middle-class status, consumption patterns changed to reflect this new marriage of religious piety with prosperity, among other consumer trends. One consequence of this process has been an intensive gentrification of many traditional neighbourhoods in Turkey's large metropolitan centres – such as Sultanbeyli in Istanbul (see Chapter 6). New apartment complexes were constructed in areas further and further from the city centres, creating massive suburban zones occupied by middle-class and wealthy families. These new suburban housing developments (*siteler*) were largely segregated along religious-secularist lines, so that entire developments would be occupied by religiously orientated families, such as the Khalidi-Nakşibendi community described by Ayşe Saktanber (see Chapter 4), while others would house self-identifying Kemalist families. The gentrification of entire religious neighbourhoods occurred rapidly in the 1990s and 2000s. For example, the small city of Sincan (near Ankara), where I did my research in the 1990s, went through an astonishing transformation in the early 2000s. I completed my research in 1999 and did not return until 2004 to visit friends, and I was astonished by the changes in evidence everywhere I looked. The minibus ride I had taken so many times during my fieldwork from Ankara to Sincan had taken me through various shabby suburbs and *gecekondu*s before the bus would wind its way through the dusty roads of Sincan itself. But by 2004, many of the open fields around Sincan and the *gecekondu*s and old apartment buildings had given away to tracts of brand-new apartment complexes and housing developments, each surrounded by manicured parks, new shops and even swimming pools with ladies' days and men's days in order to preserve gender segregation norms important to devout Muslims.

In the large cities, *gecekondu* districts were gradually replaced with high-rise development complexes, and older, smaller apartment blocks were removed to make way for newer, more modern high-capacity apartment buildings. Many of these development projects were planned and implemented by municipal governments in order to refurbish and 'clean up' economically depressed urban areas with the goal of creating world-class cities. As Istanbul aspired to attract tourists from around the world and establish itself as the 2010 European Cultural Capital, city officials went about abolishing traditional neighbourhoods and 'cleaning up' others in order to project the city as both culturally unique (the old capital of the Ottoman Empire) and modern and sophisticated (Potuoğlu-Cook 2006). But these gentrification efforts often pushed out and excluded the poor and working-class residents of the refurbished neighbourhoods. Most famously, the Roma ('Gypsy') community who had lived in the historic Sulukule district of Istanbul for centuries were forced to move out, and their iconic neighbourhood was replaced by expensive apartment buildings. In Ankara, a well-established *gecekondu* community near Ankara airport was demolished not only to make room for a major highway, but also so that the journey from the airport to Ankara would not be blemished by unsightly *gecekondus*. Though many *gecekondu* residents resisted the destruction of their neighbourhood, the then mayor of Ankara and JDP member Melih Gökçek pushed through the project, promising the residents apartments in the complexes in exchange for land – though the apartment ownership terms were not always favourable.[3]

Consumerism and the commodification of pious lifestyles and tastes

Turkey's economic growth was also accompanied by a rise in conspicuous consumption among the many practising Muslims who had joined the middle class. The process of 'going Islamic in the market' (Yavuz 2009: 60) refers to the fact that producers and markets began to cater more extensively to the tastes and lifestyles of the devout sector of the Turkish population. For example, some hotels serving pious clients opened gender-segregated beaches, where women could swim in the sea behind a physical barrier that kept out the gaze of unrelated men. These beach offerings might be part of a holiday package marketed to pious families, in which the holidaymakers could visit locations and events that would provide venues free of alcohol, dancing and immodest dress.[4]

Family-friendly parks and recreational zones became more common as well. One of the most fascinating spectacles I witnessed on my return to Sincan in 2004 was the development of a new family amusement park, called *Harikalar Diyarı* ('Fantasy Land'), on the north-west side of the town. This park featured amusement rides, a large man-made lake, performance stages, picnic areas and, most impressively, giant models of figures from popular culture and from Turkish and other folk tales, including a huge statue of Gulliver being captured by the Lilliputians. Even beyond the rapid real-estate development, this park seemed to signify most clearly Sincan's process of gentrification – this huge complex existed solely for the purposes of (wholesome) pleasure and was geared towards families with disposable income and conservative values. It also seemed to signify Sincan's increasing political moderation. Sincan had been a deeply conservative, even radical neighbourhood that was targeted by the military in the lead-up to the 1997 soft coup. Like the residents of Sultanbeyli described by Tuğal (in Chapter 5), the Sincan community seemed to have experienced a 'passive revolution' and appeared to be much more moderate in its outlook. A public venue such as 'Fantasy Land' provided a place in which families and couples could mix openly, enjoy recreational activities and participate in concerts and amusements that emphasised both Turkish nationalism (through the displays of Turkish folk heroes) and Western and Turkish-style displays and concerts.

Another important change in consumption patterns that developed in the 2000s was the softening and elaboration of clothing styles of religiously observant women. The women's *tesettür* style during the 1990s had been somewhat standard: a long, loose overcoat with a large draping headscarf that covered the hair, neck and shoulders (see Figure 5.6). But when I visited Sincan and similar neighbourhoods in 2004 and subsequent years, the stern overcoats had given way somewhat to everyday long skirts and loose tops, accompanied by a smaller headscarf often stylishly coordinated with the clothes. Certainly, overcoats could still be found as well, and some women associated with certain *cemaat*s wore the black *çarşaf* (chador), but the new modest stylishness had become the norm. These changes in women's modest clothing consumption in Turkey was accompanied by a rapid growth of the veiling fashion industry. Research by Banu Gökarıksel and Anna Secor (2010a, 2010b, 2012) traces the emergence of this industry and how it is involved in the production of Islamic distinctions in Turkey (see also Navaro-Yashin 2002a, 2002b; White 2002b). An impressive number of companies (over 200) developed a niche market that purveys colourful and constantly changing *tesettür* styles, complete with large-scale advertising campaigns, glossy catalogues and fashion shows that feature both everyday wear and the latest in haute couture (Figure 7.4). Over the course of the 2000s, women's fashion shops in conservative areas of Ankara or Istanbul increasingly came to display elaborate costumes for sale to women with the cash and inclination to dress themselves in chic outfits that were supposedly both fashionable and modest according to Islamic standards (Figure 7.5).

Some of the pious women consumers interviewed by Gökarıksel and Secor understood the contradictions embedded in products that simultaneously highlight female beauty (and wealth) and uphold Muslim norms regarding modesty. Indeed, 'bringing together veiling and fashion destabilises the veil as an Islamic reference', in that fashionable veiling allows women to display their physical beauty – though women's attractiveness is supposed to be what modest clothing conceals. Still, the women enjoyed participating in the new clothing trends, especially since modest fashion allowed women to have fun within the bounds of their understanding of proper Muslim dress (Gökarıksel and Secor 2010b: 328–9; see also Gökarıksel and Secor 2012). Islamic haute couture was, in fact, well outside the experience and budget of most pious women. Rather tasteful, modest but up-to-date clothing available at local clothes shops meets the needs and desires of most middle-class, religiously observant women.

Figure 7.4 A billboard advertising modest clothing, Istanbul, 2012 (photograph by author)

Ottomania

Another development in Turkey's popular culture and consumer markets has been renewed (and transformed) interest in the Ottoman Empire. Or, more precisely, Ottoman history is a fertile fantasyland that has given rise to interesting forms of popular culture and consumer products. Imagined versions of Ottoman-style clothes and jewellery have become fashionable, particularly in portrait studios. Books and magazines about Ottoman personalities or events have proliferated since the 1990s, and Ottoman-themed hotels and refurbished hamams (Ottoman-era bathhouses) attract more and more customers. Ottoman court music, food traditions, artistic practices and imperial artifacts, such as the Ottoman imperial standard and the various *tuğra* (Sultanic signatures designed to resemble a bow) are practised or displayed in middle-class houses as signs of taste and distinction.

Elif Batuman, a Turkish-American author, wondered at the display of what

Figure 7.5 A display in a shop selling modest clothing, Fatih, Istanbul, 2010 (photograph by author)

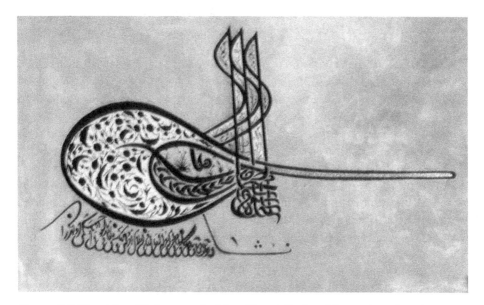

Figure 7.6 The *tuğra* of Suleyman the Magnificent displayed in a private home (photograph by author)

is often called 'Ottomania' in Turkish popular culture in an article in the *New Yorker* (17 and 24 February, 2014). She commented especially on the commercialisation of that nostalgia, observing that it was

> manifested in such diverse phenomena as Burger King's Sultan meal combo (a 2006 TV spot featured a Janissary devouring a Whopper with hummus), a proliferation of Ottoman cookbooks, Ottoman-style bathroom consoles, wedding invitations with Ottoman calligraphy, and graduation gowns and flight-attendant uniform designs inspired by caftans and fezzes. In the past ten years, there have been increasingly elaborate commemorations of the Ottoman conquest of Constantinople, in 1453, along with the construction of new Ottoman-style mosques and the renovation of old Ottoman buildings, some of which have been repurposed as hotels and malls.

Turkey's Ottomania is perhaps most evident in the great popularity of *Muhteşem Yüzyıl* (*The Magnificent Century*), a soap-opera-style dramatisation of the activities of the court of Süleyman the Magnificent (d. 1566). The series was beautifully made and included lavish costumes. Many scenes were shot in the actual Topkapı Palace, the imperial palace of the Ottomans throughout the Empire's golden age (fifteenth to early seventeenth centuries). Not only was this series widely viewed within Turkey by people of all political views, but it had a large following in other countries as well, most notably in countries that had once been under the imperial rule of the Ottomans. Bulgarians, Greeks, Egyptians and others have watched the series in great numbers, seeming to forget – at least for the moment – the past experiences of their respective regions of Ottoman domination. In Turkey, the influence of *The Magnificent Century* could be seen especially in the development of clothing styles, such as the costumes boys wear during circumcision ceremonies (Figure 7.7).

This commercial and cultural trend has flourished since the 1990s, even though attitudes towards Turkey's Ottoman background vary considerably depending on each individual's understanding of Turkey's present political and cultural configuration. Many secularists have been critical of the Ottoman Empire for its supposed backwardness, its over-reliance on religion as a governing principle, and its failure to Westernise, modernise and democratise. For such people, the Ottoman past is a burden, and the Empire made mistakes for which Turkey is still paying (Ergin and Karakaya 2017: 54–6). The Ottoman Empire was a mere prelude to the Turkish Republic, the development of which liberated the Turks to form a modern, rational nation that could compete with the advanced nations of Western Europe. Some of these secularists look with nostalgia at the period of Kemalist domination after the establishment of the Republic and see the emergence of Islamist politics as a fall away from that utopian past (Özyürek 2006, 2007). These same secularists also readily participated in the wave of neo-Ottoman nostalgia that pervaded Turkey, but for many of them, the Ottoman Empire was fine as a source of art and beauty, but good riddance to its politics and religion.

Figure 7.7 Boys in Ottoman-style circumcision costumes, Ankara, 2014 (photograph by the author)

By contrast, many pious Turks looked to the Ottomans not as a mere prelude to Turkish modernity but as an idealised manifestation of a state in which religion could be wedded to tolerant, multi-cultural governance to create a force to be reckoned with. Many pious Turks who saw the Kemalist regime of 1990s Turkey as a source of oppression and suffering expressed deep – and highly romanticised – nostalgia for the Ottoman Empire when Muslims were supposedly free to practise the religion as they pleased and the Empire was the defender of the Muslim faith against those who would disrespect it and the Turkish people (Ergin and Karakaya 2017). Such people support the JDP's increasing emphasis on events of the Ottoman imperial past, such as the enhanced annual celebration of the conquest of Istanbul (29 May 1453) and a new panorama museum in Istanbul that recreates the events of the conquest by Fatih Mehmet II (d. 1491). Just as many secularists nostalgically viewed Atatürk and the Kemalist government as a beacon of enlightenment emerging out of the dark Ottoman past, so do many pious Turks look to the Ottoman Empire as a source of pride and nostalgia. In both cases, 'people look to the past rather than the future for their utopias' (Özyürek 2007: 7).

The transformed *cemaat*s

Economic liberalism affected not only markets, socio-economic class structure and consumption patterns. It also led to transformations in the scope and

influence of Turkey's many *cemaats*, especially those with the resources to implement influential programmes and organisations within Turkey and beyond.
Certain *cemaats*, such as the Nakşibendis and the Nurcus, grew and became
more and more involved in different sectors of Turkish society, including in
education, media and civil society. As discussed in Chapter 4, many *cemaats*
already had a foothold in these various sectors, but the power and influence of
some *cemaats* grew to a breathtaking extent in the JDP era.

The success of the larger *cemaats* was not a foregone conclusion, since they
had to contend with the complex political developments of the late 1990s and
early 2000s. The soft coup that brought down the WP brought all the *cemaats*
and religious communities under increased scrutiny from the NSC. One of the
NSC's goals in the 28 February 1997 process was to get rid of all independent
sources of Islamic expression (other than the Diyanet) in order to keep the
'fundamentalists' at bay. After the soft coup, the NSC included the *cemaats* in
the 'Red Book' of security threats, designating them as reactionary (*irtacı*) and
forms of political Islam that were a threat to the secularist order. This action
affected some *cemaats* more than others. Some orders, such as the Süleymancıs,
had been less politically involved, and by keeping to themselves, they were able
to continue to gather and conduct activities outside the spotlight of the military.
Other *cemaats*, though, met with considerably more hostility and experienced
important changes that affected the course of their development, at least at first.[5]

Esad Coşan and the Nakşibendi community of İskenderpaşa mosque

One of the most influential *cemaats* in modern Turkey has been the Nakşibendi-
Khalidi *cemaat* based at İskenderpaşa mosque in Istanbul. Many political leaders
associated with Necmettin Erbakan's NOM, which provided the core membership of the Welfare and Virtue Parties and (later) the JDP, were closely associated
with the İskenderpaşa community, even if relationships between the political
and *cemaat* leaders were not always harmonious. Though the links between the
politicians and the *cemaats* were never formal, historic association between *cemaat*
and party led many *cemaat* members to fear reprisal from the military after the
1997 soft coup. In response, Esad Coşan and some of his followers left Turkey
permanently, establishing a Nakşibendi community in Australia. Even with the
departure of the leader, the Nakşibendi-Khalidis of the İskenderpaşa mosque
remained a robust and active community. They continued to produce publications, radio and television programmes, and eventually websites that promoted
Muslim piety. These productions provided a platform by which Coşan could
continue giving *sohbet*s to his community, though from the other side of the
world. The programming was not always identified as distinctly Nakşibendi, but
was produced as general programmes for the cultivation of authentic Islamic
belief and practice (Silverstein 2011: 111).

In 2001, Esad Coşan and his son-in-law were killed in a car accident in Australia, dealing a severe blow to the İskenderpaşa *cemaat*. His body was returned to Turkey for burial at the Eyüp mosque in Istanbul – Eyüp has always been an important pilgrimage site, and the presence of Coşan's grave there has only increased the popularity of the mosque. The leadership of the *cemaat* passed to Coşan's son, Nureddin Coşan, but this development was problematic. Like his father, Nureddin had some formal training in the Islamic sciences – he had attended an *imam-hitap* secondary school and studied in the theology faculty at Ankara University. But he had then earned an MBA in the United States. He had confined his involvement in the *cemaat* to the management of the community's holding group. His lack of experience in religious leadership invited criticism from within the community. Some critics were particularly concerned by the fact that Nureddin was a 'cradle sheikh', that is, a sheikh who was appointed 'not according to qualities like how deserving they are or according to their competence and authority but rather merely because they are someone's son or grandson'. Such appointments had led to the disintegration of the Sufi lodges at the end of the Ottoman Empire, these critics believed (Silverstein 2011: 181–3). Despite these concerns, Nureddin became the sheikh of the Iskenderpaşa community, a position he retains as of this writing, and the *cemaat* continued to have a substantial presence in Turkey, especially with the rise of the JDP.

The Gülen movement and Gülen's exile
In the months after the soft coup of 28 February 1997, Fethullah Gülen and his *cemaat* received some declarations of allegiance from the leaders of the coalition government that replaced the WP government. It had helped that Gülen maintained a political position in the 1980s and 1990s that focused as much on Turkish nationalism and economic development as on religious concerns. Because of Gülen's positive relationship with Prime Minister Turgut Özal, some well-educated members of the Gülen movement were able to get positions in the state bureaucracy. Gülen took advantage of the economic and political liberalisation process to increase the movement's business and media presence to 'bring "religious" perspectives into the public sphere on social and cultural issues' (Yavuz 2013: 40). But Gülen was always careful to present a face of religious moderation in the public sphere. For example, when girls were required to remove their headscarves in order to attend college, Gülen proclaimed that education was more important for a girl than wearing a headscarf, so if she must, a female student should remove her headscarf and go to school, rather than forgo school because of the headscarf issue. In response to the 1997 coup, Gülen controversially supported the military's actions against the WP and did not oppose the NSC condemnation of the various *cemaats*. Such appeasement is what earned Gülen support from some members of the Kemalist government, who saw Gülen's moderation as a potential bulwark against more radical forms of Islam.

But that support was not enough. Even before the 1997 coup, many detractors of the movement were suspicious of its wealth, expanse and power, and they suspected that Gülen's religious goals were not as moderate as they first appeared – that is, Gülen was using *takkiye* (the Islamic idea that one can use righteous deception in order to promote religion) to hide his anti-secularism. After the 1997 coup and despite the movement's attempt at appeasement, the Kemalist military sought to bring Gülen down. Beginning in June 1999, media outlets controlled by the military mobilised a fierce propaganda campaign against Gülen by branding him a reactionary and fundamentalist threat to the Turkish state. The accusers supported their position by producing a video of one of Gülen's sermons in which he suggested that his organisation was gaining power within the Turkish government (Gülen claimed the remarks were taken out of context). After this sermon was published in the *Hürriyet*, a Kemalist newspaper, the military issued an arrest warrant for Gülen on charges that he was attempting to overthrow the state by establishing a secret organisation (Yavuz 2013: 42). By then Gülen had gone to the United States for medical treatment and elected to stay there rather than face arrest. He now lives permanently in a small compound in eastern Pennsylvania, though he has maintained an active worldwide following.

The military's attack on Gülen consisted of a propaganda campaign against the movement, including its schools, foundations and media outlets. But the Gülen media fought back, launching a counter-propaganda campaign that defended the movement and its activities. As Yavuz has commented (2013: 43), 'For his part Gülen had learned a painful lesson that obsequiously catering to the centre of military power can breed contempt as much as it does forbearance.' In the end, the growing strength of Islamic political parties and the acceleration of liberalising policies meant that the Gülen movement remained popular in Turkey, able to build ever more schools, found ever more media channels, and create larger and larger civil society organisations.

Muslim civil society

The Gülen movement was by no means the only entity to establish more and more civil society organisations. The period of economic growth during the 1990s and 2000s was accompanied by a marked expansion of civil society in Turkey. Social theorists define 'civil society' as those institutions and practices that act as a 'third sector' – an arena of action and power between the state on the one hand and the private individual and family on the other hand. Civil society includes NGOs, community groups and other types of voluntary associations by which people can collectively assert their will or carry out projects separate from or even against state institutions. In both Ottoman and Turkish Republic history, religious foundations or endowments, known as *vakıfs* (Arabic:

waqf), played significant social roles. During the Ottoman period, endowments provided for the construction of mosques and religious schools, and supported social service institutions, such as hospitals, hostels, public fountains and soup kitchens, among other things (see, for example, Singer 2002, 2008). The Turkish Republic abolished many of the Ottoman foundations, and the state took over some of their social functions. Those foundations that survived into the republican era were legally transformed into secular institutions that furthered the Republic's developmental goals, such as the advancement of health, education and cultural arts, as well as the care of the poor (Zencirci 2015a).

But, as with so much else in Turkish society, the rise of neoliberalism changed the nature and scope of Turkey's foundations. As the state withdrew its governance and economic involvement in many aspects of social life, NGOs and voluntary associations stepped in to develop programmes and initiatives once left to the state. Constitutional revisions in 1995 making it easier to form associations led to an explosion in the number of civil society organisations. The 1997 soft coup slowed down that expansion, but the election of the JDP government led to the reopening of this process. Many of these new NGOs and associations were secular in nature, but others – many others – emerged from groups with religious motivations and concerns (Zencirci 2015a: 546). In previous chapters, I discussed some of the NGOs that served different Alevi communities, and Turkish Sunni groups, especially the various *cemaats*, have also had a wide variety of civil society organisations. One example of a *cemaat*-based civil society organisation would be the various dormitories associated with the Süleymancı *cemaat*, such as the Beykoz boys' dormitory described in Chapter 6. These dormitories are non-profit ventures that provide religious education to boys from pious families and are supported by donations from the *cemaat* and from fundraising activities – such as the mixed bake and flea market sales (*kermes*) that are popular in Turkey – organised for the specific benefit of the dormitories.

The Gülen movement has made masterful use of the opportunities available in Turkey's growing civil society (Walton 2017). Some of the movement's institutions have been profit-making businesses (businesses are generally not thought of as civil society organisations): some of the private schools, publishing and media enterprises, and the various holding companies associated with the movement are explicitly profit-generating. But other undertakings of the Gülen movement were strictly charitable, such as the dialogue and peace centres established in Turkey and elsewhere, and most especially *Kimse Yok Mu* (KYM), the international aid organisation. KYM was founded in 2002 in response to the massive 1999 earthquake in the Istanbul area. (*Kimse Yok Mu* translates as 'Is anyone there?' which was supposedly a cry heard from a woman trapped in the earthquake rubble.) It was a large Red Cross-like organisation with many branches in Turkey and elsewhere. It operated especially in response to disasters and conflict, sometimes acting in conjunction with state organisations. It also had initiatives where Turkish volunteers would go to other countries to assist with special projects, such as the construction of wells, programmes for orphans and a cataract programme in African nations where Turkish ophthalmologists volunteered to do cataract and other eye surgeries for free. There have arisen other similar organisations that serve populations both within and outside of Turkey. One especially influential organisation is the IHH, the acronym for the Foundation for Human Rights and Freedoms and Humanitarian Relief (*İnsan Hak ve Hürriyetleri ve İnsani Yardım Vakfı*). This foundation is based on conservative religious principles, and its volunteers are mostly devout Muslims who provide national and international assistance to those in need. The IHH garnered international attention when it assembled a flotilla of ships to bring humanitarian aid to Palestinians living on the Gaza Strip who were suffering under Israel's embargo. But when the ships approached (but had not yet entered) Israel's territorial waters, Israeli forces attacked the ships and killed nine Turks.

The religiously inspired civil society organisations have represented a significant challenge to the Kemalist state's assertive style of secularism, as the civil society arena opened up space for religious expression and action outside state control (Walton 2017: 3). Many of the devout Turkish citizens who have become involved in these civil society organisations extol them as spheres of religious freedom where pious citizens could express their religious beliefs and carry out authentic religious practices. Yet there are paradoxes engrained in the notion of religious freedom promised by civil society organisations. As Walton and others have pointed out, civil society organisations may not be arms of the state, but that does not mean they do not assert significant political power in the public arena. That is, many civil society organisations, such as those of the Gülen movement, may view 'civil society as an apolitical domain of authentic desires and identities, entirely separate from the messy turf of political society'. But in reality civil organisations enact 'a distinctive modality of politics', where they are involved in politics without necessarily aspiring to govern formally (Walton 2013: 183–4). These organisations may promote a set of values and activities that would ideally create a particular type of society and a particular kind of citizen. Such activities are still political, even if they operate outside traditional political parties (see also Zencirci 2015b).

Transformations of state institutions and policies

The effects of the European Union accession process

As the economy liberalised and non-state institutions and actors became more influential in society, the Turkish state also evolved in terms of policy and institutional organisation. At least during its first decade in power, JDP politicians were careful not to defy Turkey's secularist norms since they were well aware that the secularist military would step in – possibly with violence – if the JDP government went too far in accommodating the wishes of the devout population. They displayed a level of political liberalism, accommodating various political and social constituencies that avoided major conflicts with the Kemalist establishment. Another important factor that compelled the JDP to remain politically liberal (that is, accommodating to the views of friends and foes alike) was the European Union (EU) accession process whereby Turkey negotiated for full membership in the EU. It had long sought to join the EU, given the economic opportunities and political power associated with membership. But it wasn't until 2005 that the accession talks formally began with the recognition that at least a decade of negotiations would be required to reach an agreement that would be acceptable to all parties.

The accession process required that Turkey rework legal codes, expand human rights – including those of women and minorities – and further liberalise its markets in order to bring it into legal, political and economic alignment with the EU. Early in the 2000s, Turkey did make significant amendments to its penal and civil law codes. For example, improving women's legal rights required changes to the original Turkish 1926 Civil Code, which contained laws that placed familial authority and decision-making powers in the hands of the husband and deemed husbands to have ultimate authority over children. In fact, a husband's permission was required for a wife to work outside the home or to travel abroad with children. All of these provisions were eliminated in 2001 when the country's civil code was amended (Levin 2007: 205–9). Similar progressive changes were made to the Turkish penal code in 2005. The previous penal code had defined rape as a crime against public decency rather than against the individual, thereby configuring women's bodies to vessels of public morality rather than thinking of women as rights-bearing individuals (Ecevit 2007: 200). The 2005 changes redefined rape as a crime against the individual, and also introduced more than thirty amendments to advance the cause of gender equality and protect the bodily and sexual integrity of Turkish women (Levin 2007: 210). The 2005 Penal Code defined domestic violence as a crime that can be punished by incarceration. Not surprisingly, some religious conservatives opposed these legal changes because they saw them as threats to the traditional family structure, but the codes were successfully modified nonetheless.

Legal and political requirements of the EU accession process also compelled the Turkish government to be more accommodating to ethnic and religious minorities, including the Kurds (Soner 2010). The Turkish government subsequently eased up on some anti-Kurdish policies: Kurdish language rights were expanded, a Kurdish television station opened, Kurdish naming rights were restored and political use of the Kurdish language was permitted. While Kurdish citizens reacted positively, in reality the changes were minimal and other oppressive anti-Kurdish policies continued, including arrests and jailings for even tepid support of Kurdish interests (White 2013: 13–14; Yavuz 2009: 185–99). Nevertheless, the human rights requirements of EU membership made the accession process an attractive prospect for many Kurdish citizens.

Alevis, too, viewed the EU accession process as a way to improve their situation in Turkey, and the 2000s did offer some glimmers of hope. In 2007 the JDP developed a programme that came to be called the 'Alevi Opening' in which Erdoğan's party attempted to extend an olive branch to the Alevi minority. Erdoğan became the first Turkish prime minister to visit a *cemevi* and he offered a public apology for the 1938 massacre of thousands of Alevis at Dersim in the province of Tunceli (see Chapter 1). The JDP government hosted 'Alevi *iftars*' to celebrate the end of fasting during the Islamic month of Muharrem.[6] These dinners were largely attended by Sunnis, however – less than half of the participants at the first *iftar* on 11 January 2008 were Alevis and of the 279 Alevi associations that were invited, only six chose to attend. While Alevi imagery was a part of the *iftars*, the events included a reading of the Qur'an – not all Alevis use the Qur'an as part of their rituals. These *iftars* have remained controversial for many Alevis, who saw them as political theatre rather than an earnest attempt at reconciliation. As Derya Özkul put it:

> Labelling the dinner as iftar, emphasizing the similarities between groups with inclusive language (despite the fact that there are great philosophical differences between Sunni and Alevi beliefs), as well as reading the Quran, were all attempts by the government to pull Alevism toward their [Sunni] history and perception of the world, in the hope of making the 'Alevi issue' more manageable and controllable. (2015: 84)

Another JDP initiative of the Alevi Opening consisted of a series of workshops in 2009 and 2010 that invited journalists, academics and Alevi representatives from various organisations. The purported goal of these workshops was to discuss ways in which to accommodate Alevi demands about a range of issues. Should the state support Alevi religious activities in the same way as it supports the Sunni majority, or, alternatively, should the state abolish the Diyanet and remove its involvement in religion altogether? Should the state abolish the Religious Culture and Ethics classes, or exempt Alevi students from taking them, or, alternatively, include representations of Alevis in the courses? Should the state recognise and financially support the *cemevi*s to the extent that Sunni mosques, churches and synagogues are supported, through provision of free electricity, free water and the allocation of free property to build on? Should the state provide support for the *dede*s in the same way as the imams and *hatip*s are supported? And, finally, should the Madımak Hotel be converted into a museum commemorating the 1993 massacre of Alevis in Sivas (Dressler 2013: xii–xiii)?

The report that resulted from the workshops outlined the Alevis' various demands, which was remarkable given that previous Turkish governments had been so unwilling to recognise them in the past. The report's author, sociologist Necdet Subaşı, recommended that the state end regulations, laws and policies that discriminated against the Alevis. This included bringing to a close the state's attempt to homogenise the population, letting the Alevis themselves define what Alevism is, making sure the Diyanet accommodated the Alevis positively, securing legal status for the *cemevi*s and recognising the Madımak Hotel as a marker for an event that was devastating to the Alevi community. But actual policy changes were minimal. There was no major change in the Diyanet, so that Sunni Islam remained the de facto state religion. Only some municipalities (but not the state) recognised *cemevi*s as 'houses of worship'. And while the Madımak Hotel was made a public entity in 2010, it was eventually transformed into the Sivas Science and Culture Centre, whose website provides no information about the 1993 massacre itself (Özkul 2015: 90).

The Religious Culture and Ethics courses continued to be a source of contention. In 2006, even before the 'Alevi Opening', an Alevi Turkish citizen, Hasan Zengin, initiated a lawsuit against the Turkish government at the European Court of Human Rights (ECHR), suing to have his daughter, Eylem, excused from the Religious Culture and Ethics course because of its Sunni orientation. The complainant wanted all Alevis to be exempt from the requirement, even if they were not a formal religious minority as recognised in the Treaty of Lausanne. The ECHR ruled in favour of the complainant, saying that the Religious Culture and Ethics courses did not adequately accommodate the different religious communities in Turkish society.[7]

The Turkish state's response was not to allow Alevi students exemption from the religion courses; instead, however, the Ministry of Education attempted to include some material about Alevis in the religion courses at secondary-school level. Yet the Religion Culture and Ethics course books presented Alevism in a way that attempted to downplay its difference from Sunni Islam. In the 2008 edition of the book, for example, Alevism (*Alevilik*) was presented as a branch of Sufism – in this case Bektaşism (*Bektaşilik*) – and was thus within the scope of 'acceptable' Islam.[8] The books emphasised that Alevis know and obey the Qur'an and that the basic principles of *Alevilik-Bektaşlik* follow the 'straight path' of (Sunni) Islam. As Manami Ueno (2018: 392) points out, 'Although these descriptions positively evaluate the *Alevilik-Bektaşilik* beliefs, Alevis did not regard the description as properly reflecting their beliefs. The target readership of the textbook was the majority – Sunni Muslims.' One of the great problems with this particular outcome is that it is the state that then articulated who the Alevis were in the context of these courses and in other venues. Here – and in the Alevi Opening as a whole – the JDP government attempted to turn Alevism into a homogeneous, manageable form of Islam and failed to recognise that Alevism is a whole complex of traditions about which Alevis themselves are not in agreement (Hurd 2014). Whatever hopes Alevis had invested in the Alevi Opening ended in disillusionment as Alevi organisations realised that the Opening was really an assimilationist policy (Massicard 2016: 85).

The expanding Diyanet

Even as the JDP government shortchanged the Alevis, it oversaw a substantial increase in the size of the Diyanet, in terms of both personnel and budget. From 2006 to 2015, the Diyanet's staff doubled, while its budget increased 400 per cent, expanding its share of the government's spending by one-third (Lepeska 2015). In fact, by 2018 expenditure on the Diyanet exceeded that of the entire Department of Education. As a result of this rapid growth, mosque construction accelerated so that by 2015, there were almost 87,000 mosques in Turkey, including some new grand mosques constructed in the large cities. Religious education expanded, such that the Diyanet's summer courses for school-age children educated almost 2 million children in 2009. Qur'an courses for adults – men and women in roughly equal numbers – increased ninefold by 2014 (Kaya 2018: 55).

The emergence of the internet and the growth of the broadcast and publishing industries affected the extent to which the Diyanet conveyed religious knowledge and the modes it used to do so. The Diyanet had been providing television and radio programming since the 1970s, but by the mid-2000s, Diyanet-sponsored programmes regularly appeared on both public and private television and radio stations. Keeping with the times, the Diyanet built an extensive website, available in a number of languages, and now has dedicated live-streaming radio and TV channels. It has a Facebook page and two Twitter accounts, both with thousands of followers. Furthermore, it issued an increasing number of publications, conference reports and programmes aimed at various aspects of Islamic belief and practice. The opening up of publishing and broadcasting to all kinds of content producers and the 'lawlessness' of the internet also created problems for the Diyanet. In this free-for-all media world, anyone – expert or not – could make religious claims and gather followers to any cause, including those that clashed with the Diyanet's religious philosophy. In response, Diyanet officials, such as the head of the Diyanet publications department, Yüksel Salman, proclaimed that the institutional mission of the Diyanet television station was to combat the 'pollution of information' – meaning, alternative interpretations of Islam that had proliferated in independent publication and broadcast arenas (Salman 2008: 315, 318). Along similar lines, Mehmet Görmez (who became head of the Diyanet in 2012) stressed that any 'Muslim organisation, community, and practice outside the orbit of the DIB [Diyanet] are preemptively defined as either mere "culture" or mere "politics"'. Any manifestation of Islam outside of the Diyanet 'necessarily lacks theological authority and legitimacy from the state's perspective' (Walton 2017: 54). That is, it isn't Islam if the

Diyanet does not say it is. So while the size and scope of the Diyanet expanded under the JDP, its official mission largely remained unchanged. The Diyanet continued its objective of transmitting to the Turkish people a singular version of Islam that would fit the needs of the state.

In the late 2000s, however, the Diyanet seemed to loosen some of its controls over how Islamic knowledge was propagated, especially as it relates to Friday sermons. Prior to 2006, a central office in the Diyanet wrote Friday sermons that local preachers were required to deliver – whether local preachers actually did deliver those sermons is a different matter, and certainly preachers could extemporise in contexts outside that of the formal Friday sermon. In 2006 this process was decentralised, and local mufti offices would compose the sermons, though under the supervision of the central Diyanet. This change was supposedly to allow the sermons to address issues important to local communities and regions, but given the control the central Diyanet still exerted over the sermon-writing process, the local sermons tended to match the Diyanet in content and tone. Furthermore, the content of the sermons has not changed significantly under the JDP. As before, they tend to focus on general topics, such as 'national solidarity, loyalty to the state, and a rationalistic Islam devoid of folk traditions' (Watters 2018: 366–7).

In 2010, for the first time in forty-five years Turkish lawmakers altered the organisation and bureaucratic status of the Diyanet, enlarging its influence on Turkish society. Act 6002, passed in January 2010 to replace the 1965 Law (633),[9] elevated the Diyanet from the status of a general directorate to the undersecretary in the prime ministry, while nine of the fourteen department chairmanships within the Diyanet were raised to the level of general directorate. The law placed the ownership (not just the management) of all new mosques directly under the control of the Diyanet – mosques built before the 2010 law would be allowed to remain under the ownership of their respective foundations. The change in mosque ownership status signifies increased Diyanet control and authority over institutional religious practice at the local level.

The 2010 law also increased the educational requirements of Diyanet personnel, thereby elevating the technical professionalism of the Diyanet cadre. These enhanced requirements paired with the creation of new career pathways in the Diyanet. Before there were preachers and imams, but after 2010 the Diyanet added positions such as 'expert-preachers' and 'chief-imams' – positions available to those who attained the appropriate education and, in some cases, passed exams qualifying them for the higher positions. One result of these changes was an immediate increase in the Diyanet personnel numbers – 7,500 more positions were added after 2010 – accompanied by salary increases (Kaya 2018: 103–4).

Women in the Diyanet

One of the most interesting developments in the Diyanet in the 2000s was the increasing presence and authority of women. Women had been able to serve as state-appointed preachers (*vaize*) since the 1960s, when the Diyanet began to train female students who had graduated from the theology faculties to become preachers. Women could not preach to a general congregation but could give sermons to other women. The admittance of female students to the *imam-hatip* schools beginning in 1976 – and the fact that girls attended these schools in increasing numbers during the 1980s and 1990s – meant that more and more women were qualified to enter the Diyanet as preachers. Women were increasingly recruited into the Diyanet after the 1997 soft coup, as the subsequent government attempted to tamp down on unauthorised forms of Islam in Turkey. After 1997, women were able to serve not only as preachers but also as religious specialists (*din hizmeti uzmanı*) who could organise seminars, teach Qur'an courses, design holiday programmes in mosques and issue *fetvas*.

The number of women serving in the Diyanet grew even more rapidly with the emergence of the pro-Islam JDP and the expansion of the Diyanet enabled by the JDP government. There were only thirty-four state-certified female preachers in 1991 for the whole country, but by 2010, there were 403, representing almost one-third of Turkey's official preaching workforce. By 2014, there were 727 female preachers, and the number continues to increase (Hassan 2011: 457; Maritato 2017: 542 n. 3). According to Fikret Karaman (2008: 287), the vice-president of the Diyanet in the 2000s, an important reason for employing more women was that the Diyanet was seeking to expand its services to women. Female citizens could speak more freely about both religious and personal matters with female religious experts, and personnel changes reflected this belief. To this end, in 2002 the Diyanet also established the Bureau of Family Religious Guidance (*Aile İrşat ve Rehberlik Büroları*), which would provide counselling and moral guidance services to both men and women. The growing presence of women in the Diyanet also indicated that there were more and more opportunities for advanced religious education for women. The female preachers in the 2000s and beyond were apt to have not only diplomas from *imam-hatip* secondary schools, but also undergraduate or advanced degrees from university theological faculties. Like all employees of the Diyanet, female preachers' competencies are tested through competitive national examinations, and they take part in ongoing education and certification programmes as well.

Both male and female preachers follow a fixed schedule as designated in a 2002 Diyanet Directive.[10] The directive required that a preacher working in Istanbul would give sermons once or twice a week, spend two days a week giving Qur'an interpretation lessons and seminars, and provide counselling one day a week in the local mufti offices associated with the Bureau of Family Religious Guidance (Kocamaner 2019; Maritato 2015: 436–7). In this capacity, people could make appointments or call in to talk with preachers to seek guidance on personal and family issues that affected them, often issues around divorce, family friction, childcare and so on – topics typical of family counselling or chaplaincy services in other parts of the world. One of the most interesting job requirements of all Istanbul preachers – men and women – is that they must work at least twice a year issuing *fetva*s (religious decisions) from *fetva* call centres, such as Alo Fetva 190 in Istanbul. This is a service provided by the Diyanet where people from Turkey or from abroad may call in with questions or submit questions through a dedicated website. In response, the specialist will draw on Islamic knowledge and law to issue the *fetva*. Questions may be about proper religious practice, for instance about fasting during Ramadan or giving alms (*zekat*). Or they may deal with personal issues, such as the permissibility of divorce or healthcare decisions (Maritato 2015). Of course, these are not legally binding decisions. As stated in Chapter 1, the *fetva*s issued by the Diyanet act as advice or recommendations relating to religious conduct or private decisions, but they do not have the force of law.

Diverse media choices and religious values

The expansion of the Diyanet and of Turkish civil society led to a rapid proliferation of religiously oriented publications, internet sites, and radio and television stations that attracted ever larger audiences. As mentioned above, the Diyanet increased its media productions in order to combat the 'pollution' of religious knowledge and to convey 'proper' Islam – that is, the form of Islam that does not challenge the state's religious and governmental priorities.

Simultaneously, as the various *cemaat*s grew in size, many expanded their media offerings. The media offerings made available by the Iskenderpaşa Nakşıbendis have allowed the community to remain active and influential, even as the leadership is now based in Australia. Similarly, the Gülen movement, whose leadership is based in the US, put out an increasing number of newspapers, magazines and books, and published the many works by and about Fethullah Gülen in multiple languages. The movement increased its presence on radio and internet sites, and added five more TV channels in Turkish and in English to their older Samanyolu station that they initiated in the 1990s. The programming on these channels and other religiously oriented channels included traditional presentations about religious matters, such as holiday celebrations and stories about the Prophet and other significant figures in Muslim history. They also provided children's programming on both religious and non-religious themes, family discussion shows and programmes with 'wholesome' content.

Televangelism has become a staple of Turkish religious television and radio broadcasting, with popular preachers espousing various approaches towards religious practice. Due to broadcasting requirements, these television preachers do not promote radical messages, such as encouraging the replacement of the secular state with one based on *Shari'ah*, but most focus on religious study, family matters and conducting a moral life. Many of these preachers have some affiliation with the Diyanet or with a faculty of divinity. For example, televangelist Mustafa Karataş is a professor of divinity at Istanbul University and hosts a popular television program, *The Gate of Affection*. In this programme, Karataş discusses traditional family values and how to resolve contemporary problems of family life. Other television preachers may not have credentials such as those of Karataş, but have wielded their own charisma to promote messages that appeal to devout audiences.

These types of programmes are part of a larger trend in Islamic broadcasting in which television stations have dedicated programming designed to 'strengthen the family' and create an Islamically moral society. Anthropologist Hikmet Kocamaner (2017) studied family programming on Islamic television channels and analysed the increasing number of television programmes dedicated to solving family problems and creating stronger family units. These shows consist of discussion panels or 'expert' advisors who address common family problems, such as divorce, wayward children, domestic violence, adultery and the like, with the goal of using religious principles to resolve these problems and strengthen family ties. The discourse in the shows focuses on individual responsibility and familial duty as the foundations of effective civic and religious moral life, and the programmes serve as guidance to make sure families are coherent and functional. As Kocamaner argues, this type of programming serves the interests of the neoliberal order under the JDP, since the JDP government sees families as the centre of its social policies. In the party's view, it is the family – composed of responsible and moral individuals – that should provide social welfare (childcare, and care of the elderly, the mentally ill, the drug-addicted and the disabled), not the state. In keeping with the logic of neoliberalism, this type of Islamic programming serves as a 'technology of governance' that instructs families how to resolve their own problems without appealing to defunded state institutions.

Final comments

This chapter has focused on the process of growth and change in Turkey over the tenure of the JDP government. In describing this era, I used and re-used words such as 'increase', 'expansion', 'opening', 'proliferation', 'transformation' and 'broadening'. And when I think of Turkey in the first decade or so of the twenty-first century, I think of a country that became brighter, more open and filled with possibility and opportunity, though the withdrawal of welfare protections has left some sectors of Turkish society vulnerable. Despite the often heavy-handed politics of Erdoğan and the JDP, the dynamism of this era should not be underestimated. It helps us to understand the enduring appeal of the JDP government, even as the conditions in Turkey have darkened in the second decade of the century. Though the JDP continues to dominate at the ballot box, many former supporters have become disillusioned by the political developments in Turkey in the 2010s. Despite the diversification of the media and commercial enterprises, the expansion of educational opportunities and the general economic improvement of Turkey in the last decades, Erdoğan and his JDP allies have nevertheless been as top-down and controlling as the Kemalist governments that came before. As Dressler notes (2013: xvi), critics of the JDP government

> maintain that the dismantling of the old patriarchal, corrupt political elite, which was ideologically committed to the nationalist and secularist politics of Kemalism and institutionally engrained in the military, judiciary, bureaucracy, has been replaced by a new system of overt and hidden networks of power, organised mainly along religious and economic interests, that is equally if not more oppressive and increasingly less willing to tolerate opposition and dissent.

The growing authoritarianism of the JDP government and its effects on religious life will be explored in the final chapter.

Notes

1. The dome architectural style is common of mosques in all the territories once within the realms of the Ottoman Empire. But mosques can take any shape – they really only require a *kibla* and room to pray.
2. As with all important social scientific concepts, there is some debate about how to define neoliberalism, and subsequently there is a vast social scientific literature on the concept. My discussion of it draws from David Harvey's *A Brief History of Neoliberalism* (2005).
3. Those *gecekondu* dwellers who owned the title to their land were given a standard apartment in the new complexes, but many felt that they could have got more property in exchange for the titles if they had worked through an independent real estate contractor, rather than through the city government. Those without deeds to their properties were given an option of buying a standard apartment with a state-backed fifteen-year mortgage – a financial burden many could not take on.
4. The literature on changing lifestyles and tastes among upwardly mobile, religiously observant Turks includes works by Navaro-Yashin (2002b), Çınar (2005), White (2002a, 2013), Gökarıksel (2012), and Gökarıksel and Secor (2010a, 2010b).
5. To be clear, the NSC had been hostile to the *cemaat*s long before the rise of the 28 February process. While the Turkish-Islamic Synthesis provided an opening for Sunni religious activities, the Kemalist state remained uneasy about the growing popularity of the various organisations, including the moderate, pro-development ones such as the Nakşibendi-Khalidis and the Gülen movement. Kemalist powers, such as the military, were suspicious that even those religious orders that maintained an apolitical or moderate stance were in fact practising *takkiye* (deception used to promote religion) and were hiding a political goal to bring down the secular state in favour of one based on *Shari'ah*.

6. As mentioned in Chapter 3, if Alevis fast at all (and many don't), it is usually during the Islamic month of Muharram – when the Alevi commemoration of Ashura takes place – rather than during Ramadan.
7. *Hasan and Eylem Zengin* vs *Turkey*, Application No. 1448/04, Judgement of 19 October 2007.
8. At this point during the tenure of the JDP, 'Sufism' as a general category received positive treatment in the Religious Culture and Ethics secondary-school course books, though the books discreetly omitted all discussion of the specific *Tarikat*s and their abolition in the early years of the Republic. See Ueno (2018).
9. See www.diyanet.gov.tr/en-US/Content/PrintDetail/1
10. Diyanet İşleri Başkanlığı, *Görev ve Çalışma Yönergesi*, 80, 10 December 2002.

CHAPTER 8

The latest chapter

In many ways, the dynamism that characterised Turkey at the beginning of the twenty-first century persists to the present day, though the energetic character of the 2000s has given way to distinct pessimism, due to the increasing authoritarianism in the Erdoğan government. This is not to say that the first ten years of JDP power was consistently optimistic. As we saw in the last chapter, the JDP government operated in top-down fashion, often ignoring or even denigrating those in opposition and those who criticised the excesses of the party. Erdoğan himself revelled in his reputation as a *kabadayı* (literally, 'rude uncle'), a Turkish word that refers to a bully who uses his toughness to push other people around. While his supporters appreciated his use of power to satisfy their own political desires, his opponents were often given little voice in the changes that were taking place in the country. Furthermore, the opposition was disorganised and lacked strong leadership, and Erdoğan and the JDP proved expert at exploiting that weakness to push for legal and constitutional changes that would serve their own interests. These changes have implications for the practice of Islam in Turkey, in part because Erdoğan made regular use of religious language and symbols in his political discourse and in part because the proposed changes expanded the power of Islamic institutions in Turkish society.

One of the most significant achievements of the JDP government was the passage, on 12 September 2010, of a national referendum introducing amendments to the Turkish constitution. The constitution had been formulated under the direction of the military government that was established after the 1980 coup. The JDP had long wanted to draw up a new constitution, seemingly in order to accommodate EU accession requirements. Some of the proposed amendments were indeed aimed at enhancing the democratic character of Turkey by improving the rights of workers, women and children, and making it harder for the courts to close down political parties (Ciddi 2011: 41). But many feared that the amendments would also allow the ruling party to enhance its own power. Specifically, the amendments allowed the president, who at the time was JDP leader Abdullah Gül, to control appointments to the highest judicial bodies, including to the Supreme Board of Judges and Prosecutors, which oversees the appointment of lower-level judges and prosecutors. In a word, the amendments had the potential to decrease the independence of the judiciary, allowing a dominant ruling party like the JDP to pack the courts with supporters. The amendment package did not get enough votes in parliament to pass on its own, so Gül called for a national referendum. Tellingly, the Higher Electoral Council (*Yüksek Seçim Kurulu*) chose 12 September as the date for the 2010 referendum because it fell on the thirtieth anniversary of the 1980 coup. Despite the various reservations about the amendments, the referendum passed with broad support, reflecting the popularity the JDP maintained at the time.

Projecting strength

The growing strength of Erdoğan and the JDP corresponded with an increase in Islamic symbols and institutions in Turkey's public spaces. At the same time that the Diyanet was expanding in size and power (see Chapter 7), mosque-building accelerated as well. Not only did the number of mosques increase, but the JDP government also pushed for the construction of often controversial grand mosques. The most extravagant of these is an enormous mosque built at Çamlıca Park. In Chapter 5, I described the controversies over Çamlıca that emerged in the 1990s when Erdoğan was mayor of Istanbul. Many Turks viewed Çamlıca as a traditionally secularist space, but Erdoğan launched a programme to remake the site into an alcohol-free family garden replete with neo-Ottoman symbolism. While the effects of this transformation were really quite lovely and attracted both domestic and foreign tourists, secularists were troubled by the turn towards Islamic symbolism this transformation brought about, and the construction of this new mosque further disturbed the Kemalist sector of society. The Çamlıca mosque was inaugurated in 2016 and is designed to be the largest mosque in Turkey, 'larger than anything built by the sultans', as one foreign correspondent observed (Christie-Miller 2016). According to the *Daily Sabah* (July 13, 2016), the mosque was supposed to have female-friendly features and special accommodations for the disabled, a platform for visitors to watch prayers, a museum, an Islamic art gallery and a library.[1] Yet, when I visited the mosque in the summer of 2019, only the mosque itself was open, while none of the other features were available for public viewing. I was startled to see that the only way one could approach the mosque was by car, given its location on the side of the hill, and a special tunnel had been built to allow vehicle access to the mosque. As some devout friends pointed out to me, this feature of the mosque showed that it was built primarily as a 'display' mosque to use for official functions, not as a mosque to serve the people in the surrounding community.

The Çamlıca mosque was just one in a series of 'megaprojects' undertaken by the JDP government. Another was the construction of a new airport for Istanbul, purported to be the world's largest. This 'Istanbul New Airport' replaced the older Atatürk Airport on the European side of Istanbul near the Sea of Marmara. But it has faced a series of problems from the very beginning.

Figure 8.1 Çamlıca mosque front entrance, 2019 (photograph by author)

Construction was repeatedly delayed and even suspended, especially after the deaths of many construction workers since the beginning of construction in May 2015.[2] According to some engineers associated with the project, the land chosen for the airport was inappropriate for such a structure. It had been the site of coal mines, wetlands and coastal sand dunes, making for a very unstable and uneven surface that would require continual maintenance. The area is also in the path of major bird migrations, creating further dangers for aeroplanes and disrupting sensitive ecosystems (Tremblay 2019). Even with all these difficulties and delays, the new airport finally opened on 29 October 2018, on the ninety-fifth anniversary of the founding of the Republic. The airport is far from the city centre (50 km, or 30 miles) and, as of 2019, no transport infrastructure was in place to shuttle passengers to and from the city. The only options were to drive oneself or pay for a very expensive taxi ride. The overall effect, it seemed, was to create an airport that served as a transfer hub, but not one that served the people of Turkey. Indeed, the gates for domestic flights were delegated to the lower floor of the enormous terminal, far away from the high-end shops and fancy food courts that seemed to be designed for international travellers.

Another megaproject the JDP implemented was the construction of a third bridge crossing the Bosporus Strait where it meets the Black Sea. The bridge was intended to shunt lorry traffic away from the two other trans-Bosporus bridges, a welcome development to ease Istanbul's notorious traffic congestion. But the new bridge was the cause of several controversies. One was that the construction of the bridge and the major roads leading up to it required the destruction of protected forests in north Istanbul, contributing to Erdoğan's long-time reputation for anti-environmental policies. Secondly, the JDP government chose to name the bridge the Yavuz Sultan Selim Bridge, after Selim I – known as 'The Grim' in English – the Ottoman sultan who reigned from 1512 to 1520. Sultan Selim is best known for his military victories that led to a dramatic increase in the size of the Ottoman Empire. He gained the territory of much of what is now the Middle East, as well as Egypt and other areas of North Africa. He also secured military victories over the neighbouring Safavid Empire, but these battles have a sectarian dimension. Many Alevis and others believe that Selim ordered the slaughter of thousands of Alevis, whom Selim suspected of aiding the enemy. When the government chose to name the bridge after Sultan Selim, Alevis saw it as a further sign of Erdoğan's disrespect for the religious minority.

Another project is the construction of a 'second Bosporus'. Erdoğan envisaged digging a canal, called 'Canal Istanbul', through Thrace in parallel to the Bosporus in order to allow more shipping from the Black Sea into the Mediterranean. The cost of such a project and the potential environmental impacts (which Erdoğan has dismissed) have prevented this project from coming to fruition, at least so far.

These megaprojects, even the ones that were completed, have created enduring financial problems for the Turkish government. For example, the third Bosporus bridge immediately underperformed. When it was opened, it charged very high tolls in order to pay the promised revenues to the private company that had partnered with the Turkish government to build it. The tolls were so high that many travellers, including lorry drivers, avoided the bridge to save money, which defeated the purpose of the bridge being constructed to ease traffic on other roadways. Furthermore, the building projects often involved corrupt relationships between contractors and the JDP political elite, relationships that were geared towards enriching all those involved.[3] The Ministry of Environment and Urban Planning, established in the wake of the 2010 referendum, essentially rubber-stamped these often questionable developments under the umbrella of 'urban transformation' (Kentel 2016: 140).

These projects, along with rapid urban development and gentrification that excluded many poorer Turks, elicited much criticism. Concerns about the environment or questions about the actual need for these expensive projects were either ignored or openly derided. Many commentators both within and outside Turkey saw Erdoğan's push for ever more construction as, at best, an insistence that Turkey's economy is robust, despite clear signs that it is not, and, at worst, Erdoğan's attempt to remake himself in the image of the Ottoman sultans who left monuments in their wake. As Erdoğan quipped at the inauguration of the Çamlıca mosque, 'When a horse dies it leaves behind its saddle, when a man dies he leaves behind his works. We will be remembered for this.' In essence, many saw the megaprojects as less about creating great and useful monuments and more about boosting Erdoğan's ego. Even some of his traditional political base expressed concern that so much money was being spent on the projects, funnelling funding away from other important public institutions. To give one example: Melih, the former student of the Süleymancı boys' school discussed in Chapter 6, one day escorted me around the grand neo-Ottoman Mimar Sinan mosque, newly constructed on the Asian side of Istanbul. After we had toured the enormous structure with its elaborate interior design, I commented that it was a beautiful mosque and so big. He looked at me with a frown, and said, 'Sister, Erdoğan goes too far' (*Kim abla, Erdoğan abartıyor*).

Gezi protests

Even before the completion of these megaprojects, the over-development of Istanbul and Erdoğan's dismissal of his critics created tensions that reached breaking point in the spring of 2013. Erdoğan planned to transform the Kemalist-oriented Taksim Square by constructing a mosque and razing the Gezi Park there in order to build a shopping mall modelled on the Taksim military barracks that had been torn down in 1940. Environmentalists protested the removal of the old trees in Gezi Park, which would have eliminated one of the few green spaces in central Istanbul. These protests turned violent when, on 27 May 2013, construction workers and bulldozers began to chop down trees in the Gezi Park space, and environmental activists tried to stop the destruction. At first, the protests were limited to the area around Gezi Park, but when the police used excessive violence to disperse the protestors, thousands joined in, and protests against the JDP government erupted all around the country. These 'Gezi protests' provided opportunities for participants – who came from various sectors of Turkish society – to voice grievances about many different issues, such as the overdevelopment of Istanbul, economic inequality, the increase in JDP's socially repressive practices, and the eroding of secularist principles in the Turkey.

I happened to be in Istanbul at the time of the protests, and even though I was staying in an area away from the city centre, people out in the Istanbul neighbourhoods were taking to the streets, banging pots and pans and chanting protest slogans. I later travelled to Izmir and Ankara. In Izmir, every night at 9 o'clock, those who supported the Gezi protests blinked lights on and off in their houses and banged pots or honked horns. In Ankara, I visited a friend whose children had been participating in the protests. I went with the young people first to Kızılay, Ankara's city-centre square, and walked with them up Atatürk Boulevard to Kuğlu Park in Çankaya, a middle-class neighbourhood. Kızılay was littered with broken glass and tear-gas canisters, and my eyes burned from the tear-gas residue that had settled into the metro station underneath the square. Kuğlu Park had become the epicentre of the Gezi protests in Ankara, and the whole area had been remade into a small tent city, complete with a public kitchen, a first-aid station, a library and activity areas. The atmosphere was quite festive and vendors sold Guy Fawkes masks to protesters, as well as face masks and goggles for protection against tear gas (see Figures 8.2 and 8.3).

Figure 8.2 Vendor selling face masks, goggles and Guy Fawkes masks, Ankara, 2013 (photograph by author)

Figure 8.3 Young Gezi protestor in a Guy Fawkes mask, Ankara, 2013
(photograph by author)

Alongside the party atmosphere, though, there was definitely an undercur-
rent of anger. Signs and graffiti in and near the park criticised or made fun of
Erdoğan and the JDP government.

    While the Gezi protests were not primarily about religious issues, religion
played into the conflicts. Erdoğan's increasing authoritarianism and unwill-
ingness to compromise with the opposition played into old divisions between
Kemalists and pious Muslims. Secularists and many others publicly and privately supported the Gezi protestors and enjoyed the wit and humour displayed

by protestors in their signs, graffiti and social media posts. But supporters of the JDP were, unsurprisingly, critical of the protests. Pro-government media person-alities denounced the protestors for their violence and argued that the changes the protestors wanted should be made through the democratic process. This last point ignored the fact that it was the riot police who were most often violent, and that the democracy in Turkey was a winner-take-all system in which those in power could do whatever they wanted while the political minority had little ability to realise their own political aspirations (this had sometimes been true in the Kemalist era, too).

In some ways the Gezi protests were successful, in that Gezi Park remained intact and the shopping mall was never built. But Taksim Square ended up being paved over with a great expanse of cement that curtailed traffic through it, ruining some of its traditional beauty. More tellingly, the long-planned Ottoman-style mosque was constructed in Taksim Square right across from the Republican monument that has traditionally been the focal point of the square. And the suppression of opposing voices and movements continued in Turkey, even intensifying in subsequent years.

The Gezi protests also put the Alevi population in a vulnerable position. While Alevis had been optimistic about their position in Turkey due to the JDP's initiation of the 'Alevi Opening' (see Chapter 7), it quickly became clear that Erdoğan and his supporters were never committed to recognising Alevis as a rights-bearing minority. Many Alevis had opposed the 2010 referendum process because they feared it strengthened the Sunni character of the government, and rather than addressing their grievances, Erdoğan began to denigrate Alevis in speeches he gave during the referendum campaign processes. The president of the opposition RPP, Kemal Kılıçdaroğlu, was Alevi, and Erdoğan would sometimes allude to Kılıçdaroğlu's Alevi identity to criticise the opposition, sug-gesting the RPP was treacherous in the same way that Alevis supposedly were. In the case of the Gezi protests, Alevis were disproportionately victims of police violence. Even though protesters came from many different backgrounds, seven of the eight people killed in the violence were Alevi. This death toll became a tool by which the JDP could allege that the protests were really just an 'Alevi affair', thereby finding another way to dismiss the concerns of the protestors. Simultaneously, for many Sunni supporters of the JDP, Alevis could 'be easily politicised as the rioter "Other"' (Özkul 2015: 91).

The Syrian civil war and Syrian refugees

Even before the Gezi protests, the Alevis found themselves used as political pawns in Turkey's growing conflict with its neighbour to the south, Syria. When Syria's civil war broke out in 2011, Turkey's government aligned itself with the Syrian Sunni Muslim opposition forces who were fighting to oust the regime of President Bashar al-Assad. Assad is Alawite – Alawite Islam overlaps with Shi'ism and has some resemblance to Turkish Alevism. In Syria, the Assad regime had favoured the Alawite community over and against the Sunni major-ity, an issue that had long provoked Sunni resentment. While Turkey was con-templating entering the Syrian civil war, the official discussion in Turkey cast the Syrian Alawites as an external threat and, by association, cast the Turkish Alevis as an internal threat. Pro-JDP media coverage even made allegations that Turkish Alevis supported the Assad regime in Syria (Özkul 2015: 91).

The escalating violence in Syria resulted in a massive influx of refugees into surrounding countries, including Turkey – 3.6 million by 2019.[4] Refugee camps sprang up all along the Turkish border with Syria, and many more refugees scattered into Turkey, some of whom attempted to cross into Greece and Bulgaria (both EU countries). The Red Crescent, the United Nations High Commissioner for Refugees (UNHCR) and some other aid agencies worked in conjunction with the Turkish government to support the refugees. In fact, KYM – the aid organisation associated with the Gülen movement – acted as a primary organisation that brought direct food aid and other support to the refugees in Turkey's south-east, especially those refugees living outside the refugee camps. In 2014 I accompanied a KYM fact-finding mission to Kilis, a border city in Turkey's south-west that is hosting many refugees (refugees had doubled the size of the town's population). This mission was accompanying a United Nations delegation that was trying to understand the situation of refugees outside the refugee camps. Many of the Syrian families were unregistered and unwilling to go to the refugee camps (where they would be registered) because they were afraid of being exposed to agents of the Syrian intelligence services or of others who might threaten them. The fact that many refugees were unregistered meant that it was difficult to know what kind of aid unregistered refugees were receiv-ing, whether or not their children were attending school (most were not) or how health needs could be met. The refugees had attempted to set up makeshift tent homes and had established an informal school for refugee children (Figure 8.4). The classrooms were mostly filled with girls, since boys would be out trying to earn money for their families. My short visit to Kilis revealed how chaotic the situation was and how vulnerable the refugees were. Even with these various organisations trying to help, the stress of the refugees on Turkey's infrastructure has been intense, and reports of increased crime rates and ethno-religious con-flicts transplanted from Syria into Turkey became common.

The Syrian situation also inflamed ethnic and religious conflicts within Turkey. Not only did the pro-government discourse insinuate Alevi linkages to the Alawite regime of Assad, but the Turkish government resettled some Syrian refugees near Alevi villages.[5] That is, the Syrian Sunni refugees, fleeing bombing from the Alawite regime, were settling in refugee camps near Alevis, who Sunnis often identify with Alawites. Whether or not this is the result of direct policy

Figure 8.4 Informal school for Syrian refugee children in Kilis, 2014; note that most students are girls (photograph by author

decisions of the Turkish government, these situations have sparked considerable apprehension among the Alevis, who feared reprisal from the refugees.

The conflict has also reignited hostilities between Turkey's government and the Kurdish minority, especially those Kurds living on the border with Syria. One set of opposition groups fighting the Assad regime from the north has been composed of Kurdish fighters active along the Turkish-Syrian border. Turkey's traditional allies, the US and others, had long supported some of these Kurdish fighting groups, seeing them as especially well situated to combat the Syrian regime. But Turkey maintained that these Kurdish fighting groups, especially the People's Protection Units known as the YPG (Kurdish: *Yekîneyên Parastina Gel*), were extensions of the Kurdish separatist PKK and therefore represented a direct threat to Turkey. The Turkish military regularly attacked Kurdish villages along the border and even bombed Kurdish towns in Syria itself, provoking some of the old hostilities between the Turkish military and the Kurdish minorities. In fact, when US President Donald Trump cut off support to the Kurdish fighters of the YPG in northern Syria in 2019, Turkish troops and mercenaries under Turkish leadership intensified military activity in Syria, which has greatly exacerbated the refugee crisis in Turkey and elsewhere.

The failing relationship between the JDP and the Gülen movement[6]

Of particular importance to understanding some of the more recent political developments involving Islam in Turkey is the changing relationship between the JDP government and the Gülen movement. During its first ten years in power, the JDP could rely on strong and stable support from Gülen movement members. The interests of the movement and those of the party closely aligned in many essential ways, especially in terms of economic issues and the promotion of Islamic ethics. Both the JDP and the Gülen movement generally supported the melding of market capitalism with Islamic piety and were strongly anti-socialist and anti-communist. Under the JDP government, many well-educated members of the Gülen movement joined the government bureaucracy, dominating some government branches such as the police and the judiciary. The most famous (or infamous) example of cooperation between the party and the movement was the so-called 'Ergenekon affair'. This was an investigation of an alleged network of military and civilian actors who were accused of planning a series of high-profile murders and attacks on public and international targets designed to destabilise and topple the JDP government. Over 500 people were arrested in this investigation. Many observers accused the JDP government of turning the Ergenekon affair into a witch hunt to silence political critics. The Ergenekon trials and related investigations took special aim at the military, in particular its leadership, as high-ranking officers were accused of treason and were jailed. The once-powerful military was defanged and lost much of its traditional authority over civilian matters. It was later revealed that Gülen-affiliated prosecutors supported by the JDP government had fabricated the accusations against these military personnel. The government later dismissed the charges against most of the accused, but the damage to the power of the military was already done. Supporters of democratisation of Turkey had long criticised the overwhelming tutelary role of the military in the country, but they also recognised that sham trials and fake evidence were an undemocratic way to bring the military more fully under civilian control.

Even though the Gülen movement and the JDP have historically shared political interests and goals, there have been some points on which the movement and the party have disagreed. For example, as the Gülen movement gained public visibility and had a greater and greater role in the government, the JDP grew wary of the potential influence that the movement had on politics and policy-making. Besides the presence of pro-Gülenist bureaucrats in the government, members of the movement have been publicly lobbying on several issues, such as the Kurdish issue and the EU accession process. This lobbying activity has upset members of the JDP, not only because the JDP sees the movement as a potential political rival, but old-style Turkish politicians are simply not used to policy input from civil society organisations (Yavuz 2013: 218–19). For them, political influence from the recently emerging civil society is not seen as part of the normal give and take of actors in the public sphere but as interference in matters best left to the bureaucracy. That is, the top-down style of the JDP politics was threatened by more bottom-up civil organisations, such as the Gülen movement and other groups.

Furthermore, members of the JDP were threatened when actors within the government – presumably supporters of the Gülen movement – engaged in covert activities that targeted Erdoğan, fellow party members and even members of Erdoğan's family. In December 2013, unauthorised wiretapping of phone conversations and political meetings were released to internet sites, and these seemed to reveal illegal actions on the part of Erdoğan and his son, Bilal (though the authenticity of the wiretapping recordings is questionable). Other revelations relating to both domestic politics and foreign relations seemed to be geared towards undermining Erdoğan's legitimacy. Erdoğan reacted by accusing Gülen's supporters in the government of being a 'parallel structure' that must be expunged from the government bureaucracy, judiciary and security forces.

One reason why the December 2013 release of the recordings was linked to the Gülen movement was because in the previous month, Erdoğan had begun to force the closure of the many test-preparation schools (*dershane*) that were common around Turkey. Thousands of Turkish students attended these schools in order to prepare for the high-stress, high-stakes examinations for entrance into select secondary schools and universities. Students from middle- class or lower-class backgrounds especially relied on these schools, since children from wealthier families could always engage private tutors. The closing of the preparatory schools was a blow to families who were seeking upward mobility through the education of their children. The excuse for the closures was that the schools operated as a secondary educational system and were against the Union of Education law passed after the founding of the Turkish Republic. But the actual target seemed to be the many schools run by Gülenists, which accounted for 25 per cent of the total. The *dershane*s were where the movement recruited many of its members and were a major source of revenue, and so they functioned as an important engine in the growth of the Gülen movement. The general media and many Gülen followers saw Erdoğan's action as an effort to limit the power of the movement by cutting off its resources, even though many other educational institutions were also forced closed.[7]

The tensions between movement and party increased when on 2 December *Taraf* newspaper released documents revealing that in 2004 the JDP and the military had signed an agreement to bring down the Gülen movement. JDP officials stated that such an agreement was necessary when the military was still powerfully involved in the political process, but this did not help ease the already strained relationship. It was in this context that the events of 17 December took place as a possible retribution against the actions of the JDP: some of Gülen's followers in positions of authority in the judiciary system charged the sons of three JDP ministers with corruption and implicated a number of businessmen with links to Erdoğan and his son, Bilal. The investigators uncovered millions of dollars in cash found in shoe boxes in a wardrobe belonging to the chief executive of a bank, while extra-legal business ties to Iran were brought to light. They also revealed extensive bribery within government circles and in various construction projects. In response, Erdoğan sought to assert greater personal control over legal processes and the media, sometimes making calls to media outlets about what stories to run. He ordered the blockage of popular social media sites, such as Twitter and YouTube, because these had been the platforms on which some of the most damaging revelations had aired. The government also reassigned hundreds of police officers and removed judges – all of whom were presumably followers of Fethullah Gülen – on charges that they formed a disloyal political block that threatened the integrity of the JDP government. Both Gülen and Erdoğan, and their respective followers, issued statements of intense criticism and mutual suspicion.

The electoral victories of the JDP in 2014 clearly indicated that the party had gained the upper hand, at least in the context of Turkish domestic politics. The local elections of 30 March 2014 – considered by many to be a referendum on the JDP party after the scandals of the previous months – delivered more than 40 per cent of the votes to JDP candidates, indicating that the party had not lost significant support. It was clear that the Gülen movement members had seriously miscalculated the electorate's reaction when they uncovered the corruption and financial misdeeds of the JDP and its associates. Instead of damaging Erdoğan's reputation (and, by extension, the party's reputation), many of Erdoğan's traditional supporters actually backed him more fervently because of the scandals that the Gülen movement actors exposed. Erdoğan was able to present the release of wiretaps on the internet as a conspiracy or 'foreign plot' against the government that was perpetrated by a 'parallel state', just as he was able to persuade many that the bans on Twitter and YouTube were reasonable actions to take against traitorous entities (Middle East Monitor, 7 March 2014). Thus, his followers rallied to his and the party's defence.

The 2016 failed coup

The political situation seemed to go from bad to worse in the second decade of the twenty-first century. Before the scandals and internecine attacks recounted above had a chance to die down, a bloody attempted coup took place in Turkey in July 2016, an event that has shaped the nature of politics and religion in Turkey ever since. On the night of 15 July – seemingly out of the blue – a division of the military launched a coordinated operation in several major cities with the hope of bringing down Erdoğan and the JDP government. Soldiers and tanks appeared in the streets of Istanbul and Ankara, setting off explosions. Turkish fighter jets dropped bombs on the parliament building in Ankara, and the chairman of the Joint Chiefs of Staff, Hulusi Akar, was kidnapped. News of the attempt spread not only by social media, but mosques also broadcast calls to the citizenry to defend the government against the coup. Thousands of citizens gathered in streets all over the country, resisting tank fire and air bombardments. The attempted coup was over in just a few hours but in the end, 241 people were killed and 2,194 others were injured.

Very quickly, Erdoğan accused Gülen and his allies in the military of masterminding the coup and was able to take control of the national narrative to paint the entire Gülen movement – all of its hundreds of thousands of members – as traitors guilty of trying to overthrow the Turkish government. I will not try to sort out who was really behind the attempted coup, since it is under dispute. Erdoğan and the Turkish intelligence agencies claim to have evidence that associates of Gülen masterminded the incident. Gülen himself and his supporters deny involvement, though they are in no position to demonstrate their supposed innocence. The fact that Erdoğan and his allies have been able to control the 'Narrative of 15 July' in Turkey so completely (Altınordu 2017), it is hard to accept their account of events without scepticism. We have already seen that both the JDP and members of the Gülen movement have been willing to instigate criminal trials and fabricate evidence to bring down political opponents in pursuit of their own goals. Perhaps a clearer picture of the events surrounding the attempted coup will eventually emerge, but I am sceptical about that as well.

In any case, what followed was an extraordinary purging of supposed Gülenists from many sectors of Turkish life. Thousands of military officials, pilots, police officers, civil servants, academics and even teachers were sacked from their jobs for supposed links to the Gülen movement. The media outlets and publishing houses affiliated with the movement were forced to close, and all of the Gülen schools and universities were seized by the state. Those who could flee the country did so, and, as of 2017, 50,000 people were arrested and by 2020 more than 130,000 people were fired from their jobs, often having their property confiscated as well. The government deemed the crackdown necessary to 'root out all coup supporters from the state apparatus' (Al-Jazeera 2017).

In the end, Erdoğan was able to eliminate many of his opponents simply by accusing them of association with the Gülen movement, no matter how tenuous the evidence. Journalists, opposition politicians, doctors, academics and anyone deemed a danger to the regime faced accusations of affiliation with the 'terrorist' Gülen movement. Also in 2016, a group of more than a thousand academics had signed an 'Academics for Peace' declaration, which denounced the conflict with Kurds in south-east Turkey. In the aftermath of the attempted coup, most of the signatories lost their positions – others fled the country – and remained unemployed, even though the Constitutional Court ruled in July 2019 that the academics' rights had been violated. Some of the academics even lost access to pensions and social security, as well as normal banking and financial services (Cupolo 2020). The effect of these dismissals and jailings has been the hollowing out of many crucial institutions, such as schools and hospitals (teachers and many healthcare providers are civil servants).

Only Erdoğan was further able to consolidate power by holding a referendum in 2017 regarding a proposal to dissolve the office of the prime ministry. It would be replaced with a presidential system in which great power would be invested in the office of the president while the influence of the *meclis* (parliament) would be reduced. After a biased campaign – the opposition was only afforded a fraction of the media space the JDP was given – the referendum passed by a narrow margin. Erdoğan is now the president of Turkey with extraordinary powers, and there are no institutions or branches of government left that can check that power. In sum, the 2017 referendum reduced the power of the parliament, while the 2010 constitution reforms authorised the president to appoint members of the judiciary, making the courts essentially a handmaiden to the president. Journalists, academics and opposition leaders have been jailed or are in exile, while most media outlets, universities and government offices are populated either by Erdoğan loyalists or those who have remained strategically silent in the face of the political developments. At least in terms of its public and political spaces, Turkey seems to belong to Erdoğan.

Turkey in the twenty-first century

This picture of modern Turkey is no doubt grim. Erdoğan's Turkey is set up only for those whose interpretations of Islam align with the Turkish-Sunni Islam promoted by the state. It is certainly easier to study in the many *imam-hatip* schools and divinity faculties that have emerged, to pray in the bigger and more ubiquitous mosques, to take the many courses and seminars offered by the expanding Diyanet and so on. However, if in public one does not conform to the state's version of Islam, one must prepare for the consequences. To be honest, this situation may not be that different from the days of the one-party rule under Atatürk and his successor, İsmet İnönü (1884–1973). They too tried to create a version of Islam that would serve the needs of the Turkish state. It seems that Erdoğan has borrowed from Atatürk's playbook to promote a particular type of Islam, too, but as Erdoğan and his supporters envisage it.

Yet in my visits to Turkey since the attempted coup, I can see that most people do not live their daily lives according to the ebbs and flows of political developments, though the turbulence of the last years has certainly captured the public's attention. People continue to work, relax, socialise and pray as they always have, even if they are more careful about what they say in public and to whom. For example, in my visit to Turkey in June 2019, I visited the new Çamlıca mosque with Maryam, her husband and children. Afterwards, we wandered through the Hidiv Park, a lovely wooded zone on the Bosporus that housed the estate of the Ottoman *khedive* (the viceroy of Egypt in the years from 1867 to 1914). It was wedding season, and newlyweds were posing in various scenic spots to take photos. The *khedive*'s mansion was open to visitors, but it was hosting a rather lavish wedding, and we were shooed out as the caterers began bringing in food. Reluctant to leave this marvellous spot, we ordered tea at an adjoining café and watched the wedding preparations. Even as we appreciated these experiences, though, we acknowledged that many could not take part in such enjoyment – they had lost jobs, fled the country or been jailed. We could only hope that the political oppression would end, but it is unlikely as long as Erdoğan is in power. So we sat quietly, drank tea and watched the wedding guests begin to arrive, wondering what would happen next.

Notes

1. www.dailysabah.com/religion/2016/06/14/camlica-mosque-largest-in-turkey-opens-in-honor-of-ramadan
2. The Turkish Ministry of Labour said that twenty-seven workers had died during the construction of the airport, but others have reported as many as 400 deaths (Sonmez 2018).
3. For example, the IGA business consortium won the bid to build the Istanbul New Airport. IGA consists of five major companies (Cengiz, Limak, Mapa/MNG, Kolin and Kolyon), all of whom have close ties to the Turkish government and are often awarded favourable tenders (Tremblay 2019).
4. https://data2.unhcr.org/en/situations/syria/location/113
5. https://medium.com/@lorenarios/the-village-of-terolar-in-the-province-of-kahramanmara%C5%9F-in-southeastern-turkey-looks-idyllic-a9ff1213ee51   www.hurriyetdailynews.com/turkish-villagers-rally-against-refugee-camp-plans-citing-fear-of-sunni-extremists-97458
6. This section is derived from 'Pragmatic politics: the Gülen movement and the JDP' (Shively 2016).
7. The *dershane* closures were also a tit-for-tat move against the movement for an earlier incident. In 2012, a Gülen-affiliated prosecutor, Sadrettin Sarikaya, attempted to question Hakan Fidan, chief of Turkey's National Intelligence Organisation (MIT), about his negotiations with the PKK. Sarikaya probably would have had Fidan and others arrested and removed from power, but the Erdoğan government prevented this. Sarikaya was instead removed from his position, and the law was amended to protect MIT officials from any similar action.

Bibliography

Abadan-Unat, Nermin (1998). 'Gamalı Haçtan Türbana', Editorial. *Cumhuriyet*, 8 December, 2.

Abenante, Paola and Vicini, Fabio (2017). 'Interiority Unbound: Sufi and Modern Articulations of the Self'. *Culture and Religion*, 18(2), 57–71.

Adanali, Ahmet Hadi (2008). 'The Presidency of Religious Affairs and the Principle of Secularism in Turkey'. *The Muslim World*, 98(2/3), 228–41.

Adaş, Emin Baki (2006). 'The Making of Entrepreneurial Islam and the Islamic Spirit of Capitalism'. *Journal for Cultural Research*, 10(2), 113–37.

Agai, Bekim (2003). 'The Gülen Movement's Islamic Ethic of Education'. In M. Hakan Yavuz and John L. Esposito (eds), *Turkish Islam and the Secular State: The Gülen Movement* (pp. 48–68). Syracuse, NY: Syracuse University Press.

Agai, Bekim (2007). 'Islam and Education in Secular Turkey: State Policies and the Emergence of the Fethullah Gülen Group'. In Robert W. Hefner and Muhammad Qasim Zaman (eds), *Schooling Islam: The Culture and Politics of Modern Muslim Education* (pp. 149–71). Princeton, NJ and Oxford: Princeton University Press.

Altan, Mehmet (2010). *Kent Dindarlığı*. Istanbul: Timaş Yayınları.

Altınay, Ayşe Gül (2004). *The Myth of the Military-Nation: Militarism, Gender, and Education in Turkey* (1st edn). New York and Basingstoke: Palgrave Macmillan.

Altınordu, Ateş (2017). 'A Midsummer Night's Coup: Performance and Power in Turkey's July 15 Coup Attempt'. *Qualitative Sociology*, 40(2), 139–64.

Al-Jazeera (2017). 'Turkey's Failed Coup Attempt: All You Need to Know', 15 July. Available at: https://www.aljazeera.com/news/2016/12/turkey-failed-coup-atte mpt-161217032345594.html

Anscombe, Frederick F. (2014). *State, Faith, and Nation in Ottoman and Post-Ottoman Lands*. Cambridge: Cambridge University Press.

Arat, Yeşim (2005). *Rethinking Islam and Liberal Democracy: Islamist Women in Turkish Politics*. Albany, NY: State University of New York Press.

Asad, Talal (2003). *Formations of the Secular: Christianity, Islam, Modernity*. Stanford, CA: Stanford University Press.

Ata, Ulvi (2008). 'The Educational Services of the PRA and its Contribution to Religious Education in Turkey'. *The Muslim World*, 98(2/3), 302–12.

Bardakoğlu, Ali (2008). 'The Structure, Mission and Social Function of the Presidency of Religious Affairs (PRA)'. *The Muslim World*, 98(2/3), 173–81.

Batuman, Bülent (2018). 'Appropriating the Masculine Sacred: Islamism, Gender, and Mosque Architecture in Contemporary Turkey'. In Alexandra Staub (ed.), *The Routledge Companion to Modernity, Space and Gender* (pp. 270–87). London and New York: Routledge.

Batuman, Elif (2014). 'Ottomania: A Hit TV Show Reimagines Turkey's Imperial Past'. *The New Yorker*, 17 and 24 February.

Birge, John Kingsley (2015). *The Bektashi Order of Dervishes*. New Delhi: Cosmo Publications.

Bowen, John (1993). *Muslims Through Discourse*. Princeton, NJ: Princeton University Press.

Çağlar, Ismail (2013). *From Symbolic Exile to Physical Exile: Turkey's Imam-hatip Schools, the Emergence of a Conservative Counter-Elite, and Its Knowledge Migration to Europe*. Amsterdam: Amsterdam University Press.

Çakır, Ruşen (1995). *Ayet ve Slogan: Türkiye'de İslami Oluşumlar* (2nd edn). Istanbul: Metis Yayinlari.

Çarkoğlu, Ali and Toprak, Binnaz (2007). *Religion, Society and Politics in a Changing Turkey* (trans. Çiğdem Aksoy Fromm). Istanbul: TESEV Publications.

Christie-Miller, Alexander (2016). 'Bridge, Mosque, Airport: Can Turkey Afford Erdoğan's Mega-Monuments?' *The Christian-Science Monitor*, 9 September. Available at: www.csmonitor.com/World/Middle-East/2016/0909/Bridge-mosque-airport-can-Turkey-afford-Erdogan-s-mega-monuments

Ciddi, Sinan (2011). 'Turkey's September 12, 2010, Referendum'. *Middle East Review of International Affairs (MERIA)*, 15(4), 39–49.

Çınar, Alev (2005). *Modernity, Islam, and Secularism in Turkey: Bodies, Places, and Time*. Minneapolis, MN: University of Minnesota Press.

Cumhuriyet (1998). 'Şeriata giden yolda türban ilk adımdır'. *Cumhuriyet*, 6 December, 1.

Cupolo, Diego (2020). 'Years after Coup, Purged Civil Servants Feel Trapped in Turkey'. *Al-Monitor*, 13 January. Available at: www.al-monitor.com/pulse/originals/2020/01/turkey-coup-dismissed-civil-servants-fight-rights.html

Dağı, İhsan (2006). 'The Justice and Development Party: Identity, Politics, and Human Rights Discourse in the Search for Security and Legitimacy'. In M. Hakan Yavuz (ed.), *The Emergence of a New Turkey: Democracy and the AK Parti* (pp. 88–106). Salt Lake City, UT: The University of Utah Press.

Davison, Andrew (2003). 'Turkey, a "Secular" State? The Challenge of Description'. *South Atlantic Quarterly*, 102(2/3), 333–50.

Delaney, Carol (1991). *The Seed and the Soil: Gender and Cosmology in Turkish Village Society*. Berkeley, CA and Los Angeles: University of California Press.

Delibas, Kayhan (2015). *The Rise of Political Islam in Turkey: Urban Poverty, Grassroots Activism and Islamic Fundamentalism*. London: I. B. Tauris.

Dressler, Markus (2008). 'Religio-Secular Metamorphoses: The Re-Making of Turkish Alevism'. *Journal of the American Academy of Religion*, 76(2), 280–311.

Dressler, Markus (2013). *Writing Religion: The Making of Turkish Alevi Islam*. Oxford: Oxford University Press.

Ecevit, Yıldız (2007). 'Women's Rights, Women's Organizations, and the State'. In Zehra F. Kabasakal Arat (ed.), *Human Rights in Turkey* (pp. 187–201). Philadelphia, PA: University of Pennsylvania Press.

Eligür, Banu (2010). *The Mobilization of Political Islam in Turkey*. Cambridge: Cambridge University Press.

Er, İzzet (2008). 'Religious Services of the PRA'. *The Muslim World*, 98(2/3), 271–81.

Erdem, Gazi (2008). 'Religious Services in Turkey: From the Office of Şeyhülislam to the Diyanet'. *The Muslim World*, 98(2/3), 199–215.

Erdemir, Aykan (2005). 'Tradition and Modernity: Alevis' Ambiguous Terms and Turkey's Ambivalent Subjects'. *Middle Eastern Studies*, 41(6), 937–51.

Ergin, Murat and Karakaya, Yağmur (2017). 'Between Neo-Ottomanism and Ottomania: Navigating State-Led and Popular Cultural Representations of the Past'. *New Perspectives on Turkey*, 56, 33–9.

Erman, Tahire (2011). 'Understanding the Experiences of the Politics of Urbanization in Two Gecekondu (Squatter) Neighborhoods under Two Urban Regimes: Ethnography in the Urban Periphery of Ankara, Turkey'. *Urban Anthropology and Studies of Cultural Systems and World Economic Development*, 40(1/2), 67–108.

Erol, Ayhan (2010). 'Re-Imagining Identity: The Transformation of the Alevi Semah'. *Middle Eastern Studies*, 46(3), 375–87.

Faroqhi, Suraiya (1981). *Der Bektashi Orden in Anatolien*. Vienna: Verlag des Instituts für Orientalistik der Universität Wien.

Fernando, Mayanthi L. (2010). 'Reconfiguring Freedom: Muslim Piety and the Limits of Secular Law and Public Discourse in France'. *American Ethnologist*, 37(1), 19–35.

Gök, Fatma (1995). 'Women and Education in Turkey'. In Şirin Tekeli (ed.), *Women in Modern Turkish Society: A Reader* (pp. 131–40). London: Zed Books.

Gökarıksel, Banu (2012). 'The Intimate Politics of Secularism and the Headscarf: The Mall, the Neighborhood, and the Public Square in Istanbul'. *Gender, Place and Culture*, 19(1), 1–20.

Gökarıksel, Banu and Secor, Anna (2010a). 'Between Fashion and Tesettür: Marketing and Consuming Women's Islamic Dress'. *Journal of Middle East Women's Studies*, 6(3), 118–48.

Gökarıksel, Banu and Secor, Anna (2010b). 'Islamic-ness in the Life of a Commodity: Veiling-fashion in Turkey'. *Transactions of the Institute of British Geographers*, 35, 313–33.

Gökarıksel, Banu and Secor, Anna (2012). '"Even I Was Tempted": The Moral Ambivalence and Ethical Practice of Veiling-Fashion in Turkey'. *Annals of the Association of American Geographers*, 102(4), 847–62.

Göle, Nilüfer (1996). *The Forbidden Modern: Civilization and Veiling*. Ann Arbor, MI: University of Michigan Press.

Göner, Özlem (2005). 'The Transformation of the Alevi Collective Identity'. *Cultural Dynamics*, 17(2), 107–34.

Green, Nile (2012). *Sufism: A Global History*. Oxford: Wiley-Blackwell.

Gülen, M. Fethullah (2006). *Toward a Global Civilization of Love and Tolerance* (trans.

Mehmet Ünal, Nagihan Haliloğlu, Mükerrem Faniküçükmehmedoğlu, Mustafa Mencütekin, Hakan Yeşilova and Korkut Altay). Somerset, NJ: The Light, Inc.

Gumuscu, Sebnem (2010). 'Class, Status, and Party: The Changing Face of Political Islam in Turkey and Egypt'. *Comparative Political Studies*, 43(7), 835–61.

Harmanşah, Rabia, Yanyeri-Erdemir, Tuğba and Hayden, Robert M. (2015). 'Secularizing the Unsecularizable: A Comparative Study of the Haci Bektaş and Mevlana Museums in Turkey'. In Elazar Barkan and Karen Barkey (eds), *Choreographies of Shared Sacred Sites: Religion, Politics, and Conflict Resolution*. New York: Columbia University Press.

Harvey, David (2005). *A Brief History of Neoliberalism*. Oxford: Oxford University Press.

Hassan, Mona (2011). 'Women Preaching for the Secular State: Official Female Preachers (Bayan Vaizler) in Contemporary Turkey'. *International Journal of Middle East Studies*, 43(3), 451–73.

Hendrick, Joshua D. (2013). *Gülen: The Ambiguous Politics of Market Islam in Turkey and the World*. New York: New York University Press.

Hobsbawm, E. J. (1990). *Nations and Nationalism Since 1780: Programme, Myth, Reality*. Cambridge: Cambridge University Press.

Hurd, Elizabeth Shakman (2014). 'Alevis under Law: The Politics of Religious Freedom in Turkey'. *The Journal of Law and Religion*, 29(3), 416–35.

Imber, Colin (2002). *The Ottoman Empire, 1300–1650: the Structure of Power*. Basingstoke and New York: Palgrave Macmillan.

Introvigne, Massimo (2006). 'Turkish Religious Market(s): A View Based on the Religious Economy Theory'. In M. Hakan Yavuz (ed.), *The Emergence of New Turkey: Democracy and the AK Parti* (pp. 23–48). Salt Lake City, UT: The University of Utah Press.

Kaplan, Sam (2002). 'Din-u Devlet All Over Again? The Politics of Military Secularism and Religious Militarism in Turkey Following the 1980 Coup'. *International Journal of Middle East Studies*, 34(1), 113–27.

Kaplan, Sam (2006). *The Pedagogical State: Education and the Politics of National Culture in Post-1980 Turkey*. Stanford, CA: Stanford University Press.

Kara, Gazi (2009). *Altın Kitap Alevilik: İnancımız – Yolumuz – İbatetimiz*. Izmir: Kanyılmaz Matbaası.

Karaman, Fikret (2008). 'The Status and Function of the PRA in the Turkish Republic'. *The Muslim World*, 98(2/3), 282–90.

Karamustafa, Ahmet T. (2007). *Sufism: the Formative Period*. Berkeley, CA: University of California Press.

Kaya, Emir (2018). *Secularism and State Religion in Modern Turkey: Law, Policy-Making and the Diyanet*. London and New York: I. B. Tauris.

Kaymakcan, Recep (2006). 'Religious Education Culture in Modern Turkey'. In Marian de Souza, Gloria Durka, Kathleen Engebretson, Robert Jackson and Andrew McGrady (eds), *International Handbook of the Religious, Moral and Spiritual Dimensions in Education* (pp. 449–60). Dordrecht: Springer.

Kentel, Ferhat (2016). 'The Right to the City during the AK Party's Thermidor'. In Ümit Çizre (ed.), *The Turkish AK Party and its Leader: Criticism, Opposition and Dissent* (pp. 132–65). London and New York: Routledge.

Kılıçbay, M. Ali (2005). 'Fethullah Gülen Okulları'. In Toktamış Ateş, Eser Karakaş and Ilber Ortaylı (eds), *Barış Köprüleri: Dunyaya Açılan Türk Okulları* (pp. 67–71). Istanbul: Ufuk Kitaplari.

Kinzer, Stephen (2001). *Crescent and Star: Turkey between Two Worlds*. New York: Farrar, Straus and Giroux.

Kocamaner, Hikmet (2017). 'Strengthening the Family through Television: Islamic Broadcasting, Secularism, and the Politics of Responsibility in Turkey'. *Anthropological Quarterly*, 90(3), 675–714.

Kocamaner, Hikmet (2019). 'Regulating the Family through Religion: Secularism, Islam, and the Politics of the Family in Contemporary Turkey'. *American Ethnologist*, 46(4), 1–14.

Kreinath, Jens (2014). 'Virtual Encounters with Hızır and Other Muslim Saints: Dreaming and Healing at Local Pilgrimage Sites in Hatay, Turkey'. *Anthropology of the Contemporary Middle East and Central Eurasia*, 2(1), 25–66.

Kuru, Ahmet T. (2003). 'Fethullah Gülen's Search for a Middle Way Between Modernity and Muslim Tradition'. In M. Hakan Yavuz and John L. Esposito (eds), *Turkish Islam and the Secular State: The Gülen Movement* (pp. 115–30). Syracuse, NY: Syracuse University Press.

Kuru, Ahmet T. (2009). *Secularism and State Policies Toward Religion: The United States, France, and Turkey*. Cambridge: Cambridge University Press.

Lepeska, David (2015). 'Turkey Casts the Diyanet: Ankara's Religious Directorate Takes Off', 15 May. Available at: www.foreignaffairs.com/articl es/turkey/2015-05-17/turkey-casts-diyanet

Levin, Yasemin Çelik (2007). 'The Effect of CEDAW on Women's Rights'. In Zehra F. Kabasakal Arat (ed.), *Human Rights in Turkey* (pp. 202–13). Philadelphia, PA: University of Pennsylvania Press.

Lewis, Bernard (1961). *The Emergence of Modern Turkey*. London: Oxford University Press.

Lewis, Geoffrey (1999). *The Turkish Language Reform: A Catastrophic Success*. Oxford: Oxford University Press.

Lewis, Reina (2015). *Muslim Fashion: Contemporary Style Cultures*. Durham, NC and London: Duke University Press.

Mahmood, Saba (2005). *Politics of Piety: The Islamic Revival and the Feminist Subject*. Princeton, NJ and Oxford: Princeton University Press.

Mardin, Şerif (1982). 'Turkey: Islam and Westernization'. In C. Caldarola (ed.), *Religions and Societies: Asia and the Middle East* (pp. 170–98). New York: Mouton Publishers.

Mardin, Şerif (1989). *Religion and Social Change in Modern Turkey: The Case of Bediüzzaman Said Nursi*. In *SUNY Series in Near Eastern Studies* (pp. ix, 267). Available at: http:// navigator-cup.passhe.edu/login?url=http://hdl.handle.net/2027/heb.00915

Mardin, Şerif (1994). 'The Nakşibendi Order in Turkish History'. In Richard Tapper (ed.), *Islam in Modern Turkey: Religion, Politics and Literature in a Secular State* (pp. 121–42). London: I. B. Tauris.

Maritato, Chiara (2015). 'Performing Irşad: Female Preachers' (Vaizeler's) Religious Assistance Within the Framework of the Turkish State'. *Turkish Studies*, 16(3), 433–47.

Maritato, Chiara (2017). 'Compliance or Negotiation? Diyanet's Female Preachers and the Diffusion of a "True" Religion in Turkey'. *Social Compass*, 64(4), 530–45.

Markoff, Irene (1995). 'Introduction to Sufi Music and Ritual in Turkey'. *MESA Bulletin*, 29(2), 157–60.

Massicard, Elise (2013). *The Alevis in Turkey and Europe: Identity and Managing Territorial Diversity*. London and New York: Routledge.

Massicard, Elise (2016). 'Alevi Critique of the AK Party: Criticizing "Islamism" or the Turkish State?' In Ümit Cizre (ed.), *The Turkish AK Party and its Leader: Criticism, Opposition and Dissent* (pp. 75–102). London and New York: Routledge.

McMeekin, Sean (2012). 'World War I and the Establishment of the Republic'. In Metin Heper and Sabri Sayari (eds), *The Routledge Handbook of Modern Turkey* (pp. 35–43). London and New York: Routledge.

Meeker, Michael E. (1991). 'The New Muslim Intellectuals in the Republic of Turkey'. In Richard Tapper (ed.), *Islam in Modern Turkey: Religion, Politics and Literature in a Secular State* (pp. 189–219). London: I. B. Tauris.

Meeker, Michael E. (2002). *A Nation of Empire: The Ottoman Legacy of Turkish Modernity*. Berkeley, CA: University of California Press.

Mèlikoff, Irène (1998). 'Bektashi/Kızılbaş: Historical Bipartition and Its Consequences'. In Tord Olsson, Elisabeth Özdalga and Catharina Raudvere (eds), *Alevi Identity: Cultural, Religious and Social Perspectives* (vol. 8, pp. 1–9). Istanbul: Swedish Research Institute in Istanbul.

Moudouros, Nikos (2014). 'The "Harmonization" of Islam with the Neoliberal Transformation: The Case of Turkey'. *Globalizations*, 11(1), 1–15.

Mutluer, Nil (2016). 'The Looming Shadow of Violence and Loss: Alevi Responses to Persecution and Discrimination'. *Journal of Balkan and Near Eastern Studies*, 18(2), 145–56.

Navaro-Yashin, Yael (2002a). *Faces of the State: Secularism and Public Life in Turkey*. Princeton, NJ: and Oxford: Princeton University Press.

Navaro-Yashin, Yael (2002b). 'The Market for Identities: Secularism, Islamism, Commodities'. In Deniz Kandiyoti and Ayse Saktanber (eds), *Fragments of Culture: The Everyday of Modern Turkey* (pp. 221–53). New Brunswick, NJ: Rutgers University Press.

Norton, John (1997). 'Faith and Fashion in Turkey'. In Nancy Lindisfarne-Tapper and Bruce Ingham (eds), *Languages of Dress in the Middle East*. Richmond: Curzon.

Nursi, Bediüzzaman Said (2010). *The Words: The Reconstruction of Islamic Belief and Thought* (trans. Hüseyn Akarsu). Clifton, NJ: The Light, Inc.

Öcal, Samil (2008). 'From "the Fetwa" to "Religious Questions": Main Characteristics of Fetwas of the Diyanet'. *The Muslim World*, 98(2/3), 324–34.

Öniş, Ziya (2004). 'Turgut Özal and his Economic Legacy: Turkish Neo-Liberalism in Critical Perspective'. *Middle Eastern Studies*, 40(4), 113–34.

Özal, Korkut (1999). 'Twenty Years with Mehmed Zahid Kotku: A Personal Story'. In Elisabeth Özdalga (ed.), *Naqshbandis in Western and Central Asia: Change and Continuity* (vol. 9). Istanbul: Swedish Research Institute in Istanbul.

Özdalga, Elisabeth (1999). 'Education in the Name of "Order and Progress": Reflections on the Recent Eight Year Obligatory School Reform in Turkey'. *The Muslim World*, 89(3–4), 414–38.

Özdalga, Elisabeth (2003). 'Following in the Footsteps of Fethullah Gülen'. In M. Hakan Yavuz and John L. Esposito (eds), *Turkish Islam and the Secular State: The Gülen Movement* (pp. 85–114). Syracuse, NY: Syracuse University Press.

Ozgur, Iren (2012). *Islamic Schools in Modern Turkey: Faith, Politics, and Education*. Cambridge: Cambridge University Press.

Özkul, Derya (2015). 'Alevi "Openings" and Politicization of the "Alevi Issue" During the AKP Rule'. *Turkish Studies*, 16(1), 80–96.

Özyürek, Esra (2006). *Nostalgia for the Modern: State Secularism and Everyday Politics in Turkey*. Durham, NC: Duke University Press.

Özyürek, Esra (2007). *The Politics of Public Memory in Turkey* (1st edn). Syracuse, NY: Syracuse University Press.

Pacaci, Mehmet and Aktay, Yasin (1999). '75 Years of Higher Religious Education in Modern Turkey'. *The Muslim World*, 89(3–4), 389–413.

Pak, Soon-Yong (2004a). 'Articulating the Boundary between Secularism and Islamism: The *Imam-hatip* Schools of Turkey'. *Anthropology and Education Quarterly*, 35(3), 324–44.

Pak, Soon-Yong (2004b). 'Cultural Politics and Vocational Religious Education: The Case of Turkey'. *Comparative Education*, 40(3), 322–41.

Potuoğlu-Cook, Öykü (2006). 'Beyond the Glitter: Belly Dance and Neoliberal Gentrification in Istanbul'. *Cultural Anthropology*, 21(4), 633–60.

Raudvere, Catharina (2002). *The Book and the Roses: Sufi Women, Visibility, and Zikir in Contemporary Istanbul*. Bjarnum: Bjarnums Tryckeri AB.

Rutz, Henry J. and Balkan, Erol M. (2010). *Reproducing Class: Education, Neoliberalism, and the Rise of the New Middle Class in Istanbul*. New York: Berghahn Books.

Sağlam, Burcu (2017). 'A Discussion on the Myth of Mevlana in Modern Turkey'. *Journal of Intercultural Studies*, 38(4), 412–28.

Saktanber, Ayşe (2002). *Living Islam: Women, Religion and the Politicization of Culture in Turkey*. London and New York: I. B. Tauris.

Saktanber, Ayşe (2006). 'Women and the Iconography of Fear: Islamization in Post-Islamist Turkey'. *Signs: Journal of Women in Culture and Society*, 32(1), 21–31.

Salman, Yüksel (2008). 'The Publishing Activities of the PRA'. *The Muslim World*, 98 (April/July), 313–23.

Schimmel, Annemarie (1975). *Mystical Dimensions of Islam*. Chapel Hill, NC: The University of North Carolina Press.

Şeni, Nora (1995). 'Fashion and Women's Clothing in the Satirical Press of Istanbul at the End of the 19th Century'. In Şirin Tekeli (ed.), *Women in Modern Turkish Society* (pp. 25–45). London: Zed Books.

Shankland, David (2003). *The Alevis of Turkey: The Emergence of a Secular Islamic Tradition*. London and New York: Routledge.

Shissler, A. Holly (2004). 'Beauty Is Nothing to Be Ashamed Of: Beauty Contests as Tools of Women's Liberation in Early Republican Turkey'. *Comparative Studies of South Asia, Africa and the Middle East*, 24(1), 107–22.

Shively, Kim (2005). 'Religious Bodies in Secular States: The Merve Kavakçı Affair'. *Journal of Middle East Women's Studies*, 1(3), 46–72.

Shively, Kim (2008). 'Taming Islam: Studying Religion in Secular Turkey'. *Anthropological Quarterly*, 81(3), 683–712.

Shively, Kim (2009). 'The Sharp Edge of a Razor: Negotiating Religious Identity in Turkey'. *Vis-à-Vis: Explorations in Anthropology*, 9(1), 75–80.

Shively, Kim (2013). 'Defining (and Enforcing) Islam in Secular Turkey'. In Sherine Hafez and Susan Slyomovics (eds), *Anthropology of the Middle East and North Africa: Into the New Millennium* (pp. 203–22). Bloomington, IN and Indianapolis, IN: Indiana University Press.

Shively, Kim (2016). 'Pragmatic Politics: The Gülen Movement and the AKP'. In Ümit Çizre (ed.), *The Turkish AK Party and its Leader: Criticism, Opposition and Dissent* (pp. 183–204). London and New York: Routledge.

Silverstein, Brian (2011). *Islam and Modernity in Turkey*. New York: Palgrave Macmillan.

Singer, Amy (2002). *Constructing Ottoman Beneficence: An Imperial Soup Kitchen in Jerusalem*. Albany, NY: State University of New York Press.

Singer, Amy (2008). *Charity in Islamic Societies*. Cambridge: Cambridge University Press.

Soileau, Mark (2017). 'Hızır Pasha Hanged Us: Commemorating Maryrdom in Alevi Tradition'. *The Muslim World*, 107(3), 549–71.

Sökefeld, Martin (2008). *Struggling for Recognition: The Alevi Movement in Germany and in Transnational Space*. New York and Oxford: Berghahn.

Soner, B. Ali (2010). 'The Justice and Development Party's Policies Towards Non-Muslim Minorities in Turkey'. *Journal of Balkan and Near Eastern Studies*, 12(1), 23–40.

Sonmez, Mustafa (2018). 'Istanbul's New Airport: A Looming Black Hole'. *Al-Monitor*, 9 March. Available at: www.al-monitor.com/pulse/originals/2018/03/turkey-istanbul-airport-black-hole-in-public-finance.html

Tambar, Kabir (2014). *The Reckoning of Pluralism: Political Belonging and the Demands of History in Turkey*. Stanford, CA: Stanford University Press.

Tarlo, Emma (2010). *Visibly Muslim: Fashion, Politics, Faith*. Oxford: Berg.

Toprak, Binnaz (1981). *Islam and Political Development in Turkey*. Leiden: Brill.

Tremblay, Pinar (2019). 'Is Erdogan's Airport Dream Turning into Nightmare?' *Al-*

Monitor, 6 March. Available at: www.al-monitor.com/pulse/originals/2019/03/
turkey-erdogan-third-airport-project-may-be-stillborn.html

Tuğal, Cihan (2006). 'The Appeal of Islamic Politics: Ritual and Dialogue in a Poor District of Turkey'. *The Sociological Quarterly*, 47, 245–73.

Tuğal, Cihan (2009). *Passive Revolution: Absorbing the Islamic Challenge to Capitalism*. Stanford, CA: Stanford University Press.

Turan, Ömer (2008). 'The Turkish Diyanet Foundation'. *The Muslim World*, 98 (April/July), 370–84.

Tütüncü, Fatma (2010). 'The Women Preachers of the Secular State: The Politics of Preaching at the Intersection of Gender, Ethnicity and Sovereignty in Turkey'. *Middle Eastern Studies*, 46(4), 595–614.

Ueno, Manami (2018). 'Sufism and Sufi Orders in Compulsory Religious Education in Turkey'. *Turkish Studies*, 19(3), 381–99.

Van Bruinessen, Martin (1994). 'Genocide in Kurdistan? The Suppression of the Dersim Rebellion in Turkey (1937–38) and the Chemical War against the Iraqi Kurds (1988)'. In George J. Andreopoulos (ed.), *Conceptual and Historical Dimensions of Genocide* (pp. 141–70). Philadelphia, PA: University of Pennsylvania Press.

Van Bruinessen, Martin (1996). 'Kurds, Turks and the Alevi Revival in Turkey'. *Middle East Report, 200: Minorities in the Middle East: Power and the Politics of Difference* (July–September), 7–10.

Vicini, Fabio (2013). 'Pedagogies of Affection: The Role of Exemplariness and Emulation in Learning Process – Extracurricular Islamic Education in the Fethullah Gülen Community in Istanbul'. *Anthropology and Education Quarterly*, 44(4), 381–98.

Vicini, Fabio (2014). '"Do Not Cross Your Legs": Islamic Sociability, Reciprocity and Brotherhood in Turkey'. *La Ricerca Folklorica*, 69(1), 93–104.

Walton, Jeremy F. (2013). 'Confessional Pluralism and the Civil Society Effect: Liberal Mediations of Islam and Secularism in Contemporary Turkey'. *American Ethnologist*, 40(1), 182–200.

Walton, Jeremy F. (2017). *Muslim Civil Society and the Politics of Religious Freedom in Turkey*. Oxford: Oxford University Press.

Watters, Samuel W. (2018). 'Developments in AKP Policy Toward Religion and Homogeneity'. *German Law Journal*, 19(2), 351–74.

Watts, Nicole (2000). 'Relocating Dersim: Turkish State-Building and Kurdish Resistance, 1931–1938'. *New Perspectives on Turkey*, 23(1), 5–30.

White, Jenny B. (2002a). *Islamist Mobilization in Turkey: A Study in Vernacular Politics*. Seattle, WA: University of Washington Press.

White, Jenny B. (2002b). 'The Islamist Paradox'. In Deniz Kandiyoti and Ayse Saktanber (eds), *Fragments of Culture: The Everyday of Modern Turkey* (pp. 191–217). New Brunswick, NJ: Rutgers University Press.

White, Jenny B. (2013). *Muslim Nationalism and the New Turks*. Princeton, NJ: Princeton University Press.

Wilson, M. Brett (2009). 'The First Translations of the Qur'an in Modern Turkey (1924–38)'. *International Journal of Middle East Studies*, 41(3), 419–35.

Wilson, M. Brett (2014). *Translating the Qur'an in an Age of Nationalism: Print Culture and Modern Islam in Turkey*. London: Oxford University Press, in association with the Institute of Ismaili Studies.

Yavuz, M. Hakan (2003). *Islamic Political Identity in Turkey*. Oxford: Oxford University Press.

Yavuz, M. Hakan (2009). *Secularism and Muslim Democracy in Turkey*. Cambridge: Cambridge University Press.

Yavuz, M. Hakan (2013). *Toward an Islamic Enlightenment: The Gülen Movement*. Oxford: Oxford University Press.

Yazıcı, Seyfettin (1997). *Temel Dinî Bilgiler*. Ankara: Diyanet İşleri Başkanlığı.

Yılmaz, Hale (2011). 'Learning to Read (Again): The Social Experiences of Turkey's 1928 Alphabet Reform'. *International Journal of Middle East Studies*, 43(4), 677–97.

Yilmaz, Hale (2013). *Becoming Turkish: Nationalist Reforms and Cultural Negotiations in Early Republican Turkey, 1923–1945*. Syracuse, NY: Syracuse University Press.

Yılmaz, Ihsan (2005). 'State, Law, Civil Society and Islam in Contemporary Turkey'. *The Muslim World*, 95(3), 385–411.

Yuval-Davis, Nira (1997). *Gender and Nation*. London: Sage Publications.

Zencirci, Gizem (2015a).' From Property to Civil Society: The Historical Transformation of Vakıfs in Modern Turkey (1923–2013)'. *International Journal of Middle East Studies*, 47, 533–54.

Zencirci, Gizem (2015b). 'Illusory Debates: How the "Sadaka Culture" Discourse Masked the Rise of Social Assistance in Turkey'. *Asian Journal of Social Science*, 43, 125–50.

Zürcher, Erik Jan (2004). *Turkey: A Modern History* (3rd edn). London and New York: I. B. Tauris, distributed by St. Martin's Press.

Index

Note: n indicates notes, *italic* indicates images

CPSIA information can be obtained
at www.ICGtesting.com
Printed in the USA
JSHW040143301220
10592JS00001B/2